NINETEENTH CENTURY PHILOSOPHY

Wladyslaw Tatarkiewicz

University of Warsaw

translated by
Chester A. Kisiel

Wadsworth Publishing Company, Inc.
Belmont, California

Die Hauptideen, die in manchen Schriften herrschen, sind oft so schwer harauszubringen, dass sie der Verfasser selbst oft nicht herausfinden und ein Anderer ihm manchmal besser sagen kann, was die Hauptidee war.

Immanuel Kant
Welt und Menschenerkenntnis

Puisqu'on ne peut être universel en sachant tout ce qui se peut savoir sur tout, il faut savoir peu de tout. Car il est bien plus beau de savoir quelque chose de tout que de savoir tout d'une chose; cette universalité est la plus belle.

Qu'on ne dise pas que je n'ai rien dit de nouveau: la disposition des matières est nouvelle; quand on joue à la paume, c'est une même balle dont joue l'un et l'autre, mais l'un la place mieux.

Blaise Pascal
Pensées, no 42 et 65

Tota methodus consistit in ordine et dispositione eorum ad quae mentis acies est convertenda, ut aliquam veritatem inveniamus.

René Descartes
Regulae ad directionem ingenii:
Regula V

ISBN-0-534-00140-8

L. C. Cat. Card No.72-93474

Printed in the United States of America

1 2 3 4 5 6 7 8 9 10---76 75 74 73

To keep the price of this book as low as possible, we have used an economical means of typesetting. We welcome your comments.

Introduction to the English Edition

These two volumes were written during the Second World War and brought the story up to that point; so this history of philosophy ended before the year 1945. Since that time more than a quarter of a century has passed, and, of course, many philosophical ideas have been born since that time. The publication of an English edition after a few decades presents an opportunity to make additions: not only to add information that historians have discovered about philosophy before 1945, but also to discuss what happened in philosophy *after* 1945. However, the author did not add such a chapter.

He feels that the years of World War II were a great turning point not only in political and social areas but also in philosophy, and that it is correct to end the narration with this crucial date. What has been taking place since that date is the beginning of an era not yet closed, one that is still unclear and insufficiently understood. Later historians will be better able than we to understand the distinctness of this era. It is still too early to treat the period of philosophy after 1945 in the same manner and method by which the years 1830 to 1945 were treated. And should anyone seek information about presently important topics like phenomenology and linguistic analysis, he will find their foundations in these books: the first in the period 1900 to 1918, the second in 1930 to 1945.

These volumes are prefaced by three mottos. The author included them in the belief that the statements of great thinkers would help explain why histories of philosophy like this one are published. All three mottos are by philosophers. The first is taken from Kant's lectures at the University of Königsberg in 1790/1, which were published after his death. In translation the motto reads: "The main ideas contained in many works are often so difficult to bring out that the author himself cannot find them, and someone else is frequently better able to tell him what the main idea was." This "someone else" is, above all, the historian. Kant's assertion brings the true purpose of the efforts of the historians of philosophy into clear focus. It also strongly suggests that the individual who wishes to become familiar with the great thinkers must do more than study their original texts; he is advised to supplement them with the commentaries of historians.

The second motto is from Pascal's *Thoughts*. In English the motto is: "Since we cannot be universal and know all that is to be known of everything, we ought to know a little about everything. For it is far better to know something about everything than to know all about one thing." This text of Pascal's also justifies the work of the historian of philosophy. It explains why some histories of philosophy, including this one, discuss so many diverse trends and positions. Although among the many philosophical trends and positions, some are less important and less inventive, their multitude and diversity shows us what the human mind is capable of and how many different possible solutions there are to the most general philosophical problems.

Somewhat later Pascal writes: "Let no one say that I have said nothing new: the disposition of the content is new. When one plays ball, the same ball is tossed from one to another, but one is more skilled in tossing it." This text also expresses the conviction that the activity of the historian of philosophy is not passive, that he does more than just dig out the thoughts of former philosophers.

The third motto is from Descartes' *Rules for the Direction of the Mind*. The Fifth Rule is: "Method consists entirely in the order and disposition of the objects toward which our mental vision must be directed if we would find any truth." This means that only the method of "analysis," or the dissection of abstruse matters, can make them clear and simple. It will be readily apparent to the reader that the author of this history of philosophy has attempted to make use of the analytical method.

Contents

Introduction

Contemporary Philosophy

The philosophy that we call "modern" (in the widest sense of the term) has its beginning about the year 1830. What came before that date already belongs to the past and seems, if not foreign, at least distant to us. It is connected only indirectly with current thought. What has come after 1830, however, either belongs to contemporary thought or has directly influenced it. The ideas of Comte, Mill, and Marx, which were born shortly after 1830, have lived into our times. The ideas of the twentieth century have developed either in agreement or disagreement with their views. Some of their ideas are still current, while others, even if they have receded into the past, are still linked directly to the thought of our times.

The period after 1830 comprises a whole that can be divided into two parts: the period that is our immediate past; and the period that we call the present. The immediate past is the nineteenth century—strictly speaking its midpoint to its end. The present, broadly speaking, denotes those years of the twentieth century which have passed.

Limits of the Period

Around 1830 a radical change took place in philosophy and in all of European thought. Enthusiasm for romanticism and idealism was waning, and a more positive method of thinking, which would characterize the rest of the century, was being developed. The limits of the period are clear. Hegel died in 1831, and from this time forth no outstanding affirmative, metaphysical, idealistic philosophical work appeared. The first volume of Comte's *Course of Positive Philosophy* was published in 1830. The philosophical developments of the first three decades of the century suddenly became distant and foreign.

1

There is a tendency to consider the characteristics of the period beginning in 1830 as typical of the whole century. We seem to think of the philosophy after 1830 as the real philosophy of the nineteenth century. It has even been stated, somewhat paradoxically, that the nineteenth century did not really begin until 1830. This view is not entirely correct. The first three decades of the century, although unlike the rest of the century, exhibited features different from those of the eighteenth century, and for this reason cannot be linked with it. Precisely in 1830 began a return to the spirit of the eighteenth century, to its minimalism, realism, and utilitarianism. Comte only reverted to the position of d'Alembert.

It would be more precise to say that in the nineteenth century two succeeding philosophies prevailed which were totally divergent. First came the bold philosophy of great systems, and after 1830, a moderate and cautious philosophy; first a Hegelian philosophy, and then a philosophy on the style of Mill and Comte. The latter has lasted longer and is closer to us; therefore, it seems like the real philosophy of the nineteenth century. The former we consign to the past; the latter broadly speaking, is current.

The Splendors and Misfortunes of Nineteenth-Century Philosophy

The philosophy of the nineteenth century, particularly its second phase, developed in a different way than earlier philosophy. Above all, it developed at a far quicker pace. One after another ideas emerged, giving way rapidly to their diametrical opposites. This phenomenon had its source in the new conditions of public life, its increased tempo, its new technology, its more highly developed organization. Completely new means of communication facilitated the exchange of ideas. Never had there been so many institutions of higher education or so many possibilities of discussing and hearing lectures on philosophy. Never before had the number of philosophical publications been so great. Not only would the flood of books have transcended the imagination of previous centuries, but a new phenomenon also appeared—the scholarly journal. Almost at once it became one of the main outlets for philosophical work, thus influencing a transition from larger publications to articles, smaller contributions, and notations, all of which led to a quicker exchange of ideas.

The results of these new conditions, of this new tempo, were not entirely positive. Greater access to knowledge contributed to its superficiality. There were more professional philosophers, but there were also more dilettantes. Ease of publication permitted the printing of lesser works, which in an earlier age would have remained manuscripts at no great loss.

Furthermore, although philosophy in itself profited, it suffered by comparison with the gains of other sciences. It lost to the natural and historical sciences its preeminence in the total number of scholarly works, which it had enjoyed in previous centuries. It declined in relative productivity and also in social importance compared with natural science and history. This happened gradually, yet only a few years separate the time of philosophy's greatest triumphs from the time when, in the eyes of many, it had become anachronistic and even superfluous.

Philosophy retreated not only before the individual sciences, but before *belles lettres* as well. Many philosophical works appeared; yet, in the beginning of the century, still more poetry was published and, later, even more prose. The eighteenth century had been called "philosophical." The nineteenth century was described as "scientific" and "literary," "technical" and "political." More than once the spirit of the age found its fullest expression in poetry and prose rather than in a philosophical system. Although philosophy continued to influence the individual sciences and *belles lettres*, they now influenced philosophy in turn. What is more, philosophy tried to imitate them, approaching in style either the individual sciences or *belles lettres*. Philosophers either wrote essays bordering on prose stories, or, again disregarding their previous distinctness, strove to convert philosophy into one of the individual sciences. Philosophy wavered between these poles—between literary creation and scientific analysis. For the first time in its history it faced two dangers at once, losing its identity on the one side to the individual sciences and on the other to *belles lettres*.

Philosophy prospered by widening its range of problems. Knowledge of its past history increased considerably. In this century for the first time philosophy was independent, unhampered by traditional, moral, or religious considerations. Yet a peculiar phenomenon manifested itself. The leading figures of the century began to scorn philosophy, asserting that it could be no science, and even considered it harmful because it drained attention from true science. To some extent they thought as did Pascal, that to renounce philosophy is true philosophy. They wished to renounce it for science, just as Pascal had wished to renounce it for religion.

National Differences

Advances in communications brought nations and peoples closer together; curiosity about foreign ideas also affected this process. Translations signaled this coming together of peoples and would later even accelerate it. Never had so many philosophical works been translated as in the second half of the nineteenth century. The large number of translations resulted from the proximity of nations, which in turn intensfied communication still further.

Positivism, that most characteristic philosophical attitude of the era, was the joint product of at least two nations, France and England. It originated from the "positive philosophy" of Comte and from the empiricism of Mill. The mutual influence of these two countries was not an isolated instance. First, German idealism influenced other countries; later, the positivism of other countries influenced Germany. There was no hegemony of any one country. For one generation at the beginning of the century, it might have seemed that Germany, which until Kant had been last among the nations of Europe in philosophy, had suddenly captured first place. However, this superiority was dubious, or, in any event, transient. The main current of the epoch, positivism, took shape and prevailed without Germany's participation.

In spite of everything—the ease of communication, the hawking of books, the exchange of ideas—national differences in philosophical emphasis remained. They proved stronger than all external, unifying factors. Finally, philosophy in every country developed differently during the nineteenth century. In England different positions were elaborated and debated than in France, and in Germany and Poland still others. In each country different problems were stressed. The rhythm of development was also different. In England and France opposing theories lasted side by side throughout the century, while in Poland and Germany they took precedence successively and mutually disavowed one another.

England began the century with the debate between the philosophers of "common sense" and those of "philosophical radicalism," and to the end of the century remained the battleground for the two doctrines which these groups represented—intuitionism and empiricism.

France also (from Biran and Comte) was the scene of struggle between two opposing tendencies, but ones different from those in England, namely, spiritualism and positivism.

In Germany, still other doctrines contended with one another—criticism, materialism, and idealism. However, they came to the forefront in succession. German philosophy, beginning from criticism, quickly passed to metaphysical idealism. In the 1830s however, it impetuously turned to materialism, only to return, by the 1860s, to a position of criticism.

Poland, too, in the course of the century shifted from one extreme philosophical position to another. She began with

positivism, turned to messianic metaphysics after the 1831 revolution, and returned to positivism after the 1863 rebellion.

The Period of Criticism and Enlightenment

The main feature of the period comprising the middle and
end of the nineteenth century was the great variety of philosophical positions. New positions were formulated while old
ones still retained supporters. Anti-metaphysical doctrines
were elaborated at the same time that metaphysical views were
being rehabilitated. This renewal of earlier views, this
growth in the number of systems, this division of philosophy
into mutually opposing schools, makes this period similar to
the Hellenistic and medieval periods of "schools."
Not all of the philosophical schools and doctrines of the
nineteenth century enjoyed the same recognition, however. Predominant and typical were schools that limited their final objectives in order to achieve them in a careful, precise, and
sure manner. Such theories make up the main philosophical
thread of the times. Theories of the other type, however, proclaimed by the messianists, neo-Scholastics, or spiritualists
such as Ravaisson or Fechner, were, at best, an opposing minority. Again, this period shows a similarity to earlier periods,
those in which the main slogans were criticism and enlightenment.
This philosophic attitude was undoubtedly in tune with
contemporary social and cultural conditions. These were conditions of unusual peace, prosperity, well-being, and ease of
life. These advantages were available only to privileged
classes, but it was precisely from these classes that the majority of philosophers were recruited. It was to be expected
that these classes would produce naturalists and empiricists,
willingly occupying themselves with existing reality and not
thinking of renouncing it for speculative fantasies about a
truer or better existence. On the other hand, the well-being
of the nineteenth century, which produced empiricism, did not
bring forth an optimistic philosophy. To be sure, the classical positivists asserted that they were satisfied with life as
it was, and the evolutionists were at least meliorists who
believed that the world was moving inexorably toward a better
future. But, at the same time, the pessimistic teachings of
Schopenhauer became rather widespread, and the bitter views of
von Hartmann and Renan were formulated. This shows that
philosophical theories are sometimes not so much an expression
of the thinking of the masses as a complement to it or the
expression of an opposing minority.

Two Types of Philosophy

Since the beginning of recorded history there have been differences in the tone of philosophical inquiries—in some boldness is prevalent, and in others caution prevails. In the nineteenth century, this opposition intensified. Two diametrically opposed types of philosophy contended with one another. One can call them maximalistic and minimalistic types.

Maximalistic philosophy sets vast objectives for itself and tries to achieve them at all cost. Of course, it tries to achieve them in as certain a manner as possible, but, failing this, it is satisfied with uncertain results. Minimalistic philosophy, however, considers only that which is certain. It poses and tries to solve only problems that it can handle with complete certainty. Maximalistic philosophy is primarily guided by the goal it has in mind, minimalistic philosophy by the means at its disposal. The first is the philosophy of ambition, the second the philosophy of prudent abstention.

The difference that can be observed in the aims of these two types of philosophy also appears in their results. In all philosophical questions there exists a minimum about which everyone more or less agrees. The debate centers on whether one can and should assert something beyond this minimum. Everyone agrees on the existence of probable statements—but do completely certain propositions also exist? We possess knowledge about phenomena—do we also have knowledge of things in themselves? We have knowledge of our ideas about reality—but do we also know this reality itself? We know its fragments—but do we also possess knowledge of the whole? We possess empirical knowledge—do we also have a priori knowledge? We get to know the world through sense impressions—but can we also know it through intellect and intuition? A world of matter exists—but is there also a separate world of spirit? Nature exists—but is there also a supernatural world? Real objects exist—do ideal objects also have existence? The actions of people are aimed at direct satisfactions—but do they also have other aims? The good for man is pleasure—but are there also other goods for him?

Minimalistic philosophy recognizes only the minima, only such theses as phenomenalism, empiricism, subjectivism, utilitarianism. Maximalistic philosophy is inclined to recognize certain transcendental, a priori, intuitive truths over and above these minima. It recognizes a spiritual, ideal, and supernatural world. It acknowledges other drives, goals, and goods in addition to exclusively utilitarian ones. For the cautious mind, these minima seem sufficient to describe our world, knowledge, and behavior. Everything else seems illusory or, at any rate, uncertain. The results of minimalistic philosophy have been various forms of scepticism, relativism, sub-

jectivism, empiricism, sensualism, and hedonism. The opposite
results have generally stemmed from a maximalistic view.

In antiquity Pyrrhonism was undoubtedly a minimalistic
philosophy and Neoplatonism a maximalistic one. Scholasticism
in the thirteenth century was a maximalistic philosophy, and
in the fourteenth century it became a minimalistic one. In
more recent times, Spinoza represents the first type of philosophy, Locke or Hume the second. The time of "great systems" as
a whole belongs to the first type, the period of "criticism and
enlightenment" to the second. In earlier times this opposition
did not have particular import. Indeed, maximalism and minimalism are extreme views, and extreme positions do not exhaust
all philosophical possibilities. Intermediate positions still
remain. Boldness and caution can also be balanced in philosophy, as most great philosophers have done. It would be incorrect to consider Aristotle as either a maximalist or a minimalist. Descartes and Leibniz are similar cases. They strove
to achieve the same goal as the maximalists. They wished to
discover most important and most difficult things such as the
existence of God, the soul, and freedom. Their methods of reasoning and proof, however, approached those of the minimalists.
With Kant, too, these tendencies balanced. In the eighteenth
century, however, the break between the two types of philosophy
began to appear more clearly. The views of the encyclopedists
were decidedly minimalistic, and Wolff's school was decidedly
maximalistic.

In the nineteenth century this breach became complete.
Philosophers no longer talked of balancing these two tendencies. They now said: either-or, either all or nothing. And in
the course of the century, both types of philosophy came to the
fore in succession. In the first part of the century maximalism was predominant, reaching its peak in idealism. Minimalism
was predominant for a much longer time, reaching its zenith in
positivism. This is the main reason for dividing the philosophy of the nineteenth century into two periods—before and after 1830.

Of course, after 1830 other ways of thinking also made
their appearance. Marxism was not one-sided minimalism. Precisely for that reason, however, it was not as popular then as
it later became.

The Prevalence of Minimalism

The minimalistic tradition of the Enlightenment remained
vital in England and France until the beginning of the nineteenth century. Only then did it begin to wane. Shortly after
1830 came another wave of minimalism. Auguste Comte's *Course
of Positive Philosophy* and J. S. Mill's *The System of Logic*

initiated the new period in both countries. These two books were the philosophical foundations of the epoch. The next generation laid a third foundation—Herbert Spencer's *Synthetic Philosophy*.

French positivism from the fourth decade of the nineteenth century, English empiricism from the fifth, and evolutionism from the sixth together created a minimalistic philosophy that became the authoritative mode of thinking in almost all of Europe. It drew from all three sources, but it most frequently took its name from Comte and called itself "positivism." The middle of the century (1830 - 1860) was the period of its formulation and the end of the century (1860 - 1900) the time of its predominance. In the second phase, certain variations of minimalism, more or less similar to positivism, appeared; in the seventh decade neocriticism, represented by F. A. Lange; and in the eighth the empiriocriticism of Avenarius.

At that time one view was proclaimed from all sides: we acquire knowledge through the senses and only through the senses. The only source of knowledge is experience; the only method of science is induction; the only objects of inquiry are facts. No absolutes, no metaphysics, are allowed, for these produce errors and insanity. Aims may be limited and results relative as long as the work is sober and honest. Knowledge, if it is not scientific, is worth nothing. One can come to philosophy only through science. Art should be based on the results of science. Science confirms the laws of nature on which everything else depends, not excluding man and his works, his morality, economy, religion, and art, for even these are creations of nature.

This was the leading doctrine of the nineteenth century. It was characterized by intellectualism, indifference to metaphysics, and naturalism. Because science corroborates necessary relationships, the nineteenth century defended determinism—although in practice it fought for freedom. It explained the characteristics of individuals in terms of their surroundings, thus subordinating the individual to the environment—although in life it fought for the rights of the individual. It explained phenomena *retrospectively*, as having been caused by factors which took effect slowly and by stages—although in life it was *prospectively* inclined and believed in rapid progress. It explained the organization of the world historically, as the work of time which created ever new forms of existence—although it imagined (or at least its most typical representatives did) that after the realization of its social ideals time would cease, and there would be no more history.

Other Philosophical Positions

Minimalism was the representative position of this period, yet it was not the only one. It attracted many but not all progressive thinkers. Then, too, philosophical reactionaries still existed. In Germany, the Hegelian right wing did not become extinct. One of its representatives, C. L. Michelet, professor at the University of Berlin, lived until 1893. The French attended schools of philosophy which, until the end of the century, were based on the program of Victor Cousin. The English, who until the beginning of the century had never passed through a phase of idealistic metaphysics, now began to take an interest in it. T. H. Green in 1874 exhorted English youth to close their Mill and Spencer and to open Kant and Hegel, but he was appealing to a philosophy which, on the continent, already belonged to the past. And in Poland, in the days of positivism, the most active philosopher, Henryk Struve, a "real idealist," was an opponent of positivism.

Metaphysicians of another type also appeared, those who deprecated all previous metaphysics and wished to create a new brand of metaphysics. They even appeared among thinkers who were pioneers of the empirical sciences. In Germany, H. Lotze, a pioneer of natural psychology, also announced a metaphysical system (1841, 1879). G. T. Fechner, founder of psychophysics, was also the author of a spiritualistic metaphysics in phantastic poetical guise (1879). In France, the spiritualism of Maine de Biran was intensified by F. Ravaisson who, having wide influence as inspector of higher education, was able to disseminate this view. C. Secretan, professor at the University of Geneva, and E. Vacherot, professor at the University of Paris, also developed spiritualistic doctrines. In England, F. H. Bradley of Oxford came out with a new idealism in 1876. These men were metaphysicians in days when metaphysics was generally disavowed. But even with them, metaphysics had the characteristic symptoms of the age. It tried to establish connections with the natural sciences, to be "scientific," "inductive" metaphysics.

The History of Problems and the History of Philosophers

In history one can observe how philosophy posed the problems it tried to solve. In solving them, however, it generated new problems, which it left to future investigators. In this way its course of development ran and still continues to run from problem to problem. One can conclude that the history of philosophy is the history of problems, and that the individual has only an executive function.

Nonetheless, such a conclusion is only partially true. Most problems still pertinent today were posed more than two thousand years ago. The centuries have advanced new solutions rather than new problems. Which of these ancient problems were solved, however, depended on the individual and his interests as well as on the needs of society. Individuals selected the problems, and, in solving them in their own ways, influenced future history. Therefore, individuals have been factors no less important in the development of philosophy than the problems themselves.

Moreover, not all philosophers began with problems. It was not always true that problems came first and then theories were constructed to solve them. Many philosophers began immediately from theories, conceptions, ideas, propositions, convictions—certain visions of the world or life. Problems arose for them only secondarily. Many handed down to posterity not problems but formed conceptions.

Rarely, however, had philosophy faced so many problems at once as it did in the 1830s. The problems posed by the rationalistic philosophy of the seventeenth century and the empirical philosophy of the eighteenth had not yet faded away; problems that had been raised by the mystics and by Rousseau were still recurring, when Kant and Hegel, ideological and radical philosophers, introduced still new ones. However, which of these problems received attention depended on the philosophers active at the time. Notwithstanding the great transformation that took place after his death, Hegel's influence on the selection of problems continued for at least another generation.

Not only loyal Hegelians were dependent on him for the selection of their problems. His opponents, too, were tied to his all-embracing system, idealistic, universalistic, abstract, intellectualistic, and synthetic. Feuerbach, then Marx and Engels, became enmeshed in its coils, for it was in combating his idealism that they created a new type of materialism. Stirner also became bound to Hegel, but he disagreed with Hegel's universalism and tried to construct a philosophy of the independent individual. Kierkegaard also was linked to Hegel, but he hated abstract philosophy and took the lead in creating a concrete philosophy of existence. Newman knew little about Hegel, whom he could not endure, but he lived in a similar atmosphere of intellectualism and, in opposition to Hegel, developed a philosophy of faith. Cousin was impressed by Hegel, but also by other currents, and against this background he constructed his eclectic philosophy. The synthetic nature of Hegel's system offended Comte and Cousin, and, in order to avoid it, they developed a system based on positive facts. This was nonetheless a *system*, and it is in fact possible to discern echoes of Hegelianism in it. Many of the theories constructed about the year 1830, then, had a similar point of departure. However, they developed in different directions.

At that time there were, to be sure, philosophers who had a different point of departure. Mill is foremost in this group. Hegelianism and all systems were alien to him. He embraced the tradition of empiricism.

In the next generation, about 1860, different problems came to the fore. Hegel was no longer in favor. Kierkegaard and Stirner found little sympathy. Mill and Comte were left in command of the field. Their positive view of the world now became the point of departure, as in the previous generation Hegel's system had been. But again, various individuals parceled up this theory in different ways, which led to different problems. Spencer made it agree with the theory of evolution, Lange with the views of Kant; Mach erected on its foundations a theory of the natural sciences, and Taine a theory of the humanistic sciences.

When a third generation had grown up about 1880, some of its representatives were still developing the problems of positivistic philosophy, while others had gone on to new problems and had begun to work on the unsatisfactory aspects of positivistic philosophy. Boutroux and Poincaré elaborated a theory of the natural sciences, Dilthey of the humanities, Brentano of the theory of knowledge, and Nietzsche of culture.

The development of philosophical problems in the nineteenth century was as dependent on the internal logic of the problems as on the individuality of the philosophers and the cultural conditions of the epoch.

Phases of Development

If we may overlook the years 1800–1830* and regard only the remaining part of the nineteenth century, considering it as one period, one can and should divide it into three phases.

The first phase, from 1830 to 1860, although indistinct and transitional, was nevertheless the most productive and abundant in new philosophical ideas. This period produced the positivism of Comte in France and the new empiricism of Mill in England. The dialectical materialism of Marx and Engels was formulated. Succeeding generations of the nineteenth century lived on the ideas produced in this period, further developing and disseminating them.

---

*The two volumes published in English, *Nineteenth Century Philosophy* and *Twentieth Century Philosophy* are part of a complete philosophical history first written in Polish [Trans.].

Moreover, this phase, in its vitality and diversity, produced views that would mature only in the remote future. The nineteenth century did not wish, or perhaps did not yet know how, to make use of them. They became accepted only in the twentieth century. Among these were ideas in the field of logic that attempted to make this most precise of all philosophical disciplines still more precise. In this period De Morgan and Boole in England gave a great impetus to mathematical logic, and Bolzano in Prague contributed new logical formulations. In Russia, Belinski, Chernyshevsky, and Dobroliubov produced a novel, realistic, and social aesthetic. In addition, ideas concerning man and his relationship to God and the world were also born, ideas which were to find a large number of supporters only much later. These views were developed by the Englishmen Carlyle and Cardinal Newman and by the Dane Kierkegaard.

The second phase of the century (after 1860) already had a rather well formulated philosophy, positivism, and during this period it was systematically and precisely cultivated. The first phase had laid the foundations, the second erected the walls. In the name of its doctrine, it tried to "parcel up" philosophy. It wanted to divorce those areas from philosophy which could become specialized sciences, empirical and naturalistic. These positivistic philosophers were convinced that science develops more successfully when it is cultivated independently from philosophy.

The majority of the philosophers and the wide mass of the intelligentsia were satisfied with positivist philosophy. They even saw in it the limit to which the development of human reason could aspire, the zenith of scientific possibilities. In the course of time, however, even some of the supporters of positivism began to subject their own doctrine to criticism.

And about 1880, a third philosophical phase began which lasted to the end of the century. It was transitional in nature, for at that time minimalistic philosophy still predominated, but arguments from all sides already began to clamor against it. These arguments led to a process of change in philosophical views that was not completed until the next century.

The First Phase: 1830-1860

Positivism, empiricism, and dialectical materialism were the most important views of this period. Positivism was initiated by Comte, empiricism by Mill, and dialectical materialism by Marx and Engels. These views refer to seemingly parallel phenomena. Each has a different character but developed from a similar base, careful and sober, anti-metaphysical and anti-idealistic. Positivism began in France, empiricism in England, and dialectical materialism among German immigrants in the West.

These views had in common a sober tone evident in all countries. "To be a philosopher," Stendhal wrote, "one must be dry, clear, and without illusions." This tone was not confined to philosophers. It became common to the entire intelligentsia. "Our age, so ill-reputed, so notoriously prosaic, our generation so repelled by reverence and faith and by idealists"—so wrote Seweryn Goszczynski in 1842.

Another doctrine of this period should also be added—the realism of Herbart. Herbart, to be sure, was a contemporary of Hegel and announced his philosophy not much later. Chronologically, therefore, he belongs to the previous period. But his doctrine became widespread and gained recognition only after 1830. For this reason he can be included in this later period, especially because the nature of his views is more akin to it in spirit.

Positivism, empiricism, naturalism, and dialectical materialism were the newest, most independent, and most vital creations of this period. This does not mean, however, that they were the most widely disseminated. Neither Comte, Mill, Marx, nor Engels occupied university chairs. The leading official philosophical posts were in other hands.

In England, Mill had to contend with the great popularity of the Scottish school in the form which Hamilton had given it. In France, eclectic spiritualism, largely shaped by Cousin, was stronger than Comte's philosophy. The Hegelians still occupied university chairs in Germany, and Schelling was still alive.

The philosophies of Feuerbach and Marx must be understood
against this background. These currents—the Scottish school,
spiritualism, and Hegelianism—were still strong, but they were
fading. They were connected with the past, not with the future.

In the first decade after Hegel's death (1830-1840), the
strength of Hegelianism was even greater than during his lifetime. It had both a right and a left wing, giving rise to reaction as well as progress. Virtually the entire philosophy of
history of those times was derived from it. The leading German
philosophers of the second half of the nineteenth century, such
as Fechner and Lotze, were nurtured in its atmosphere. New
views were formulated in polemics against it. Its main center
was Germany, but its influence spread to France, Italy, and the
Slavic countries. Among the Hegelians were I. Hanuš and F.
Palacky in Czechoslovakia; Chomaikov, Aksakov, and B. Chicherin
in Russia; and Libelt, Cieszkowski, and Dembowski in Poland.
In Germany, the doctrine receded slowly, attacked from all
sides, by the realism of Herbart and the materialism of Marx,
by naturalists and by historians. At the University of Berlin
the greatest efforts in combatting Hegelianism were made by
F. A. Trendelenburg (1802-1872; *Logical Investigations*, 1840),
who espoused the doctrines of Aristotle and arrayed them
against Hegel.

This period also produced the socio-ethical doctrines of
Carlyle and Stirner and the religio-ethical views of Kierkegaard and Newman. These views were not related to positivism
or materialism, the main currents of the period, nor were they
related to views then in decline—the philosophies of common
sense and metaphysical idealism. They had an original position,
expressing the need to account for emotions, which was not done
adequately by empiricism or naturalism.

The beginning of this period is clearly delineated. One
can only point to the year 1860 as an approximate end. The
essential fact is that in 1859 Darwin's *On the Origin of Species* brought to a close a whole series of scientific discoveries based on a positivistic, scientific view of the world. Of
course, Mill was still alive and would continue to write for a
long time, and Marx did not publish his main work until 1867.
Nonetheless, their ideas had been formulated earlier. Mill's
System of Logic appeared in 1843, the *Communist Manifesto* in
1848. Therefore, their place is in this first period.

Superficially, this period was peaceful, ingenuous, and
prosperous, without wars and historical catastrophes. Although
there were no wars, the years 1830 and 1848 produced "The
Spring of Peoples," moods of an almost chiliastic and messianic
nature, of great expectations and feverish competition. Rarely
in history had there been such intense social movements. Utopian socialism was vigorous; the "phalangists" and "phalanstery"
were developing; scientific socialism was being formulated.

Neither was there peace for the individual. The discontent of romanticism had not yet faded. Many works of this period expressed disquiet, embitterment, internal emptiness, and pessimism—*Confessions of a Child of the Century* by de Musset, *Adolph* by Benjamin Constant, "Dominique" by Fromentin. Schopenhauer, still alive and active, was gathering an increasing number of supporters. "Our generation, as its predecessor," wrote Taine, "has been touched by the sickness of the age and will never completely recover from it. We shall arrive at truth, but we shall not have peace." Against this background of political troubles and psychological disturbances the philosophical doctrines of the age must be considered—peaceful, balanced, soberly making their way to limited but certain knowledge, to a greater satisfaction with life. Philosophy is sometimes a rather accurate reflection of its epoch, but at other times—such as the middle of the nineteenth century—it is a criticism of its age and a complement to it. Positivism was only beginning at this time, but it reflected the age that was ending. Its creators and supporters might not have admitted this but although positivism had ascended to a very subtle intellectual plateau, it had lost its elasticity, its power of conquering, its faith in itself and the future. Its philosophy had to be minimalistic, because it wished to close old accounts with the world rather than open new ones.

Mill developed a theory of knowledge and Comte an encyclopedia of the sciences. Both of them treated theoretical philosophical problems, but they did not confine themselves to these problems. They also considered social and religious philosophy. They had practical intentions, to perfect people's lives through philosophy. This was even more true of Feuerbach and Marx. The former was primarily concerned with problems of religion, the latter with problems of society.

The representatives of secondary and opposition movements, however, were concerned with these problems only. The main interest of both Stirner and Carlyle was the problem of the individual's relationship with other people; for Kierkegaard and Newman it was his relationship to God. In this area they expressed their opposition to the irreligious trend of contemporary philosophy, for Kierkegaard and Newman regarded religion as the most important element in man's life. The main currents of the century, Comte's altruism and Mill's utilitarianism, evolved a social and egalitarian ethic, while Stirner evolved an asocial one and Carlyle an elitist one. In addition to these particular problems of ethics and the philosophy of religion, their opposition aimed at something deeper and more far-reaching. For instance, Carlyle's arguments were derived from ancient pantheistic and spiritualistic metaphysics; the source of Newman's propositions was the emotionalistic theory of knowledge.

Contemporaries view the philosophy of their age differently than does their posterity, which has the advantage of perspective and, living in another epoch, holds different views. Contemporaries have to overcome opposition to new ideas, whereas posterity remembers only the new ideas. After one hundred years the philosophies of Comte and Marx are seen as holding first place, because we know that succeeding generations adopted them. We rank second the philosophies of Carlyle, Newman, or Kierkegaard, because we know that their views later found only sympathy. There is hardly any mention by posterity of the pupils of Hamilton, Cousin, or Herbart, because we know that they remained mere disciples. At that time, however, current opinion was otherwise. These lesser men were the most numerous, occupying most of the university chairs and enjoying the most respect. Statistically speaking, therefore, their philosophy was the typical philosophy of the epoch. They predominated in the period that had already produced Comte, Mill, Marx, and Kierkegaard. For the time being, these latter were respected or even recognized by only a small number of contemporaries. It is important to remember this whenever one looks for the seeds of the future in the philosophy of the past. However, it is no less important to know this past as it actually was.

Philosophical views continuously make their way from the philosopher's study to the wider circles of the intelligentsia. But only parts of these views become very widely disseminated. Frequently a long time separates the origin of an idea from its wide acceptance. For this reason, in the nineteenth century the views of specialists were different from the general opinion. Specialists professed views that had not yet been accepted by the general public, and by the time these views were accepted the specialists already had new ones. The ideas of Comte and Mill, which conquered the entire intelligentsia in the next generation, were in Comte's lifetime and Mill's youth the common property of only a small group. Mill writes clearly about this in his *Autobiography*, and the ill-fortunes of Comte are well known. Of Newman's views only his religious ones scored immediate success. The social and political ideas of Marx and Engels found ready acceptance, but their philosophical views reached wider circles much later.

This situation is even more evident in the case of Boole's and De Morgan's (1848) ideas on logic and of Bolzano's theory of "truths in themselves" (1837). These concepts never spread beyond a tiny circle during the entire century. Developments in mathematical logic paved the way for the wider acceptance of the first set of ideas, and the second group owed its later success to advances in phenomenology. Notwithstanding lags, however, these views were important. Boole and De Morgan brought logic and mathematics closer together, leading to the further development of both these sciences and to a clearer explanation of the nature of the deductive sciences in general. Bolzano, on the other hand, elaborated a new position akin to non-metaphysical Platonism. He demonstrated that the analysis of our perceptions indicates that they comprise not only individual and relative propositions but also universal and certain ones. This view was neither positivism nor a reversion to the speculative metaphysics prevalent in his day. It was a third, more moderate position, for which his age had no understanding but whose apogee came later.

Above all, the historian wishes to establish when philosophy originated new ideas and when it was at its peak. But the novelty and number of philosophical ideas do not always coincide with the flowering of philosophical thought—if by flowering one means an intensified interest in spreading or reviving a general philosophical movement. Original philosophers do not write only when the general public takes an interest in philosophy. Nonetheless, during the period 1830-1860 philosophy was not flowering. At the beginning of the century, judging by occupation, the number of people interested in metaphysical systems was declining. Scholars and the masses were turning their thoughts to other matters. At just this time, however, many philosophical talents were produced, and many fundamental ideas were formulated.

The following order seems proper for presenting the views of this period: first, the most important and most representative views—those of Comte, Mill, Marx, and Engels; second, the more specialized and personal positions—those of Stirner, Carlyle, Newman, and Kierkegaard.

COMTE AND POSITIVISM

The current that began this new period in the history of philosophy was positivism, originated in France by Auguste Comte. His aspiration was to hold to facts and avoid metaphysics. He grafted this aspiration onto the epoch, although he himself realized it only partially, for he grew up in an earlier, metaphysical period and retained some of its features, in particular the yearning for a great synthesis, an all-embracing system.

Life

Auguste Comte (1798-1857) was born in Southern France, in Montpellier, and was educated in Paris in the newly opened Ecole Polytechnique. He was the first philosopher in history to complete a course of technical studies. After completing

his studies, he lived in Paris and earned his livelihood by
tutoring in mathematics. From 1818 and for more than six
years, he was closely associated with the great utopian social
reformer Saint-Simon, but later severed the association. As
early as 1826 he sketched the outline of his system in a series
of private lectures. Only a small number of persons heard him,
but this group included some outstanding contemporary scholars,
mathematicians, and natural scientists. A nervous breakdown
did not permit him to finish this course of lectures. After
two years, however, he was able to return to work. From 1832,
he was a tutor of analysis and mechanics at the Polytechnic,
and from 1837, an examiner. In spite of his efforts, he did
not gain a more important academic position, and, in 1848, lost
even this modest position. His conviction that science should
be completely reformed, and that he had been called to do so,
antagonized the official representatives of science. Later, he
lived only on what his friends and pupils gave him. From 1845,
his interests turned to social, metaphysical, and religious
problems. His aspiration to reform expanded, encompassing the
entire organization of the world. He began to expound a "religion of humanity." He was a strange person, externally modest
yet convinced of his mission. He was a positivistic scholar
and, at the same time, the archpriest of the cult he had created.

Arrangement of Philosophical Camps in France About 1830

Around 1830, when Comte introduced his positivistic theory,
French philosophy was divided into two camps. One was sensualist, close to materialism. This was the camp of the "ideolo-
gues." It was an inheritance from the eighteenth century but
was now losing strength. The second camp represented a directly opposite tendency; it was spiritualistic. It had developed
later and had the vital characteristics of a nascent movement.
Maine de Biran belonged to this group, as did Catholic traditionalists from the time of the Restoration—de Bonald, de
Maistre, and Chateaubriand. But the movement was headed by the
eclectic philosophers—Cousin and his pupils. In its eclectic
form, this spiritualism became the prevalent philosophy of
France and remained so for a long time. All new currents arising in France had to contend with it, and one must view the
origin and development of positivism against the background of
this philosophy.

Writings

Comte's main work was the six-volume *Course of Positive Philosophy* (1830-1842), written in a heavy and diffuse style. Many people in the nineteenth century adored it, but few wished to read it, preferring to draw their information about positivism from other sources. Comte expressed his views in shortened form in *Discourse on the Positive Spirit* (1844). He expressed his later social, metaphysical, and religious views in *System of Positive Polity* (4 volumes, 1851-1854).

Predecessors

Comte's views were so strikingly similar to those of some thinkers of the previous century—especially d'Alembert, but also Turgot and Condorcet—that their views are sometimes referred to by the name "positivism," a term introduced by Comte. Their philosophic position was the same as his and was maintained more consistently.

In the generation that preceded him, many thinkers had similar ideas, but for the most part they only sketched out what he elaborated in detail. Comte himself pointed to the similarity of his position and that of the mathematician Sophie Germain (1776-1831). She asserted that many errors had their source in the fact that people seek to discover the origins of the universe, wishing to reach eternal existence through knowledge of the world. Mathematics does not do this and for this reason is free from such errors. Through it one can accomplish a reform of philosophy. Above all, this reform will consist in abandoning the question "why" to enable one to inquire only "how" things are in the world.

The prehistory of positivism dates back to even earlier times. As initiators of the movement Comte mentioned Bacon, Descartes, and Galileo. He also spoke as though Newton had already grasped the idea of positivism. As his major predecessor, however, Comte correctly mentioned Hume. Renan, himself close to the position of positivism, rather grudgingly said that in general Comte only repeated in bad style what had already been written in good style by Descartes, d'Alembert, and Laplace.

Comte's views were formulated not only under the influence of scientists and philosophers, but also under those of the reformers and utopian socialists of his epoch. The most famous of them was Claude Henri de Saint-Simon, who taught him that the way to achieve universal human happiness is through industry and science. He taught Comte to consider science not only as pure theory, but also as a means of reforming the world. Saint-Simon was a pupil of the positivist d'Alembert. Without being a philosopher himself, he became a link in the develop-

ment of philosophy, namely a link between the earlier positivism of the eighteenth century and the new positivism, which
began in the nineteenth as a complete system, not only in science but also in life.

Though the philosophy begun by Comte displaced idealistic
and spiritualistic philosophy, it was related to them in many
ways. Even great turning points in thought take place gradually, and Comte's positivism is an example of this. His views
are similar to those expounded by the creators of idealistic
systems, especially Hegel. He also borrowed much from his
French opponents, the spiritualists and traditionalists. He
accepted the stress that de Maistre and de Bonald placed on the
transcendental element in society, on the notion that society
is not reducible to the individuals that comprise it, on the
idea of social authority. He benefited from them, when—to oppose the anarchy of his time—he based a conservative political
policy on science and positivistic philosophy. From them he
also took the slogan of order, which he fused with the slogan
of progress and through which he injected many conservative motifs into the positivistic movement.

Views

1. Positivistic Philosophy. Comte, in giving philosophy
the name "positive," wished to express: first, that it is exclusively concerned with real objects, avoiding the imaginary
and investigating only objects accessible to human thought, not
occult processes; second, that it considers only useful themes,
avoiding the sterile, and wishes to serve the improvement of
life and not the satisfaction of idle curiosity; third, that it
confines itself to objects about which one can acquire certain
knowledge, avoiding uncertainties, which lead to interminable
disputes; fourth, that it concerns itself with precise questions, avoiding obscure ones; fifth, that it operates posi-
tively and does not confine itself to negative criticism.

According to Comte, a positivistic philosopher is one who
understands that the natural sciences have created an incompa-
rable model for scientific inquiry, and whoever applies this
model gives up speculative philosophy for factual investigations. One who avoids absolute assertions, replacing them by
relative ones, is also a positivist.

However, these characteristics are not unique to positivism. Every minimalistic philosophy confines itself to facts
and relative assertions and stresses reality, utility, certainty, precision, and the positiveness of its inquiries. In addition to this, however, positivism asserts that knowledge is

primarily concerned with physical facts, with material objects exclusively. I cannot say—Comte was convinced—that we possess knowledge of psychic facts. We do not have this knowledge, for it is not possible to be the subject and the object of knowledge at the same time. Introspective inquiry is a chimera. How, for instance, can one investigate one's own emotions, when this investigation requires the control of the emotions? This objective, antipsychological attitude was the feature of positivism that distinguished it from other forms of minimalism. One group of nineteenth-century minimalists followed his lead, while another adopted a directly opposite position, asserting that psychic facts alone are given to us directly and, for this reason, only they can be the foundation of knowledge. Therefore, in the nineteenth century minimalism divided into two types: the antipsychological and the psychological.

One generally speaks of "positivistic" philosophy and "positivism" as having two meanings. In the wider sense it is minimalistic philosophy in general, careful, holding to facts, avoiding speculation. In the narrower sense, it is philosophy that considers external facts, material objects as the only objects of an honest science. Mill, for instance, was a positivist in the first sense only, whereas Comte was one in both senses.

2. *The Development of Humanity*. Comte thought that the positivistic conception of the world was the most perfect human creation and could have been conceived only during humanity's highest peak of development. According to Comte, humanity's intellectual development passed through three stages: the theological, the metaphysical, and finally the positive. In the first phase humanity explained phenomena by appealing to spirits and in the second by referring to abstract concepts. In the first period it was governed by feelings, in the second by the intellect. Both the intellect and the feelings create fictions: the fictions created by the feelings give rise to mythology, the ones created by the intellect lead to metaphysics. Mythology and metaphysics dominated humanity in turn, and only after freeing itself from them could it enter a further phase of development. According to Comte, positivistic philosophy, finally free from mythology and metaphysics, made this development possible. It alone states facts, explaining them neither by the soul nor by abstractions and thus forms the highest and final phase of development. Therefore, this positivist thought in a manner similar to that of the metaphysician Hegel, who also saw in his own doctrine the final, highest summit in the development of human thought.

Comte stressed the fact that, although humanity passes through three phases, at bottom the second phase differs but little from the first. Together, they contrast with the positivistic phase: both are phases of illusions in opposition to the phase of positivistic cognition. "The middle phase," he wrote, "is much more closely related to the earlier than the later phase"; "metaphysics is at bottom a kind of theology." He had less sympathy for metaphysics than for theology, for the latter can at least be a consistent faith, whereas the former is always an inconsistent philosophy.

3. *The Discovery and Anticipation of Facts.* The only things accessible to the mind are facts. The leading rule of science is not to make assertions that are not based on some fact or other. The razor of positivistic philosophy was turned against all efforts to go beyond facts, in particular against searching for the causes of facts that lie beyond the facts themselves.

However, the aim of science is not limited to registering facts; these are only the material for further inquiries. The true task of science is to elaborate and establish fixed relationships between facts, in other words, to establish laws. This feasible aim should supersede the impractical tasks that science has hitherto posed, particularly the search for causes. Nevertheless, it must be remembered that laws are nothing more than fixed relationships. They are either relationships of probability or laws of succession.

On the basis of this knowledge of laws governing facts science can anticipate further facts. *Savoir pour prévoir*, to acquire knowledge in order to predict, was the formula of Comte. His conception of prediction was broad: not only as the establishment of future facts, but also of unknown present facts, and even past ones.

Hence, true science builds on experiences. Yet, it is not composed of experiences alone. On the contrary, it strives to make them superfluous, to reach beyond them and replace them by predictions. For this reason, Comte was an opponent of empiricism, if empiricism is conceived as restricting science to simply collecting experiences. "Pure empiricism is sterile," he said. He even asserted that true positivistic philosophy is, at bottom, as far from empiricism as it is from mysticism: it should steer between these two—equally disastrous, as he thought—impracticable ways. In investigating facts, the scientist cannot be wholly passive, if only because an infinite variety of facts exists and, to orient oneself, guiding hypotheses are necessary. In a thesis that was unexpected in a follower of Bacon and Hume, Comte asserted that thought shows the way to experience, and that the final aim of science is to make experience unnecessary, to replace it with reasoning.

He did not inquire how a generalization of facts and their prediction is possible: in general, he did not pose epistemological problems, and this restriction was characteristic of positivists. They did not wish to be theorists of knowledge but only methodologists. They believed that, because we know facts objectively, it is unnecessary to pose the main problem of the theory of knowledge: how is the knowledge of objective facts possible? Hence, they saw their task not as searching for the foundations of science but—as Bacon and d'Alembert had done—as classifying its results.

4. *The Classification of the Sciences*. Above all, Comte distinguished between abstract and concrete sciences. The first deal with general laws governing the elementary facts of nature, and the second consider the ways in which these facts appear in experience. For instance, mineralogy does not deal with laws, for the laws from which mineralogy originated are general mechanical and chemical laws of physics and chemistry; it only deals with the concrete forms in which mechanical and physical laws manifest themselves in the minerals of our planet. Physics and chemistry are abstract sciences; mineralogy is a concrete one. A similar relationship holds between an abstract science such as physiology and such concrete ones as zoology and botany. Abstract sciences deal with the processes by which things change, while concrete sciences consider the things themselves. Comte believed that the concrete sciences are not yet truly formed, and that they will only be able to develop on the basis of the abstract sciences on which they depend. In his classification, Comte considered only the abstract sciences.

He listed but six of them. As the criterion of his classification he chose their lesser or greater generality. The most general science, which deals with all manner of forms, was mathematics. After this, he placed astronomy, or the mechanics of the heavens, which he broadly conceived as the science dealing with the movement of all bodies; next, physics and chemistry, which he considered less general, for they only apply to terrestrial bodies, and after these, the still less general sciences of biology and sociology, which deal exclusively with living bodies. In a manner typical of positivism, he considered mathematics as the most general inductive science, in its nature not different from the natural sciences. In sociology, however, he included all disciplines that study the abstract science of man.

In this classification all the sciences were arranged according to their generality—but also according to their complexity, for the generality of the sciences is inversely proportional to their complexity. Mathematics, the most general, considers the most simple facts, whereas sociology, the least general, deals with the most complex facts. At the same time, the sciences in this classification were arranged in the order of their mutual dependence: astronomy depends on mathematical laws, physics on astronomical ones, chemistry on physical ones, biology on chemical ones; sociology depends on all these laws.

In Comte's time the first five of these sciences were already formed and developed. Only the sixth, sociology, did not yet exist. Nonetheless, Comte postulated it, for it was necessary to his system. He had to construct it himself. In constructing it, however, he asserted—and this was his great achievement—that it is possible and necessary to extend the thesis concerning the existence of general laws from the natural sciences to the sciences that deal with humanity. He applied the historical method to sociology, reaching general conclusions by comparing historically known forms of human existence. These conclusions were then tested against biology: he conceived society as a biologist understands animals and plants, as an organism, for he believed that all components of society are mutually dependent. His sociology was divided into two parts: social statics, dealing with the social order, and social dynamics, the science of progress. These ideas of its founder determined the development of sociology in the nineteenth century.

5. *The Task of Philosophy.* Although he was a philosopher, Comte did not include philosophy in his classification of the sciences. He held that all phenomena capable of investigation are the property of the various other sciences, and that nothing is left for philosophy. He was convinced that only phenomena are real, that metaphysics has literally nothing to consider. It is impossible to inquire into causes and ends of phenomena, especially the first cause and final goal. Metaphysical debates, particularly those of the materialists and spiritualists, seemed empty to him. In his rather simplistic understanding, metaphysics was simply false interpretation of existence derived from abstractions; in particular, he maintained that the Platonic theory of ideas wholly resulted from this error.

Comte's positivism also denied the theory of knowledge. Inquiries into whether and how knowledge was possible, defined as nonsensical doubts concerning the existence of external bodies, seemed to him unnecessary. He believed that "common sense long since has given up such a philosophy." What is more, it excluded logic: abstract inquiries, separated from particular facts, seemed barren to him. Toward the end, he considered general methodology chimera. He asserted that psychology was impossible, that one cannot be both observer and observed at the same time. This denial of psychology gave positivism its distinctive character, separating it from otherwise related minimalistic trends, which also limited science to the investigation of facts. For positivism, only external facts remained.

Thus, for extreme positivism not only were metaphysical philosophical problems eliminated, but even the narrower ones—epistemological, logical, methodological, psychological—by which the newer philosophy had replaced metaphysics. Only one task remained for philosophy—the theory of the sciences. But even in this field the investigation of the assumptions or principles of science is not part of philosophy. Only the sciences themselves can deal with them. Hence, only an encyclopedic task remained for philosophy: to set down what the particular sciences have achieved. In limiting himself to this, Comte believed that he avoided the "terrible risk" of metaphysical philosophy and reached the "prudent reserve of positivism."

Positivism wished neither to assert nor deny any matters that went beyond facts. Hence, it did not become involved in atheism. It did not deny purpose in the world, even admitting that the hypothesis of purposefulness is more probable than the hypothesis of blind mechanism. Nor did its assumptions lead to materialism; Comte considered this an unscientific position, for matter, conceived of as the cause of phenomena, is not and cannot be the object of experience. He regarded "matter" as the same kind of metaphysical fiction as "soul." In addition he argued that the materialistic mechanism of his times erroneously reduced higher phenomena to lower, reduced the psychic and social to the mechanistic.

Comte's assertions did not lead to *skepticism*; he considered that position quite as unfounded and still more dangerous than absolutism. Positivism and skepticism differed in that (as one of Comte's pupils, Littré, stated it) "skepticism submits everything to doubt, while the philosophy of positivism only doubts what is beyond experience and recognizes only what is in experience." Nor did positivism imply probabilism, which proclaimed that assertions can only be probable—for science states completely unquestionable laws.

The attitude of positivism does not seem foreign to the average person. Comte asserted that it is simply the position of common sense, wholly respectful of facts. Science merely elaborates what common sense knows. It derives its first principles from that source, but it later generalizes them; this is the main difference between them.

6. *The Social Dependence of Science.*   Our knowledge of
facts and their relationships is certain but relative.   "The investigation of phenomena never leads to a nonrelative knowledge
of them; knowledge always remains dependent on our organism and
situation."   Astronomy, for instance, could never arise in a
society of blind people, nor in the presence of nonshining
stars, nor if the atmosphere were always hazy.   Finally, he
concluded that "only one thing is totally nonrelative, and that
is that nothing is nonrelative."

   "Our concepts are not exclusively individual phenomena;
they are also and even primarily social phenomena, the creation
of a continual collective evolution."   Consequently, theoretical investigations and our scientific knowledge depend not only
on individual conditions but also on social ones, on the fact
that people live and develop collectively.   For this reason,
philosophers became the victims of their own unrealistic conceptions, because in their deliberations they did not take into
account the social content and origin of their ideas.   The individual is an abstraction; the only reality is society.

   Science strives to embrace all phenomena in one unified
picture of the world, but phenomena are so diverse that they do
not permit such a picture.   In spite of this, science does not
relinquish its aim of constructing an unified picture of the
world, a synthetic system, but it can only attain this on a subjective base.   Unable to derive unity from the qualities of the
world, science derives it from the needs of man, from internal
experience.   Even sciences whose object is farthest from humanity, such as astronomy, are not exceptions.   Hence, Comte had
to introduce the subjective factor into the theory of science,
although his point of departure was wholly objective.   He also
wrote: "All theoretical considerations should be considered as
the creations of the intellect intended to satisfy our needs."
And as a result of this, in science "we must always return to
man."

7. *Positivistic Politics.*   It is natural and common for a
philosopher who has limited his theoretical aspirations to com-
pensate by extending the moral tasks of philosophy.   Comte did
this.   His underlying goal became to find a perfect social order for humanity, and positivistic philosophy was the preparatory means for achieving this goal.

   "The most important task of humanity," he wrote, "should
be the continual improvement of human nature, individual as
well as collective."   In the spirit of positivism, he stipulated that this perfecting can take place only "within the limits
set by the laws governing the real world."   The slogan of his

practical philosophy was: *vivre pour autrui*, live for others.
It implied a renunciation of certain personal rights for obligations to the whole; in its development, it led to sacrifices
by the strong for the weak and to adoration by the weak of the
strong. Consequently, this practical philosophy had similari-
ties with Christian teaching, albeit completely different foundations.

Humanity was its final end. This slogan displaced another
one, which had prevailed for centuries in Christian philosophy:
that the final end is God. To be sure, Comte did not originate
this new slogan, but he formulated it and placed it at the head
of his ethics and politics. One might have expected the representative of a careful, minimalistic philosophy to deny himself
the right of creating slogans, ideas, and goals and limit himself to a conceptual analysis of already existing slogans, ideas, and goals. But Comte was not a minimalist in this regard.
He not only investigated slogans, he also created them. At
most, his minimalism appeared in the fact that his slogans were
realistic ones.

He considered his most important contribution to positivism to be its application to practical matters, to politics.
"Up to now," he wrote,

> the struggle for power has been waged exclusively be-
> tween the representatives of theological and metaphys-
> ical philosophy; the positivistic school did not take
> part in it; now, however, it is prepared to do so.
> And it will finally solve political difficulties, for
> it alone is capable of reconciling the demands of
> order and progress.

Humanity, order, and progress were the main slogans of the practical philosophy of Comte.

The solution of political problems depended on transforming the political movement into a philosophical one, as the idealists and messianists had tried to do. He also believed that
the modern crisis can only be resolved by completely reorganiz-
ing the world on philosophical foundations. He devoted the
last part of his life to politics, to his project of improving
humanity. In this regard, he was not a minimalist, but typical
of the maximalistic epoch in which he had been born, an epoch
which sought not only a great synthesis of knowledge but also a
prompt deliverance of humanity.

*The Development of Comte and the
Last Phase of His Philosophy*

Generally, two phases in Comte's philosophy are distin-
guishable: *The Course of Positive Philosophy* belongs to the
first, *The System of Positive Polity* to the second. Only the
views of the first (which were discussed above) are considered
true positivism and a valuable contribution to philosophy; the
views of the second period are seen as a departure from positivism and as the collapse of an outstanding intellect, for in
this period his philosophy (which ended religious and metaphysical philosophy once and for all) turned into a metaphysics,
even a religion. His clear thought degenerated into oddities.
"The second half of my career," Comte wrote in the fourth volume of his *System*, "had the intention of turning philosophy into religion, just as the first changed science into philosophy."
     Yet, a more precise analysis indicates that Comte's first
phase contained the makings of the second, toward which he developed in a gradual, uninterrupted, progressive way. In part,
the change in his views was simply caused by the change in the
problems with which he was concerned. When he began to consider the problem of life, he became convinced that the principles
by which it had previously been explained were insufficient,
and that they could be further developed without the concepts
of entity and goal: only in the inorganic world is the whole dependent on the parts; in the organic world the parts are dependent on the whole. As he asserted in a letter to Mill in 1843,
this view directed him onto new paths.
     To this, he joined a second factor stemming from his inner
nature. His love for order was not less than his love for
facts. He wished to control every area of life. He could
leave no questions open; every one of them had to be solved.
This concept of knowledge ran contrary to the spirit of positivism and evolutionism. Because of this, his views often
lacked caution, that cardinal virtue of all minimalism. He was
not sufficiently impressed by the thought, which he so frequently repeated, that all scientific truths were relative. He
did not always remember that his own views were historically
conditioned, that sciences would continue to progress; he
thought that in the first half of the nineteenth century they
approached a completed state.
     Lastly, his need of absolute foundations and goals was as
strong as his need of holding to facts. He, who had renounced
the absolute, created a new absolute; he did not wish to consider God, but he elevated humanity to near divinity. He was used
to writing certain abstract nouns, such as Humanity, Nature,
and Order, with capital letters: perhaps one can justifiably de-
tect in this habit a tendency to create those "metaphysical existences" that he fought so stridently. He had a proclivity

for constructing systems from the very beginning, but with time
this became an ever stronger tendency to construct an absolute
system. Especially as he passed from scientific to political
problems, his inclination to establish controls and absolutes
intensified. Humanity became an almost suprareal object for
him; he began to call it the "Great Being," *Le Grand Être*.
More and more frequently, it replaced God in his speech.

In the end, he, who constantly repeated that he had extin-
guished the theological and metaphysical phase of humanity, created a new cult with prayers, rites, sacraments, churches, spiritual authorities, and saints. His "positivistic politics"
called not only for a religious order but also a theocratic one.
It entrusted teaching and healing to the clergy. It combated
parliamentarianism and called for a dictatorial power with inherited offices, censorship of books and of intellects, and a
fight against independent thought. It permitted scholars to
take up only such problems as had been approved by the authorities. It ordered all books that were not directly useful to
be burned. And finally, Comte, who had originally been a fanat-
ic supporter of the sciences, lost respect for them. He declared that abstract inquiries were unhealthy occupations for
people. He also began to express an antipathy for the Greeks
and a sympathy for the theocracy of the East, even for fetish-
ism, which in the end he declared to be a position close to
positivism.

Summary

Comte is considered by most historians to be the "creator
of positivism," and in a sense he was: in place of loosely connected positivistic ideas he created a great positivistic system. This is not contradicted by the fact that main ideas
of positivism had already been announced before him, that his
law of three phases is taken from Saint-Simon, and that his
classification of the sciences is little different from that of
d'Alembert.

But some historians doubt that Comte was a positivist at
all. And if one holds to his own designation, then Comte really was not a consistent and pronounced positivist, even in the
first phase of his philosophizing. Some of his predecessors,
particularly Hume and d'Alembert, and many of his followers
were more consistent positivists than the "creator of positivism." Positivism, or basing knowledge exclusively on facts,
was only one motif of his philosophy and one which he did not
wholly observe. There are even grounds for distinguishing the
philosophy of the creator of positivism from the philosophy of
positivism.

The program of limiting inquiry to things that are real, certain, precise, and positive; the conviction that all knowledge is relative, that science should be limited to facts, and that the naturalistic way of treating facts should be imposed severely on the humanities; the noninvolvement in transcendental problems, whether to support or rebut them; the stress on the social conditioning and social consequences of science, the conviction that one can arrive at a positivistic position only by stages—these are the characteristics of every positivism. The special features of Comte's positivism are that it was the third (and highest) phase of humanity's development; that the sciences must be classified according to their generality and complexity; that metaphysics, the theory of knowledge, logic, methodology, and psychology were all denied a place in his philosophy; that his ethics was based on altruism with the slogans of Humanity, Progress, and Order; that it led to a Religion of Humanity.

All these tenets were a part of positivism, but Comte blended them with other motifs that had no relationship to positivism and were even incompatible with it. He was a positivist, but he was also the son of a nonpositivistic epoch. He wrote down and propagated his system in the second third of the nineteenth century, which had already passed to minimalism, but he had already conceived this system in the first third. He can, in fact, be compared with the metaphysical idealists of that time with regard to their similar ways of philosophizing— synthetic and systematic, dogmatic, universalistic, and reformative. It is striking that this positivist considered Aristotle, St. Thomas, and Descartes to be the greatest philosophers, and deprecated Condillac. Of course, he occupies a distinctive place among the synthetic philosophers of the first half of the nineteenth century. He is distinguished by his awareness of facts, naturalism, relativism, and practical-mindedness. But despite these differences, like other synthetic philosophers, he strove to construct an all-embracing system, one that would encompass all truth and quickly save humanity. He began as a minimalist but ended as maximalist. His point of departure was positivistic, but his aspirations were similar to those of the great system builders of the nineteenth century. These aspirations caused him to stray from positivism.

Comte and Hegel have always been considered opposites—the former an extreme minimalist, the latter an extreme maximalist. Only much later did it become apparent how much they have in common: both of them aspired to a synthesis; although they were relativists, both created absolute systems; both placed the greatest stress on social phenomena; both arrived at a conservative view in politics; both imagined that the world developed in a threefold rhythm; both were convinced that they were ushering in the last epoch of history.

Influence

All the same, Comte helped make positivism the dominant philosophy of the nineteenth century. He prompted thinking in a direction that he himself observed only partially. As J. S. Mill observed, positivism was certainly not the property of Comte but of the century. Various thinkers who were close to positivism, such as Spencer and Buckle, denied that they were in any way indebted to Comte.

Mill, an original thinker himself, spread Comte's earlier philosophy in England, imparting to it a distinctive hue. And when positivism became the prevailing trend all over Europe in the second half of the nineteenth century, it perhaps had more of Mill, Buckle, and Spencer in it than of Comte.

Comte left two schools in France. One of them, headed by E. Littré, remained true to the *Course* and rejected Comte's later views as a departure from his own slogans. It was rather close to the movement started by Mill and formed an extreme minimalistic splinter group in French philosophy. It influenced such outstanding intellects of the mid-nineteenth century as Renan and Taine and imbued these philosophers with a disrespect for philosophy.

Comte's second school, however, recognized as truth everything he had ever said. At its head was P. Laffitte. It also called itself positivism, although it was of a very different species from the former. In accord with the last aspirations of its master, it was more of a religious community than a philosophical school. It proclaimed the religious "cult of humanity." Its participants considered Littré an "enemy of the master." They read Comte's writings as the Bible; they deemed it sacrilege to deny any of his views; they worshipped him not only "as a philosopher, the chief of the positivist school, but also as the creator of a universal religion and the first priest of humanity." Its communities and churches, organized for the most part in France and England, have lasted into the present. In the United States Henry Edger successfully preached the ideas of positivism. In the 1870s its communities and churches spread to South America, especially to Brazil, where the "Church of the Positivistic Apostolate" was formed with an "Apostle of Humanity" at its head and with the great "Temple of Humanity" in Rio de Janiero. Comte's slogan, "Order and Progress," was stamped on currency in the Republic of Brazil.

Littré

Emile Littré (1801-1881), although he was a philosopher only secondarily, played an important role in the history of positivism. He was more responsible for spreading it than Comte himself, and positivism in the second half of the nineteenth century bore more qualities of his intellect than of Comte's.

He was a physician, natural scientist, philologist, and historian, as well as a journalist and man of letters. He was one of the most eminent translators in France: he produced a famous translation of Hippocrates (10 volumes, 1839-1862) and translated the entire *Natural History* of Pliny, the methodological work of Herschel, the physiological writings of J. Muller, and Strauss's *Life of Jesus*. In addition, he translated Dante into fourteenth-century French. In 1838, he was elected to the Academy of Inscriptions and Belles Lettres and became one of the main collaborators of the *Literary History of France*, although this was far from his original interests. One of the great lexicographers of France, he compiled a new dictionary of the French language (1859-1871). For his huge amount of scientific work, he received great honors in his old age, a place not only in the French Academy, but also in parliament and the senate. From his authority as a scientist, he also gained philosophic authority.

He was already a famous scholar when he took up philosophy. Around 1840, he read *The Course of Positive Philosophy*, which won him to philosophy and positivism. In 1848 he expounded on the content of positivism in a series of newspaper articles. His philosophical works were exclusively discussions of Comte. In 1867, together with a few supporters, he founded the organ of the movement, *La philosophie positive*, which appeared until 1883. He did not have original philosophical interests; positivism for him was only a backdrop for scientific and educational activity; hence, it already had a different character than with Comte. Above all, he was agnostic and anti-religious, and in some measure anti-philosophical. His anti-philosophical spirit influenced the history of philosophy itself.

Littré's positivism, although intending to steer a neutral course between materialism and spiritualism, was always closer to materialism. "Human knowledge," he wrote, "is the investigation of forces belonging to matter." After his death, the younger collaborators of the periodical *La philosophie positive* were absorbed into the materialist movement.

JOHN STUART MILL AND EMPIRICISM

Empiricism was renewed in England in the nineteenth century by J. S. Mill. He ingeniously expounded its principles in all their possible aspects, and, at the same time, was ready to compromise with his opponents. He stated these principles in the spirit of humanitarianism and liberalism—considering theoretical as well as life problems. In many important particulars Mill's empiricism was distinct from Comte's positivism, but in view of its basic position was positivism's most faithful ally.

The Arrangement of Philosophical Camps in England around 1830

Empiricism was the prevalent philosophy in eighteenth-century England and produced the outstanding thinkers of the century from Locke to Hume. The "radical philosophers," from whom Mill originated, continued the empirical tradition into the nineteenth century, but by 1830 they were no longer the majority.

Another trend also originated in England during the eighteenth century: the philosophy of common sense. It was distinct from empiricism in that it accepted a priori elements in cognition; but it agreed with empiricism in recognizing only direct cognition and rejecting intellectual speculations. In the beginning of the nineteenth century, while the radical philosophers were renewing empiricism, Sir William Hamilton (1788-1856), a professor in Edinburgh from 1836, renewed the philosophy of common sense. He renewed it at great cost, however, by linking it with Kantianism. In one respect, Kantianism was its direct opposite. In the original form given it by Thomas Reid, the philosophy of common sense was characterized by: 1. realism, recognizing the existence of things independent of the intellect; 2. dogmatism, appealing to common sense to justify realism; and 3. opposition to relativism, skepticism, and phenomenalism. Kant, however, had opposed realism and dogmatism and supported phenomenalism.

Hamilton abandoned the dogmatic justification of realism. To be sure, common sense is inclined to assert that we can directly apprehend things independent of us, but the inclinations of common sense do not constitute an argument. He replaced dogmatic solutions with critical ones. Having adopted this position, he also had to admit that direct cognition is limited to a part of our consciousness, and only on this ground do we conclude that things independent of our consciousness exist.

Such a conclusion was most obviously not to be reconciled with Reid or with the original philosophy of common sense, which asserted that we apprehend things simply, without indirect links, experiences, or parts of the consciousness between them and the intellect. It asserted that our consciousness comes into contact with things, whereas Hamilton argued that it only comes into contact with their phenomena. His interpretation of the philosophy of common sense made it into phenomenalism, the very position commonsense philosophy had originally been directed against.

He also injected relativistic theory into his phenomenalism, even underscoring the relativity of cognition. He turned
it into agnosticism, excluding any kind of metaphysics and any
kind of cognition of the absolute—or, as he expressed it, of
"unconditioned" existence. In any event, he said, we cannot
become conscious of such an existence through reason; if we do
know it, our knowledge comes through faith. And finally, there
was more of Kantianism in Hamilton's philosophy with its phenomenalism and apriorism than there was of the philosophy of
common sense. Hamilton opposed post-Kantian German philosophy
but supported Kantianism at a time when, on the continent, especially in Germany, it was losing supporters. The debate between Mill and Hamilton was not so much a debate of empiricism
with the philosophy of common sense as with Kantian criticism.
Empiricism and Kantian criticism were the two great philosophical camps that, for a few decades beginning about 1839, contended for power in England.

For some time Hamilton had the advantage. He gained recognition through articles in the *Edinburgh Review* even before he
became a professor. Later, during the years of his academic activity, he published no important work (after his death his pupils published the *Lectures on Metaphysics and Logic*, 1858-60,
4 volumes); in spite of this, he was influential. This clear
and unusual thinker, who was unusually erudite for Britain, led
most of his contemporaries. In the years 1830-1860, the Scot-
tish-Kantian philosophy proclaimed by him was the prevailing
trend in England. Only in the 1860s did it come under attack
by both the empiricists and the metaphysical idealists who had
appeared unexpectedly in England at that time. In 1865 both
the empiricist Mill and the Hegelian Stirling came out against
Hamilton's philosophy. This spelled its end. However, traces
of it remained in English philosophy: Spencer derived his agnosticism from it, and in the beginning of the twentieth century
the new English realism returned to the principles of common
sense.

Still another trend played a role in English philosophy
around 1830, when Mill and Hamilton were expounding their theories: the metaphysical, irrationalistic, romantic theory. The
philosophical expression of romanticism derived its authority
from romantic German philosophy and was represented in England
by Carlyle and Coleridge. It attained no great recognition in
philosophy but exerted its force in literature. Mill demolished it in his early writings, and never returned to the theory so alien to him.

Predecessors

J. S. Mill belonged to a long line of English thinkers who proclaimed the empiricist theory of cognition, associationist psychology, and utilitarian ethics. Taine wrote that he was the "last in a series of great people, composed of Bacon, Hobbes, Newton, Locke, Hume, and Herschel."

More precisely, he was linked to Bacon by his desire to base the sciences exclusively on facts, to improve induction, to pursue sciences not only for theoretical purposes but for practical ones as well; to Hobbes by a nominalistic understanding of concepts, an atomistic comprehension of psychic phenomena, a subjectivist conception of perception, a utilitarian view of ethics, and an application of scientific methods to social problems; to Berkeley by his denial of the existence of general ideas; to Locke and Hume by his placement of the sensualist element in cognition in the foreground and his limitation of cognition to phenomena; and to Hartley and Priestly by associationism. All of this came to him through the channel of the "radical philosophers." He originated in their midst and developed the psychological ideas of James Mill, the ethical views of Bentham, and the economic thoughts of Ricardo; he became their heir and the most mature philosopher of their group.

He also benefited from the inquiries of scholars who did not belong to the empiricist movement. In particular, he profited from studies of methodology and of the theory and history of the natural sciences, which were undertaken in England during his lifetime. The most important authorities in these fields were the astronomer Sir J. Herschel (*On the Study of Natural Philosophy*, 1830) and W. Whewell (*History of the Inductive Sciences*, 1837).

He knew the writers of the continent better than most Englishmen did up to that time. He had personal contacts with Saint-Simon. Above all, however, he studied Comte and wrote a book about his views, *Auguste Comte and Positivism*, 1865; to some extent he helped link English empiricism with continental positivism. To be sure, they differed in that Mill saw the foundation of knowledge in internal facts, whereas the positivists saw it in external ones, in that Mill constructed his philosophy on psychology and the theory of knowledge, which the positivists rejected; yet they were drawn together by the cult of facts and their disrespect for metaphysics, apriorism, and irrationalism.

Mill, tolerant and moderate, also took the views of opposing camps into consideration. He even had discussions with the poet Coleridge, the most idealistic and romantic English thinker of the first half of the nineteenth century. Mill was the foremost empiricist of the nineteenth century, but he was a conciliatory empiricist.

Life

The life of John Stuart Mill (1806-1873) is set forth in
Mill's own *Autobiography* (1873). His educator and teacher was
his father, James Mill; his education was an experiment designed to bring up the boy to become a philosopher, empiricist,
and liberal. As early as his sixteenth year he read Locke,
Berkeley, Hume, Helvétius, Reid, and his father's philosophical
manuscripts. In his twenty-first year he passed through a
psychological crisis, a time of aversion to work and to the
views he had been taught. He overcame this crisis, but at the
same time he overcame his purely intellectual education, permitting him to develop the emotional factors of his mind. With
his mellow disposition and characteristic friendliness toward
both people and ideas, these factors caused the jungle of "philosophical radicalism" to lose some of its harshness and sever-
ity in him. Mill spent his life in literary activity and in
political activity in the service of liberalism. He was a
private scholar, not associated with academic schools. For a
few decades he had important practical and political matters in
his hands. As an official, and later head of India House, he
controlled the central administration of India. Between 1865
and 1868 he was a member of parliament. He was not only one of
the most interesting intellects of the century, but also one of
the most honest characters; Gladstone called him the "saint of
rationalism."

Writings

Mill's most comprehensive and most important writings are
The System of Logic (1843) and *Examination of Sir William Hamilton's Philosophy* (1865). He intended the first as the handbook
of a doctrine that derived all knowledge from experience; the
second was only supposed to be a criticism of the main opponent
of this doctrine in England, but it became an exposition of his
own theory of knowledge. Although ethical problems assumed
first place in his thinking, he devoted only *Utilitarianism*, a
small, popular treatise, to them. About this work, which later
became so famous and influential, he later wrote that he had
taken some unpublished articles from his drawer and arranged
them into a small book. It was published in a periodical in
1861 and as a book in 1863. Others of Mill's books, dealing
with economics, politics, and the theory of religion, are less
important philosophically.

Views

1. *Logic from the Standpoint of Empiricism.* Mill distinguished two basically different views in philosophy: the empirical and the a priori views of human knowledge (this latter he
called the "a priori or German view," but he asserted that
even in his times it predominated in England). According to
the first view, all truths about the external world are based
solely on observation and experience. The second also recognizes intuition and innate ideas. Mill represented the former view and resolved to demonstrate its correctness in the
field of logic.

Philosophers had always considered logic their domain but
in more recent times had paid little attention to it. To do
so would have conflicted with their convictions, first, that
logic was completely developed and further progress in it was
impossible, and, second, that it was a formal science having no
influence on the solution of philosophical problems. But Mill
perceived that the logic which enjoyed universal recognition,
namely the logic of general concepts and necessary conclusions,
conflicted with empiricism. Hence, he believed that logic
should be worked out from the beginning and reconciled with
empiricism. He did not think of seeking new laws of logic (as
De Morgan and Boole began to do during his lifetime), but he
wished to reinterpret the earlier laws.

His opponents asserted that necessary truths existed,
universal and obvious, and believed that such truths have to
have a deeper source than experience. Mill, however, postulated that their necessity, universality, and obviousness must
arise from experience and association. But if they were derived from experience and association, they were neither necessary nor universal.

Traditional logic derived general concepts from realistic
rules: it assumed that there are corresponding genera and species in reality. Mill had to deny this argument. For him, as
an empiricist, only individual things existed, and there were
no totalities, species, and genera; only expressions could be
general. His understanding of concepts could only be nominalistic. Concomitantly, he had to qualify the traditional view
of definition: according to the traditional view, definitions
acquaint us with the essence of things; according to Mill, they
merely mention the meaning that people assign to expressions.

In deduction, or deriving conclusions from general assertions, traditional logic did not sense a basic difficulty. For
empiricism, however, the difficulty was indeed a basic one:
from whence are general assertions derived? Empiricism could
not consider them as primary. We derive all knowledge from ex-

perience, and experiences are always individual. Only through induction can we arrive at general assertions. Hence, induction must come first, only then to be followed by deduction. One must first inductively arrive at general assertions to deductively derive further assertions. The syllogism is proof of a vicious circle: for it deduces the mortality of John from the fact that all people are mortal, but to know that all people are mortal one has to know, among other things, that John is mortal. The fact that John will die we surely know not through the general assertion that all people are mortal but through ascertaining that people similar to John have died. The advance of knowledge has taken place through analogy or induction; it passes from one particular to another and from these particulars to the generality.

Nevertheless, in the advance of knowledge deduction has at least a supporting role. Mill was perhaps the first to demonstrate that induction and deduction, although opposed to one another, work together in reality. In a sense one can say that he fused Bacon and Aristotle.

However, inductive reasoning, if it is to be correct, cannot be completely simple, *per enumerationem simplicem*. Mill attempted, as had Bacon, to discover special methods that would guarantee certainty to induction. Using the investigations of Herschel and Whewell, he formulated its four major methods, which he called the methods of "agreement," "difference," "residues," and "concomitant variations." This formulation was an advance in the inductive method over the achievements of Bacon and all others before Mill. This advance was essentially of a technical-logical rather than of a generally philosophical character; it belongs to the general history of methodology rather than to the history of philosophy. A somewhat deeper difference is evident in the views of these two most famous theoreticians of induction: Bacon expected that induction would permit us to ascertain the essence of things while Mill expected that through it we would arrive at causes of events.

Traditional logic assumed that certain primary general truths are apparent and require no proof; if they did not exist, then no statement of any kind could be proved, for there would be nothing on which to base it. Among these truths were logical laws and mathematical axioms. On the other hand, Mill had to deny the existence of such truths: all general truths are derivative; they are really only the combination of individual truths. Logical truths and mathematical axioms are no exception. Even they are only a generalization of experience; they are not obvious; they can and must be substantiated empirically and inductively. If they seem necessary, it is because they are based on a great number of experiences that have created indissoluble associations in our consciousness.

2. *The Theory of Knowledge from the Standpoint of Empiricism.* Mill also began anew to criticize the leading concepts of the theory of knowledge—especially causality—which had been pursued by the empiricists, beginning with Locke, Berkeley, and Hume. He did not doubt that we are all convinced of the universal validity of the law of causality, but he asked what foundations we had for this assumption. The only foundations are habit and the expectation that what many times has been true and never been false will continue to prove true. Hence, the foundation of the law of causality seems, by nature, to be exclusively psychological, subjective.

Yet, we cannot relinquish the law of causality altogether, because it is the indispensible presupposition of induction, and induction is indispensible for the progress of knowledge. Knowledge can be derived through a generalization of particular experiences, or through induction. But here we seem to encounter difficulties: how can the law of causality be based on induction if induction is based on the law of causality? Mill believed that this vicious circle was only superficial, and he resolved the paradox in the following way: a perfected induction operating by means of the four methods is based on the law of causality, but the law of causality itself is based on simple induction *per enumerationem simplicem*, which does not operate by these methods; that is, through simple induction we arrive at the law of causality and through it at a perfected induction. Simple induction is generally uncertain but, coupled with the law of causality, it has exceptionally greater certainty because of the tremendous number of experiences that continually substantiate it. Moreover, Mill, as befits an empiricist, did not recognize the complete universality of any law, and, hence, not even the law of causality; he considered it possible that unknown parts of the universe may exist in which causality is invalid. Only experience, not deduction, can decide this matter.

Mill also continued the critique of substance (begun by Locke and Hume). In accordance with the tradition of empiricism he defended not only the thesis that the only source of knowledge is experience, but also that experience is composed solely of sensations, from which we form our picture of the world. What we call "things" or, more scientifically, "substances," as well as "matter," "reality," and "the external world" are composed of them. We feel sensations independent of our will, and, for this reason, it seems to us that they exist independently of us, beyond our consciousness. This is the main source of faith in the existence of independent substances, matter, and the external world. This faith also has its origin in association, from which comes our belief in the causal connection of phenomena. What do we really know about matter?

Only that through it we continually receive sensations. Hence, Mill defined matter as a "permanent possibility of sensation."

He described the mind in an analogous fashion. He asserted, as had Hume, that "mind," "self," "soul" were essentially expressions signifying nothing more than our experiences. They only stressed the permanence of these experiences, just as the expressions "matter," "substance," "external world" stressed the permanence of our external sensations. To be sure, it seems to us that our "self" continues to exist even when we do not experience anything. But what is it that continues during such a time? The possibility of experiencing. With this idea Mill defined the mind and the self as he had defined matter. In this way, his empiricism reduced matter as well as mind to the multiplicity of sensations.

3. Ethics from the Standpoint of Utilitarianism. Mill wrote, "The difference between the two philosophical schools— one based on intuition, and the other supported by experience, is not simply a question of abstract speculation: it is full of practical consequences." Mill saw in the conviction that certain truths could be apprehended through intuition, without appealing to experience, a support both for erroneous doctrines and for bad social organization. To consider differences between people as innate and not capable of being removed was an obstacle to the rational arrangement of social affairs, and he saw the source of this conviction in intuitionist metaphysics. For this reason, too, he opposed it; he wished to apply his empirical view not just in theory but in practice.

This application is rather simple, and Bentham had already achieved it. If one holds to experience, what people really feel, then one must say that the only good is happiness, which reduces to pleasure. Hence, the only moral task is to strive for the pleasure of everyone. Mill accepted Bentham's position, but he gave his views an original tone. He tried to demonstrate the correctness of hedonism, which Bentham had accepted without proof. His proof ran as follows: all people desire only pleasure; good is what is desired; hence pleasure is the only good. Therefore, he proved ethical principles by appealing (hardly fortuitously) to psychological facts.

He also introduced some important modifications into the doctrine of hedonism. He ceased to consider it egotistically and sensually (Bentham was already inclined to do the same): only pleasure is good, but every pleasure, not just our own and sensual pleasure. He began to distinguish pleasures of a higher and lower order. He introduced the new name "utilitarianism" for his theory—and not without cause, for with these modifications it was no longer pure hedonism. Believing that

pleasures were not equal to one another, he emphatically stated
that it would be better to be a dissatisfied Socrates than a
satisfied fool. But if this were the case, then satisfaction
alone would not determine which pleasures are better: life did
not appear as simple to him as earlier hedonism had imagined it.
In Mill's hands the ethical theory of Hume lost its one-sidedness, and its hedonistic simplicity.

Summary

John Stuart Mill formulated anew the doctrines of empiricism in the theory of knowledge and logic, inductionism in
methodology, and utilitarianism in ethics. He developed these
views without going to extremes; he was not a nonconciliatory
empiricist as were his father and Bentham. He was the most
mature, and least uniform, intellect among the empiricists.

Nothing is more characteristic of his way of thinking than
that he once charged Comte, a somewhat related thinker, of not
recognizing open questions and of always wanting definitive
solutions, of dogmatically prejudging the future of science, of
having a prejudicial inclination to regulate human behavior, of
having neglected the most basic sciences—psychology and the
theory of knowledge—of having insufficiently worked out the
concepts which he used, for example, combating metaphysics
without carefully defining what he meant by it; and finally, of
admiring himself excessively. In comparison with him Mill was
much more honest, careful, and modest.

Role

Mill did not belong among those who initiated ideas, but
among those who finished them. He united the inquiries and
thoughts of many generations of empiricists, embracing in this
task such a broad range of problems as only Hume before him had
attempted. His own original ideas concerned particulars and
areas of application. Particularly in ethics, they overcame
the one-sidedness of empiricism up to that time. But even in
logic he tended to avoid extremes. Beside induction he found a
place for deduction. When James Mill, following Hobbes in the
claim that human history was exclusively dependent on material
interests, was attacked by the historians Macaulay and Mackin-
tosh, John Stuart admitted that they were right, not his father.

He seemed to have been destined to integrate the ways of
thinking of the eighteenth and nineteenth centuries, in particular the naturalistic viewpoint of the eighteenth and the historical one of the nineteenth. He concluded that the truths of
empiricism, which the philosophical radicals considered as

nonrelative and eternal, were also relative, that even they, as all truths, were the products of historical conditions.

Early in his career he worked out the most general problems of theoretical philosophy; then he turned his attention to details and practical matters. Above all, in his writings he fought for freedom. In parliament he represented uncompromising liberalism, and with unusual public courage he defended the most difficult issues. He defended empiricism not only because of its theoretical values but because he considered it the most appropriate grounds for liberal reform, for the reformer wishing to carry out changes in the social order must be convinced and must be able to convince others that the prevailing order is not sacrosanct. And indeed, empiricism teaches that nothing is sacrosanct, for reality is not governed by necessity.

Successors

The conciliatory and vital nature of Mill's views led to their wide dissemination. In the years 1850-1860 a "positivistic spirit" prevailed among European intelligentsia, a desire to free philosophy from metaphysical or "metempiristic" elements (as Lewes called them). This movement took the name of positivism from Comte, but it derived its content from Mill. Hardly anyone was familiar with the difficult works of Comte, but everyone read Mill. A large group of thinkers in England and on the continent followed in his footsteps. In England, closest to him were the psychologists A. Bain (1818-1903), professor in Aberdeen, and J. Sully (1842-1923), professor in London, the logician J. Venn (1834-1923), the historians H. T. Buckle (1821-1862), author of the famous *History of Civilization in England*, 1857-1861, and W. E. Lecky (1838-1903), a scholar of the history of rationalism. Also close to him was the moralist Henry Sidgwick (1838-1900), professor in Cambridge and author of the well-known *Methods of Ethics*, 1874.

Empiricism, allied with positivism (and soon with evolutionism), dominated the mentality of Europe for a few generations. These doctrines, making simple assumptions and operating with clear facts, were easily assimilated. To be sure, many professional philosophers did not agree with them, but the wider circles of the intelligentsia had complete faith in them, and nearly every enlightened person in the second half of the nineteenth century was a "positivist."

Opposition

However, even Mill's doctrines did not prove everlasting. Opposition appeared in England during Mill's lifetime. In the

1850s Jevons, a pupil of Boole, one of the creators of mathematical logic, sharply assaulted Mill's empirical logic. Hegelians, whose speculative and metaphysical philosophy was in greatest contrast to Mill's empiricism, also appeared in England at that time. The whole vitalistic movement, long under Mill's influence, began to be influenced by totally different, irrationalistic trends, in particular Carlyle's cult of heroes, Ruskin's cult of beauty, and Newman's cult of faith.

Three Empiricisms

The name empiricism has been given to various theories; all of them generally appeal exclusively to experience in knowledge but in their details they are quite different.

1. *Genetic*, or *psychological*, empiricism asserts that all individual human knowledge is derived exclusively from experience. All judgments are acquired; none are innate. Such was the empiricism of Locke and Condillac—radical in Condillac, who identified experience with sense impressions (sensualism), and more moderate in Locke, who also recognized internal experiences. The opposite of this empiricism is nativism, which is convinced that the individual possesses inborn judgments.

2. *Epistemological* empiricism asserts that experience is the sole criterion of genuine knowledge. An individual's judgments stem from various sources—some are innate and some are created by the imagination, but only those based on experience are authentic. Locke, who is considered a classical empiricist, was not an empiricist in this sense; he believed that all ideas, both correct and false, arise from experience, but only reason can decide which of them are true.

3. *Methodological* empiricism asserts that if science is to arrive at genuine and useful assertions, it should report only experiential facts and construct inductive generalizations from them. Francis Bacon was the classical representative of this empiricism. Descartes' methodology, which required that science base itself on obvious, certain axioms and derive further assertions deductively from them, was the direct opposite of this.

In some thinkers these three empiricisms intermingled. James Mill made special efforts to assert the primacy of psychological empiricism, stating that the two other kinds stemmed from it. J. S. Mill developed methodological empiricism. He continued the Baconian tradition in a more moderate form. With Bacon he stated that science should take its premises solely from experience, but Mill believed there was no need to limit its method to induction. Empiricism does not imply induction; it only rejects deduction from non-empirical premises. Mill's logic had places for both deduction and induction.

The name empiricism has also been given to theories requiring that experience be used in cognition, but not demanding that it be used exclusively. Aristotle's theory in psychology, Galileo's in methodology, and Kant's in the theory of knowledge are examples. This is empiricism in a very loose sense, and these theories have neither the character nor the consequences of real empiricism.

The Relationship of Other Theories to Empiricism

Three great earlier philosophical theories—positivism, Kantianism, and Aristotelianism—bear important relationships to empiricism.

The *positivism* of Comte denounced empiricism, but at the same time Comte was Mill's closest ally. Comte denounced pre-Millian methodological empiricism, for he considered deduction to be as important to the progress of science as induction. On the other hand, with Mill and the whole empiricist movement, he combated the non-empirical, axiomatic, intuitive premises of science. Here the activities of positivism and empiricism were a common effort; there can be no positivism without a reasoned empiricism.

Kantianism opposed genetic empiricism, for it recognized a priori judgments. Yet, it also was related to empiricism by the assertion that judgments are authentic only when they can be applied in experience. According to Kant, no genuine assertion concerning the world can be based on experience alone, but no such assertion is without support in experience. Kantianism accepted the negative empiricist statement "nothing without experience," but not the positive statement "everything from experience." It was not empiricism if one considered the content of knowledge, but it was empiricism if one considered its range of application.

Aristotelianism had always emphasized empiricism. All the same, empiricists had always considered it their greatest enemy. Here again the point is: Aristotle asserted the empiricists' view that only receptive knowledge is authentic. But Aristotelians assumed that the senses as well as the mind have a receptive character, and empiricism could never agree to this. Compared with Platonism, Aristotelianism stressed the empirical factor, but in a way that was unacceptable to strict empiricists.

HERBART AND REALISM

Herbart had formulated his philosophy before the 1830s, but his philosophy, based on realism and empiricism, did not

gain popularity at that time. Only after 1830 did it find supporters and play a greater role.

Life and Writings

Johann Friedrich Herbart (1776-1841) studied in Jena under
J. G. Fichte. Later he was a professor in Königsberg and Göttingen. Herbart accepted the views of Kant but opposed his successors, especially those who were the most popular in the
first years of the century—Fichte and Schelling. His acquaint-
ance with the great pedagogue Pestalozzi directed him toward
pedagogical work. He was the first lecturer in pedagogy (at
Göttingen, in 1802). He devoted his life exclusively to science and teaching, far from public matters.

The content of his writings is metaphysical, psychological,
and pedagogical: *The Science of Education* (1806); *The Science
of Practical Philosophy* (1808); *Introductory Textbook in Philosophy* (1813); *Psychology as a New Experimental Metaphysical
and Mathematical Science* (1824); *The Science of Metaphysics*
(1828). He also was a typical son of his nation: he wrote
about the ennobling influence of military service and published
a treatise *On voluntary obedience as the foundation of a genuine civic sense in monarchies.*

Predecessors

Herbart called himself a Kantian, but his actual connection with Kant was tenuous. He also departed from Kant's philosophy, but differently from most Kantians. He stressed the
realistic elements in Kant's theory. His understanding of Kant
was one-sided, and his philosophy became very different from
Kantian criticism.

He added two motifs to it: one was naturalism and mechanism, the second pluralism and individualism; the first motif
had supporters in philosophy for a long time, the second was
mainly represented by the monadology of Leibniz. Both of them
assumed a greater place in Herbart's philosophy than Kantian
motifs.

Views

1. *The Natural Picture of the World.* Herbart asserted
that cognition is based on experience, but he understood experience in a particular way. He stated that its object is not

the ideas of things, as Kant had argued, but things themselves, not a chaotic diversity that the mind must first bring to order, but a world that is spatially and temporally ordered.

He thereby returned to the view from which Kant and his idealistic successors had wished to depart. They did not take popular convictions into account, but Herbart considered these convictions as the only possible point of departure and support for philosophy. He stated that, although popular convictions are its indispensable point of departure, they are not at all similar to philosophy's final results. They are not and cannot be authentic, because they are contradictory. The task of philosophy is to replace these views with others free from contradictions.

According to Herbart, contradiction is inherent in the major concepts with which the common mind operates, above all, in the very concept of "thing." A thing is a unity, but at the same time it is a plurality if it has diverse qualities. Equally contradictory is the concept of "qualities," for qualities are dependent on the things they belong to, but at the same time they are independent of them, for they are conditioned by other factors; for example, color is conditioned by light. The concept of "self" was also contradictory for Herbart, for the self is a unity and yet is not because it is composed of many psychic states. He saw similar contradictions in other concepts that help the common mind to form our natural picture of the world.

2. *Metaphysics*. According to Herbart, metaphysics had been on a false path up to this time: it used contradictory concepts, namely the concepts of things (in naturalistic systems) and self (in idealistic systems). Herbart tried to dispose of these concepts and create a metaphysics free from contradictions. For this reason, he wished it to be as far from idealism as from naturalism.

In fact, however, he consistently opposed only idealistic systems, and his own views were not far from naturalism. The idea that formed the core of his whole system was indeed similar to the concept of thing. This was the concept of elementary, real existences, real units mutually independent of one another, which he called "reals." There are many "reals" qualitatively different from one another; Herbart's system was pluralistic. The qualitative diversity of the "reals" distinguished it from the majority of realistic systems, such as Democritus' atomistic system.

Although these real units have different qualities, we do not know these qualities. We know only the relationships occurring between them. For this reason, our knowledge of exist-

ence can deal only with relationships; it can only be formal.
This was what the metaphysics of Herbart intended.

According to Herbart, however, the fundamental relationship between these real units is that each acts to preserve
itself. But to preserve itself it works against others. The
world is structured from this action and opposition of reals,
and this structure in turn acts on the reals. Therefore, not
only is the totality of the world determined by its parts, but
the parts, in turn, are determined by the whole. This conviction differentiated the metaphysics of Herbart from other deterministic theories, which only recognized the influence of
the parts on the whole and not the reverse process.

The Herbartian metaphysical picture of the world, assuming
the multiplicity of individual components, is reminiscent of
Leibniz's monadology, but it is meager and unimaginative. It
was not the result of a vital spiritual attitude toward the
world (such as Herbart's opponents, the idealists, doubtless
possessed), but an artificial creation of conceptual combinations. Nevertheless, it turned out to be fruitful in application, particularly in the field of psychology and the allied
sciences.

3. *Psychology*. The most independent part of Herbart's
philosophy was his psychology, an application of his general
metaphysical conception. He conceived psychic life in the same
way as he viewed the external world—as a group of independent
units acting upon one another.

He considered ideas as psychic units, as elements of the
soul. Ideas strive to retain their place in the consciousness
in spite of the opposite action of other ideas that try to dis-
place them. Psychic life consists in this struggle of ideas.
Complicated psychic states are combinations of simple ideas;
they arise from the association and repulsion of these ideas.
Herbart, then, imagined psychic life as a mechanics of ideas
(Vorstellungsmechanik) analogous to the mechanics of bodies.
Just as the mechanics of bodies is subject to precise laws, so
also is psychological mechanics. Herbart tried to formulate
pyschology in precise, mathematical form; as he indicated in
the title of his book, psychology was to be based on experience,
metaphysics, and mathematics.

Herbart's psychological mechanics was only one current at
the time; another one was constructed by English psychologists.
The English associationists regarded psychic life as subject to
only one law, the law of association, but Herbart believed that
the law of apperception was also active in psychic life. According to the associationists, ideas arise to consciousness
only under the influence of stimuli and associative links with

other ideas. According to an apperceptionist such as Herbart,
however, the formation of ideas is also dependent on the mass
of ideas that has been accumulated in the consciousness. So
the formation of ideas in the consciousness depends on the individual sequences through which this consciousness has passed.
People with different pasts also have different ideas and different perceptions: even perception is dependent on apperception. Apperception plays a decisive role, particularly in some
psychic processes. This also explains why psychic processes in
different creatures operate in different ways—why, for instance, the same sight evokes different ideas in different people. Such a conception of psychology permitted Herbart to reconcile a mechanistic view of psychic life with the individuality of cognition. Nevertheless, his concept was deterministic:
all ideas are causally related, there is no place for freedom.
    Another equally essential feature of this psychology was
its intellectualism. It assumed that only ideas are primary
psychic elements and that only they determine the condition of
consciousness. Feelings and drives are only secondary phenomena, arising when the formation of ideas has for some reason or
another been obstructed.
    Nineteenth-century psychology did not retain the views of
Herbart in its further development. It attacked them for deem-
phasizing experience, for treating apperception as equal in
importance to association, and for underestimating feelings and
drives. But in combating these views, later psychology continually referred to them. Thus, Herbart's psychology played a
role in history.

    4. *Ethics and Aesthetics*. Herbart's ethics and aesthetics
were an application of his psychology. They also had a deterministic and intellectualistic spirit. Herbart's originality
was in relating aesthetics and ethics. He accomplished this to
the detriment of ethics, which he subordinated to aesthetics.
In joining them, he asserted that our relationship to good is
the same as our relationship to beauty—one of direct contact
and disinterested appreciation. Kant had defined aesthetics in
this way. Herbart, however, believed that this definition
could also be applied to moral principles.
    As did many thinkers of the nineteenth century, Herbart
narrowed the range of ethics in order to solidify its scientific position. Within such limits the task of ethics became essentially similar to the tasks of aesthetics: it had only to
determine what is pleasing and what is displeasing. Ethics became exclusively a matter of "moral taste," as aesthetics was a
question of artistic taste.

Above all, formalism characterized the aesthetics and ethics of Herbart. This was consistent with his metaphysical assumptions. He believed that we find delight only in relationships: beauty is only encountered in the proper combination of colors and sounds; morality similarly is inherent in the proper relationship of man to himself and others.

5. *Pedagogy*. According to Herbart, pedagogy is based on ethics (which indicates the goal of education) and psychology (which provides the means of education). In reality, it was based more on his psychology, which, in effect, also suggested goals. Among the most important of these goals was the creation of many-sided interests; this was supposed to protect the student from extremism, from a one-sided addiction to a single life interest and a neglect of others.

From its psychological bias, Herbart's pedagogy took on a tinge of subjectivity. From this bias it also derived the intellectualism that differentiated it so radically from another great pedagogical system, that of Rousseau. From Herbart's psychological theory of apperception his pedagogy derived the conviction that suitable intellectual preparation is the most essential part of education. From proper intellectual preparation feelings and drives then arise automatically.

Summary

Herbart's philosophy, then, was made up of: (1) realistic, pluralistic, and deterministic metaphysics; (2) mechanistic and intellectualistic psychology, using the concept of apperception; (3) formalistic aesthetics, conceived so broadly that it subsumed ethics as well; and (4) intellectualistic pedagogy.

This philosophy arose in Germany at the same time as the great idealistic systems and took their place when they declined after 1830. It was more in keeping with the spirit of the times, yet even this philosophy was not entirely suitable; it was not empirical enough. Later, more radical trends struggled with and finally defeated it.

In content and chronology Herbart's philosophy was an intermediate position between the metaphysics of the beginning of the century and later criticism and positivism. When these philosophies appeared in the last third of the century, the idealists were no longer playing a leading role—Herbart's pupils were. The attacks by the new generation were largely directed against them: in the theory of knowledge they attacked dogmatic realism; in psychology, apperceptionism; in practical philosophy, formalism.

School

History has indicated that Herbart's philosophy had features more conducive for creating a school than many another more original and outstanding philosophy. From the beginning, during the predominance of idealism, Herbart went against the main trend and did not find supporters. But this situation changed after Hegel's death. Herbart's school began to dominate German universities and was even stronger in Austria. It gained a privileged position there, thanks to the efforts of two of its members: F. Exner, Austrian Minister of Education from 1848, and F. Bonitz, a well-known historian of philosophy who advised the Minister of Education. About mid-century, Herbart's philosophy was the most widespread university philosophy in Germany. His pupils generally rejected his metaphysical doctrine, but they further developed other areas of his philosophy. Drobisch, professor in Leipzig, applied Herbart's ideas to logic; Volkmann, professor in Prague, to psychology (1853); R. Zimmermann, professor in Vienna, to aesthetics (his treatise of 1865 has remained the classical expression of formalistic aesthetics); T. Waitz, professor in Marburg, pioneered the anthropology of primitive peoples (1859), and the Berlin professors M. Lazarus and H. Steinthal pioneered ethnology and comparative linguistics. The number of pedagogues who had come from the school of Herbart was even more numerous.

Herbart's influence generally did not extend beyond the German-speaking countries. After 1870, it even began to decline there. His views retained their influence longest in pedagogy, where they dominated teachers' schools in Germany and Austria, but even in these they had to retreat before the non-intellectualistic spirit of newer times, closer to Rousseau and Pestalozzi than to Herbart.

FEUERBACH AND NATURALISM

In Germany after 1830 there was also a change in philosophy. The forerunner of these new trends was Ludwig Feuerbach. Just as Comte and Mill had done, he abandoned transcendental theories in philosophy, metaphysics, and idealism to initiate a minimalistic trend. But conditions in Germany were different from those in France or England. His philosophy, similar to their philosophy in what it opposed, was different in what it asserted: Feuerbach was a materialist.

The Arrangement of Philosophical
Camps in Germany around 1830

Idealism predominated in Germany, especially in the pan-
logical and dialectical form given it by Hegel. Already Schelling's romantic idealism was receding into the background.
There was no empiricism in Germany; but now Kantianism was also
losing supporters: nearly everyone joined the idealist movement.
A change began in the Hegelian left wing and Feuerbach was
one of its products. When he broke with idealistic metaphysics,
others followed him and the general retreat gained rapid momen-
tum.

Life and Work

Ludwig Feuerbach (1804-1872) came from a family that produced three outstanding people almost simultaneously: he was
the son of an eminent jurist and a relative of a great painter.
He first studied theology, then under the influence of Hegel
changed to philosophy, but to the end of his life religious
problems remained paramount for him. Although he later broke
with Hegel, he always retained some features of Hegelianism.
His radical philosophical, political, and religious views made
it impossible for him to pursue an academic career, so he settled in the provinces and worked independently, at first materially secure, then in difficult conditions. He was a realist
in philosophy, but an idealist in life, courageous and unselfish.
His earlier works were primarily devoted to the history of
philosophy, his later ones to the philosophy of religion. The
History of Philosophy from Bacon to Spinoza (1833), a monograph
on Leibniz (1837), and one on Bayle (1838) were the most important of the first period. Most important during the second
were: *The Essence of Christianity*, 1841, his most important and
most influential book, and *Principles of the Philosophy of the
Future*, 1843. He owed his renown to the radicalism that pre-
vented him from pursuing a career. He greatly influenced the
radical youth of that time, especially during the revolutionary
ferment after 1840, but he exerted this influence solely
through his writings, for living in the provinces, he had no
personal contact with them.

Predecessors

He began from Hegel but then changed to a directly opposite position. In 1839 he had already began to criticize Hegelianism. He came close to the views of the materialists, espe-

cially to the French writers of the eighteenth century; he was also influenced by Spinoza. He then left the confining circle of German philosophy, and the change he caused in German philosophy reflected non-German influences.

Views

1. *Opposition to Idealistic Metaphysics.* For Hegel, authentic existence consisted of general ideas, but Feuerbach, who had freed himself from Hegel's influence, returned to the natural view that existence is composed of individual things and that ideas are only abstractions. For Hegel, if thought and existence were in agreement, it was because existence agreed with thought; for Feuerbach, on the contrary, it was because thought is subordinate to the laws of existence. For Hegel, the criterion of truth consisted of concepts; Feuerbach was convinced that only phenomena could be the criterion of truth. Feuerbach completely departed from idealism.

2. *Sensualism and Materialism.* Above all, he wished to reject the speculative ideas that characterized nineteenth-century German philosophy. It was said that in him "German philosophy contradicted itself." As a matter of fact, he ceased to view philosophy and its task as most of his countrymen did; and, in opposition to them, he said "My philosophy is that I have no philosophy."

He did have a philosophy, but it was more concrete, empirical, and real. In the spirit of the emerging epoch he said: "Philosophy should again associate itself with the natural sciences, and the natural sciences should unite with philosophy." This link, based on mutual needs and internal necessity, "will be more lasting, fortuitous, and fruitful than the present inappropriate relationship of philosophy with theology."

His philosophy was quite simple. In the theory of knowledge he retreated from rationalism and returned to empiricism and sensualism. Only what is given by the senses "is clear as the sun. The secret of direct knowledge lies in sensuality." In the theory of existence, however, he passed from idealism to naturalism. His axiom was that only nature exists, that every existing thing is subject to the same natural law. "There is nothing beyond nature and man." "Any solution that seeks to go beyond the boundaries of nature and man is worthless. . . . The deepest secrets are hidden in the simplest natural objects. The return to nature is the only recourse." He was not only a naturalist but also a materialist: he was convinced that nature, which represented the only existence, is basically material. He said: "Thought from existence, and not existence from thought." From him comes the well-known saying, which was supposed to clearly express the materiality of everything, even man: "Man is what he eats" (*der Mensch ist, was er isst*).

His views—sensualism and materialism—were not novelties in philosophy, but they were unexpected in Germany in the nineteenth century and they were opposed to those prevailing at that time. The shift was vehement. To espouse such views as Feuerbach's required boldness and independence of mind. In their details, however, they were still not fully determined and elaborated. Marx and Engels owed much to him and admitted this, but they did not act in complete uniformity with him; they did not consider him a consistent materialist.

3. *Anthropologism.* Man occupied first place in his philosophy: he regarded man as its proper object and anthropology as the universal science. "God was my first thought, reason my second, and man my third and last." He passed from a theological philosophy to a Hegelian and then to an anthropological one.

By no means, however, did he oppose man and nature: he viewed man and everything that exists as a creation of nature. "The new philosophy makes man and nature, which is his base, the only universal and lofty object of philosophy." His "anthropologism" was a form of naturalism.

He considered man the most perfect creation of nature. For this reason, man was an ideal for him: a new ideal in place of the earlier supernatural ideals. In his philosophy, a process took place similar to what had occurred in the philosophy of Comte.

4. *Naturalistic Ethics.* The naturalistic assumptions of Feuerbach also appeared in his ethics. Because there is nothing beyond nature, there is nothing above it. There is no greater good than nature and one should show it the greatest reverence. "Bread, wine, and water are holy to us." And above all, man: "Man is a god to man." All the drives that nature has given man are valid. "Follow your inclinations and desires, but follow all of them: then you will not be the victim of any one of them."

Such an ethic had to be mundane. Feuerbach combated the ideas of eternity and immortality from the moral point of view: he believed that we only begin to live an authentic life when we realize that death is a reality; for then our thoughts and actions are concentrated on what is real, not dissipated on other-worldly matters. "Thought about the historical past has an infinitely greater ability to arouse man to great deeds than daydreams about theological eternity."

Yet, it was precisely in ethics that Feuerbach's materialism reached its limit. He believed that materialism teaches us what is, but not what should be; the state of nature does not give prescriptions on how man should live. He wrote: "For me materialism is the foundation of the edifice of human knowledge, but . . . it is not the building itself. Looking back, I completely agree with the materialists, but I do not agree with them in going forward."

5. *Naturalistic Theory of Religion.* Feuerbach thought about religion throughout his life. Convinced as he was that nothing is supernatural, for him it could only be a human affair. Man is not created in the image and likeness of God, but rather, God has been created by man in his own image and likeness (Xenophon once said this). Very simple needs have led man to religion: "What man himself is not and would like to be he imagines as existing in his gods: divinities are human desires, imagined as if they had been realized and transformed into real beings." Without human desires there would be no gods, and man's divinities are similar to his desires. Primarily adolescent needs find their satisfaction in religion, and, for this reason, it has meaning in the juvenile phase of humanity; afterward, education and culture, which realize the later dreams of humanity, take its place.

Nonetheless, Feuerbach believed that the needs leading to religion are eternal and, therefore, that religion is eternal. He also believed that its role is important: great eras in the history of humanity are primarily distinguished by their relationship to religion. New eras arise when the relationship of people to religion has changed. He also retained the belief that religion is noble: he said of himself, that in reducing theology to anthropology he rather raised anthropology to religion.

Influence

Feuerbach's original contributions to philosophy were not great. He used his intellectual energy combating the views of his predecessors. The naturalists of other countries, France and England, had arrived at the same results even earlier. But for his country he was a pioneer, not only in theory, but in politics as well; the idealistic doctrines of German philosophers ended in nationalistic totalism and the cult of the Prussian state, but his doctrine led to humanitarianism. From this time, everything in Germany opposing idealism and absolutism—naturalism, materialism, positivism, humanitarianism—was directly or indirectly derived from Feuerbach.

The Materialism of the Natural Scientists

Feuerbach's materialism found supporters in the Hegelian left wing. Besides the materialists with humanitarian interests, another group of materialists appeared during his lifetime, recruited from the natural scientists. Naturally, they had a different approach to these problems than did Feuerbach, who was a humanist, theologian, and philosopher by training. The natural scientists began to play an important role in the intellectual life of Germany; after the period of speculative philosophy there was a period of intensive inquiries and discoveries in the natural sciences. Confirmed materialists among them were J. Moleschott, K. Vogt, and L. Büchner. In clear formulas, they asserted that psychic phenomena are derived from physical ones, that "there is no thought without phosphorus and that, bluntly speaking, thoughts are in the same relationship to the brain as bile to the liver or urine to the kidneys." They came out with their views shortly after 1850: Moleschott's *The Course of Lives* appeared in 1852, Büchner's *Force and Matter* in 1855. In the same year, Vogt defended the materialistic position at a conference of natural scientists in Göttingen.

However, another group of natural scientists opposed materialism: the physiologist Wagner combated Vogt, and the chemist Liebig opposed Moleschott. The materialistic trend was not only a response to the flowering of the natural sciences but also a reaction to idealistic philosophy, a symptom of disrespect for it and a switch to the opposite extreme. Countries that did not have idealism in the nineteenth century did not have materialism. Moleschott, Vogt, and Büchner did not contribute to the development of materialism. On the contrary, their superficial conception contributed to the rapid reaction against it.

Further Development

Feuerbach's historical role was in forming a link between Hegel and Marx and Engels. At one time, as Engels wrote, "we were all enchanted by him and for a time we became Feuerbachians." But Marx and Engels went further. They charged Feuerbach with even having broken with what was valuable in Hegel, namely, the dialectic. They criticized him, first, for culti-

vating an old-fashioned, mechanistic materialism, and, second,
for not having derived social consequences from materialism;
they argued that his conception of society, history, and morality was, at bottom, incompatible with materialism. By not considering the dialectic and by ignoring the historical factor,
he operated with abstractions and schemata. He thought that he
was understanding man realistically but treated him abstractly,
for he took only the biological, not the social, view. He ignored the environment, which is changeable; he created a fictional "general" man. The result of this, in ethics, as Engels
wrote, was that "It was fixed for all times, all nations, all
conditions and, precisely for that reason, it could have no application in a particular time or place." This was also the
case with Feuerbach's understanding of religion. "The cult of
abstract man, which was the nucleus of Feuerbach's new religion," Engels wrote, "had to be replaced by a science of real
people and their historical development." This, beginning in
1845, was done by Marx and Engels.

MARX, ENGELS, AND DIALECTICAL MATERIALISM

Dialectical materialism was an incomparably more independent and important work of this epoch than Feuerbach's philosophy. Its creators were Karl Marx and Friedrich Engels, and it
is frequently called Marxism, from the former. It was a reaction to the predominant metaphysical idealism and an expression
of new times, as was positivism in France and empiricism in
England. But dialectical materialism went even further; it was
not only a world view, but also the basis for a revolutionary
social movement: socialism and communism.

Relationship to Hegelianism

Dialectical materialism is often represented as a simple
linking of the dialectic with materialism, of Hegel with Feuerbach. This interpretation is incorrect, however; dialectical
materialism was something more than a fusing of earlier views.
It benefited from them, but it treated them originally; its dialectic was different from the Hegelian, and its materialism
different from the Feuerbachian. For a time Marx and Engels
were supporters of Feuerbach, but later they departed from his
intermediate view, in their understanding of nature and even
more so in their understanding of history. They were also influenced by Hegel, but they quickly broke with his idealism.
The relationship of Marx and Engels to Hegel is complicated. First, they did begin from Hegelianism, they grew up in
his atmosphere, they used many of his concepts. Second, they

radically changed his position, even reversing it: Hegel was an idealist, they were materialists. It is not true, as frequently stated, that they partially changed his views, for they broke with his idealism and retained his idea of dialectic. Their dialectic is different from Hegel's. They retained the name but used it to mean something different: the law governing the development of matter, not the idea. "My dialectical method," Marx wrote in the introduction to the second edition of *Das Kapital* in 1873, "is not only different from the Hegelian, but is its direct opposite." His dialectic was created under different social conditions: the Hegelian dialectic, although a revolutionary movement became linked with it, was itself an expression of reaction. In spite of these basic differences, Marx valued Hegel highly and regarded his errors as the errors of a great mind. He even regarded Hegel as the only great thinker of the epoch worth debating. When Hegelianism appeared in England in the seventies and began to oust empiricism, Marx considered this a positive phenomenon. Engels wrote, "In spite of its deficiencies, the system of Hegel embraced an incomparably wider field than any other earlier system and developed a richness of ideas that even today is astonishing."

Other Predecessors

Many motifs—philosophical, scientific, social—flowed together in the theory of Marx and Engels. Lenin wrote that "The teaching of Marx is the legitimate heir of the best that humanity has created in the nineteenth century in the form of German philosophy, English political economy, and French socialism."

Two great lines of development that had progressed independently of one another came together in dialectical materialism. One of them was materialism: it passed from the English thinker Hobbes in the seventeenth century to the French materialists La Mettrie and Diderot in the eighteenth century to the German Feuerbach in the nineteenth century. But in Marx and Engels this line was violently changed. Hitherto, materialism had been primarily understood mechanistically; Hobbes had given it such a character, and La Mettrie had intensified it. Dialectical materialism, however, was anti-mechanistic; if it had any predecessors, they were eighteenth-century thinkers, particularly Diderot, and—going much further back—the ancient hylozoists and stoics.

A second line leading to Marx and Engels was evolutionary socialism. Socialistic ideas had already been disseminated in the eighteenth century, especially in France, but they originally had a utopian character and were associated with an idealistic view of the world. With Saint-Simon they received a positivistic philosophical base. However, Marx and Engels achieved the greatest revolution in the theory of socialism: they passed from utopian to scientific socialism, from an idealistic to a materialistic argument.

They arrived at their philosophy early. In 1844, when Engels visited Marx in Paris, they jointly formulated its theses. They not only went beyond Hegel, but also beyond Feuerbach.

Lives

Karl Marx (1818-1883) was born in Trier of a German-Jewish family. He studied law and philosophy. He was attracted to an academic career, but difficulties led him first to devote himself to journalism. For some time he was the editor of *Rheinische Zeitung* in Cologne. He was forced to leave Germany and in 1843 settled in Paris; he stayed there until he was expelled at the request of the Prussian government. In Paris he came into contact with French socialists. Above all, however, at that time he drew closer to Engels.

Friedrich Engels (1820-1895) was born in Barmen of a family of German industrialists. From his youth he took part in a literary-political movement, "Young Germany," and, like Marx, gravitated toward the Hegelian left wing. In 1842, he worked in his father's factory in Manchester, England, and he published what he observed there in 1845 in *Position of the Working Class in England*. After he met Marx, their fates joined once and for all. In 1844, he visited Marx in Paris, and they worked out their philosophical and political views in common.

In 1845, they both returned to Germany. There they wrote books and together engaged in political action. At this time, their main concern was to create the Communist party, which was to bring their slogans into reality. The year of revolution, 1848, found them in Germany. Engels took an active part in the struggles. In the time of reaction after the revolution, they both had to leave their country and immigrated to England. Marx settled in London, where he stayed until his death, writing and directing political action from there. Engels, however, returned to the factory in Manchester and worked there in order to insure his own and Marx's existence. He also settled in London in 1870. He outlived Marx by several years and, after the latter's death, continued their scientific and organizational work.

For 40 years Marx and Engels formed an unusually harmonious team; it was unprecedented for a philosophical theory to be the indivisible work of two people. They complemented one another: while Marx prepared *Das Kapital* and made his economic studies, Engels carried on studies in the natural sciences.

Engels attributed the main credit for their common theory to his deceased comrade and placed himself in the background. And the name "Marxism" as well as the belief that the theory was basically the work of Marx became firmly established. Nevertheless, Lenin determined that Engels played a more important role in the general philosophical parts of their theory than he himself had admitted.

Writings

Das Kapital (first volume, 1867; second (1885) and third (1894) volumes edited by Engels), the fundamental economic work and the foundation of socialism, was exclusively the work of Marx.

Engels was the author of several works with a philosophical character: *Anti-Duehring: Socialism, Utopian and Scientific* (1878); *Ludwig Feuerbach and the End of Classical German Philosophy* (1888).

Earlier works, which formed their view of the world, were their common effort. *The Holy Family, or Critique of Critical Philosophy* appeared in 1845, *German Ideology* was written in 1845-46 and the *Communist Manifesto* in 1848.

Views

1. *Two Camps.* Engels wrote:

The leading problem of all of philosophy is the problem of the relationship of thought to existence, of spirit to nature. According to their answer to this question, philosophers have divided themselves into two great camps. Those who asserted that spirit existed prior to nature formed the idealistic camp. Others, however, who considered nature as being prior to spirit, belong to various materialistic schools.

With Marx, Engels intentionally avoided other differences of opinion in philosophy in order to stress the most important one. While the nineteenth century, in general, developed, differentiated, and complicated the problems of philosophy, they tried to simplify them, considering only what was the most essential.

The two great camps they distinguished had existed in philosophy for ages, and the advantage had shifted continually between them. Before Marx and Engels, idealism predominated and in Germany was absolute. Only the Hegelian left wing and

Feuerbach began a reverse trend. However, Marx and Engels already found themselves in the opposite camp: they were decided opponents of idealism and supporters of materialism.

2. *The Realistic Theory of Knowledge*. These two great camps are distinct from each other in two ways, ontologically and epistemologically: they have fundamentally different theories of existence, and they imply different theories of knowledge.

The fundamental thesis of materialism, its theory of existence, can be stated as: the world in its entirety is material; or, putting it somewhat differently, the only primal and independent form of existence is matter, not spirit. Marxian materialism did not deny that spirit exists but held that it exists only in association with body, that it is a product of the development of matter and not an original form of existence independent of matter. It combated the views of Plato and Leibniz, that only spirit is the original and independent form of existence, and also the view of Descartes, that spirit and matter originated at the same time and are equally independent. Materialism called the views that opposed it idealism, although they are known in the history of philosophy by the name of spiritualism, and the antithesis is usually phrased materialism and spiritualism.

But materialism also implies a theory of knowledge, an epistemological thesis, for material objects can be understood in two ways: either as creations of the mind, or as existing independently of it. Or, it can also be stated, as Berkeley said, that to exist means nothing more than to be perceived. Another proposition is that to exist means something more than to be perceived, for perception itself points to an existence that is distinct from and has evoked perception. The first position is generally called idealism (epistemological or subjective) and the second realism. Marx and Engels preached realism against idealism, just as they had supported materialism against spiritualism. And they united this twofold antithesis in the slogan materialism versus idealism.

The thesis of realism states that the material world, which we perceive through the senses, is the real world, not just our imagination. Materialism makes this thesis more radical: "The material world, which we perceive with our senses, to which we ourselves belong, is the only real world." The spiritual world is derivative; it is matter's creation. "Matter is not a creation of the spirit, but spirit is the highest creation of matter."

Realism can be either moderate or radical. Moderate realism states that material objects exist independently of our perceptions, but that they are not wholly accessible to us; we perceive them, but we do not know whether our perceptions are similar to objects. Marx and Engels thought otherwise; their realism was radical. According to them, material things, although they exist independently of our perceptions, are accessible to perceptions. We not only know that they exist, but we know what they are. Our knowledge of the material world, based on experience and verified through the practice of life, is wholly reliable and objective.

The realistic view is the natural view of man. Yet, philosophy has departed from it repeatedly. Marx and Engels were indeed on the side of the natural view, and not on that of the philosophers who avoided it. "Practice, namely, experience and industry, is the convincing rejection of philosophical monstrosities." Industry is particularly important, for it is the best proof of the reality of things, that we can create them ourselves and order them to serve our goals. Such was the original argument of Marx and Engels and the only one they considered correct: theories of knowledge that did not appeal to practice were confusing and misleading.

3. Nonmechanistic Materialism. The distinctness and novelty in the view of Marx and Engels did not lie in materialism—there had been many materialists before them—but in their particular understanding of materialism. Earlier materialists had viewed philosophy mechanistically. They derived their views from physical enquiries of inorganic objects, dead matter, which they regarded as the real form of matter. And mechanistic philosophy became coupled with materialistic philosophy: the view became widespread that matter only exists where there is mechanism, and if nonmechanistic phenomena are found, then they must be manifestations of spirit, for they are certainly not signs of matter.

Marx and Engels came out against this understanding of matter: for them mechanism was only one form of matter. Everything real was a form of matter, whether mechanistic or nonmechanistic. Life is a form of matter. Consciousness, psychic life, is also a form of matter: it is not a mechanism; yet, despite this, it is a creation of matter just as mechanism is. All sciences investigate the movement of matter, not only mechanics. And nearly all of them investigate different kinds of movement: sound, the object of acoustical studies, is a different kind of movement from a mechanistic one; warmth, electricity, chemical, biological, psychic, and social processes are all movements of matter. As long as matter is identified with mechanism, materialism is a narrow and paradoxical theory. This new conception contains all the diversity of phenomena,

all the richness of the world. The new materialism does not
have to contradict everything that mechanistic materialism denied; it admits that the entire diversity of phenomena is real
and only asserts that all of this is linked with matter.

   4. Dialectical Materialism. Marx and Engels called their
materialism "dialectical." What they meant by this needs explanation, for they did not use the term in its usual sense.
Up to this time, the dialectic had signified a method of thinking that the Greeks had used and Hegel had revived; with the
Greeks and with Hegel, it was an exclusively intellectual method, which consisted in making conjectures without appealing to
experience. With Plato and Hegel, it was associated with idealistic philosophy. Marx and Engels accepted the name of dialectic, but their conception was so totally different that it
almost became the direct opposite of the earlier variety. Until their time it had been a property of the mind, but now it
was a property of material nature; before it had been a method
independent of experience, but now it became an expression of
experience; until now, it had been linked with idealism, but
now it was associated with materialism. Nevertheless, the
adoption of this name by Marx and Engels was not accidental.
The features of nature they considered most fundamental were
those that had formerly been observed in ideas expressed dialectically, in continual movement and development. By "dialectical" materialism they meant that only matter existed, but
that matter is continually developing, taking ever new forms.
   Speaking more precisely, the dialectic ascribed four qualities to nature: 1. nature is composed of things that are
joined together, which condition each other and are therefore
relative; 2. it is in continual movement, change, and development; 3. in development it creates new qualities; and 4. the
motor of development is the struggle between internal contradictions.
   Some earlier thinkers, particularly Heraclitus in antiquity, had had a similar view. But the majority of philosophers
had sought unity and oneness in the world, and, as a result of
this, they had a different view of nature. In particular, the
metaphysicians had postulated a unified, absolute, unchanging
form of existence, not subject to development. However, the
dialectical philosophy of Marx and Engels, appealing to experience, asserted that every form of existence is changeable, developmental, and dependent. Hence, they opposed metaphysics,
the philosophy of the absolute, with dialectics, the philosophy
of changing existence. Nothing was more characteristic of
Marxian philosophy than this contrast. Even with Hegel, the
dialectic was a method of constructing an idealistic metaphys-

ics; now it became the opposite of idealism as well as metaphysics.

5. *Concrete Man*. The slogan of the philosophy of Marx and
Engels was: hold to experience; represent things in their concrete characteristics. In particular, they wished to understand man concretely, not as an abstraction. At the same time,
they asserted that philosophy operates with abstractions; both
the idealist Hegel and the naturalist Feuerbach used them.
This was true not only for philosophy, but also for the particular sciences. Man, as represented by biology, is an abstraction, for social factors are ignored; it creates the fiction of
a man with constant characteristics, independent of time and
place, whereas people in different times and places have different characteristics. Their concrete qualities are dependent
on the social conditions in which they live, on the level of
development in which they find themselves, on the environment
that influences them. Dependent on his social conditions,
stage of development, and environment, man is different in each
case. Therefore, only in the light of sociology and history
can he be understood concretely.

6. *Historical Materialism*. One peculiarity of dialectical
materialism was that it did not confine itself to the phenomena
of nature; it also considered social phenomena. It went beyond
the materialism that had previously prevailed. Marx argued
that both nature and human events have a materialistic base,
which is subject to necessary laws. It seems otherwise only to
the person who considers the history of particular people in
abstraction. But people must be considered in a social context,
for no one lives alone; everyone lives socially. In social
life, they enter into necessary relationships, which are independent of their wills.
This view was given the name historical materialism: "historical" because it dealt with human relationships in their
historical development, and "materialism" because it explained
these relationships materialistically. This was a very independent application of dialectical materialism to social relationships. Marx discovered, in Engels' words, "a simple fact,
until now hidden under ideological stratifications, that people
have to eat, drink, have shelter and clothing before they can
pursue politics, science, art, religion, etc."

In the introduction to *Critique of Political Economy* Marx wrote:

> The whole complex of the relations of production cre-
> ates the economic social structure, the real base on
> which the legal and political superstructure is
> erected with its corresponding forms of social con-
> sciousness. The manner in which the material goods
> of life are produced conditions the social, political,
> and spiritual process in general; the consciousness
> of people does not determine their form of existence,
> but, rather, their social existence determines their
> consciousness.

This means, first, that social factors take priority among the determinants of human life. Individuals, whether they wish to or not, must conform to them. Second, material conditions occupy first place among social factors, and, of these, econom-ic factors are the most important. They determine the forms of spiritual life. This excludes a subjectivistic, idealistic view of the historical process. Subjective consciousness un-doubtedly plays a role, but it is objectively, economically conditioned.

7. The Ideological Superstructure. Speaking more precise-ly: the factor that determines development, the social order, and culture is the manner in which the means of life are ac-quired, or how material goods are produced. This means is de-termined by the productive forces, the people and their instru-ments of production, and by the social relationships in which this production takes place. Production always has a social character. People produce in common, and the relations that unite them in production can be diverse; the relationship can be either common or exploitive.
    History tells us of five basic types of productive rela-tionships: the primitive horde, the slave type, the feudal, the capitalistic, and socialistic. They are not eternal, for pro-duction is always in the process of development. Its transfor-mations have far-reaching consequences; they are not confined to the economic sphere, but they inevitably produce a change in the manner of life, thinking, and feeling, a change in the en-tire social order, ideology, political views, and cultural in-stitutions. "As is the means of production in the society, so also, at base, is the society, its ideas and theories, its po-litical and cultural institutions. Speaking more simply: as is the way of people's life, so also is their manner of thinking." Economic relationships influence people's ideas and judgments;

they create legal and political as well as religious, artistic, and philosophical forms. These forms are, as Marx said, the "ideological superstructure" on the economic base. This base—contrary to what idealists say—is always material. Every epoch has a legal system, a philosophy, and a morality that corresponds to the economic order. In this order, not in general ideas, lies the key to understanding society and its history. Once they are formed, ideas themselves act further, even influencing the economic base in turn, but this is already a secondary phenomenon.

Changes in production always begin with changes in the productive forces. Production relationships dependent on them change in turn. If changes in production do not keep pace with the productive forces, then the system of production begins to suffer; economic crises begin and are always followed by social revolutions. Conflicts between the forces of production and the relationships that do not keep pace with them find their expression in these upheavals. Marx diagnosed one conflict in his epoch: capitalism, which concentrated workers in factories, gave production a social character and, therefore, undermined its own foundations, for social production demands social ownership of the means of production. Therefore, a revolution, which will hand over power to the workers, the proletariat, must take place.

8. Philosophy and Politics. The philosophy of Marx and Engels was a view of the world and, at the same time, a foundation for political action. Materialism had value for them, not in and of itself, but as a theory of socialism. Their theory envisaged a political revolution, and they devoted their lives to its realization. Never had a philosophical theory been so closely linked with practice. "Just as philosophy has its material weapon in the proletariat, so the proletariat has its spiritual weapon in philosophy." Marx said that earlier materialists only explained the world, "whereas it is a question of changing it." The theory of dialectical materialism belongs not only to the subject of philosophy, but also to politics, to one of the stages of social struggle: for it made the workers' movement a conscious class movement.

The whole complex of results achieved by particular sciences can only be comprehended with the help of dialectical reasoning. This is a task for all of humanity in its progressive development, not for single individuals. For this reason, Marx and Engels saw in their philosophy "the end of philosophy in its former meaning."

9. The Ethics of Marxism.   In ethics, Marxism was also
directed principally against absolute, eternal, suprahistoric,
non-class morality.   Engels wrote:

> We reject any attempt to impose upon us any kind of a
> dogma of an eternal character, and therefore, an un-
> changing moral law. . . . On the contrary, we assert
> that every ethical theory up to this time has been,
> in the final analysis, the result of a given economic
> state of society.   And since society, until now, has
> developed in class struggles, morality has always
> been class morality.

Society either justified the interests of the ruling class, or
it changed to defend the interests of the struggling class.
   Such a dialectic ethics found itself outside the philosophical views that had contended with one another until this time.
Of course, it could not be reconciled with the position of
apriorists such as Kant, but it also rejected the position of
the empiricists, for their utilitarian ethic also had universalistic suprahistoric pretensions.

Summary

   Marxism was a unique materialism: anti-mechanistic, dialectical, unlike any that had previously existed.   It took special account of history, deriving social forms from economic
factors.   It was a philosophy that consciously served practice,
politics—more precisely, the politics of the proletariat,
whose certain victory it deduced from its assertions.   At the
grave of Marx, Engels said, "As Darwin discovered the law of
the development of the world, so Marx discovered the law of the
development of human history."

The Relationship of Marx to Other Philosophical Positions

   Marx sought supporters for his theory among the masses,
not among philosophers; here he entered into a duel.   He combated not only idealistic systems but even those that might have
seemed close to his position; he was contemptuous of positivism
and totally neglected intermediate and conciliatory positions.
The only opponent whom he considered as worthy of his attention
was Hegel.   The revival of Hegelianism in England about 1870 he
considered as relatively favorable, for he considered this view,
the direct opposite of his own, as better than intermediate,
half-way views.   He combated it, but in some measure derived
his own existence from it.   All of history runs from one oppo-

site to another. He wrote: "We German socialists are proud
that we come not only from Saint-Simon, Fourier, and Owen, but
also from Kant, Fichte, and Hegel."

Opposition and Influence

The association of Marxist philosophy with a political
party gave it resolute followers but also aided its opponents.
The philosophers and historians of philosophy of the nineteenth
century did not understand the tremendous importance of Marxism;
histories of philosophy hardly give it more than passing notice.
Marxism was considered a political view not a scientific-philo-
sophical one, and originally it did not have supporters outside
the party. After the death of Marx and Engels, it even began
to lose followers in the party; toward the end of the century,
its leading representatives in Germany began to disgard the
philosophical portions of the doctrine, while retaining its
economic and political theories. For the most part, they preferred to associate themselves with materialistic views that
had a better scientific position: Kantianism or the new positivism. This state of affairs lasted only a short time: the
situation changed radically with the appearance of Lenin.
The continuation and further development of Marxism was
decided by Leninism, which appeared at the turn of the century.
It will be discussed later—as a trend of the twentieth century.

INDIVIDUALISM AND ELITISM: STIRNER AND CARLYLE

The period that created positivism and empiricism was not
exclusively minimalistic. It was exuberant and many-sided;
with the minimalists, it also produced opponents of minimalism.
The latter primarily expressed their views in practical philosophy, in the philosophy of life, in the philosophy of history,
and in ethics. They comprised a common front against the prevailing philosophy, but they were quite different from one another. The ideas of Stirner were individualistic, those of
Carlyle were elitist. Neither of them belonged to the main
current of the epoch; they were precursors of trends that would
appear later.

STIRNER

Life

Max Stirner was the pseudonym of Kasper Schmidt (1806-1856) who lived a life of poverty as a teacher in boys' and girls' gymnasia in Berlin and the provinces. He spent his childhood in Chemnitz, where his father had a drugstore. He completed his studies with interruptions and passed his examination with difficulty. His marriage, to an illegitimate daughter of a midwife, made his position still more difficult. He studied in Berlin during the time of Hegel's greatest triumphs; these successes caused a reaction in him and were a factor in forming his first philosophical views. In Berlin he belonged to a group called Die Freien (The Free): reporters, economists, and philosophers, mainly from the Hegelian left wing, who gathered in wineshops for discussions. His *The Individual and His Property*, a revolutionary and sensational book published in 1845, was conceived in the atmosphere of these discussions in opposition to the despotism of the times. After its publication, he gave up teaching to devote himself to literature. But he published only *The History of Reaction*, purely contemplative and of little value. His poverty increased, and he was forced to think only of how to support himself and his family. He tried unsuccessfully to run a dairy and lived on the occasional commissions he earned. He died in poverty. His drab, poor, and difficult life was in sharp contrast to his splendid and masterful theory.

Predecessors

Although Stirner's views were in opposition to those of Marx, to some extent they share a common genealogy. Stirner also was a product of the Hegelian school; he also belonged to the Hegelian left wing and joined the opposition to Hegel; he also was influenced by Feuerbach, but considered Feuerbach's position as moderate and went beyond it. However, he followed a directly opposite line from Marx.

Views

1. *Defense of the Independence of Man.* Feuerbach freed me from dependence on God, Stirner stated. But he added: he put man in place of God, and I continued to be dependent. Feuer-

bach's position implied that I do not have to consider God, but that I am forced to consider society. If I have to consider society, then I am not free. This was Stirner's first leading thesis.

Stirner's second thesis was: If I am to be free, then I must shake off even this dependence. I can easily do this, for this relationship depends on a fiction, on something that really does not exist.

Feuerbach taught that God is a fiction, a specter—but society is also a fiction. Hence, there is no reason to obey it, just as there is no reason to obey God. Every aspect of society is a phantom: the state, the nation, the family. Everything that arises from society is also a fiction: law, morality, all truths, beliefs, faiths, all these ideas that I am supposed to obey.

These phantoms are harmful: this is the third thesis. They are harmful, because these "new highest Beings"—society, the state, the nation, the family—tyrannize me, use me, and impose obligations that burden me. Likewise law and morality, and all truths and faiths. Yet, I not only regard them as real, but as holy, and my submission is all the more complete. It might be possible to serve them, if they were either real or useful. But why should they be served, if they are neither real nor useful? Because they are harmful phantoms, one need not and should not consider them. I shall not consider society, its morality and ideology, for they make me dependent. One should realize that they are not realities; still less are they divinities.

No thought and no faith is holy; only I make them holy. Therefore, I alone am responsible for the fact that I must later serve them. I must free myself from spirit: if it is revealed that spirit is a chimera, then I shall deprive it of all holiness and divinity, and instead of serving it, I shall be able to regard it as I regard nature. I should also free myself from a truth outside myself, one that I would have to obey —there is no such truth, for there is nothing outside myself.

And if I reject all phantoms, what remains? What is real? Only I myself am real. All these other things—God, man, the state, law, morality, spirit, truth—are only my ideas. I mistakenly ascribe a higher reality and value to them than I give to myself. Therefore, I make myself dependent on them, and I live in this dependence, not as my own nature would require, but as the nature of these fictions dictates. This imposed action blinds me not only to reality but to my own interest. If these things were realities, then perhaps it might be worth sacrificing my own interest to them; or if it were in my own interest, then perhaps it might be worth ignoring reality. However, this is not the case. One should live in conformity with reality and one's own interest. This means, "One should

be an egoist, not attributing value to anything, but seeking it
in oneself."

Stirner did not combat any particular idea or value but
all ideas and values; he considered all of them a fiction. No
one went further in seeking out fictions and unreal creations
of the mind. Nor did anyone derive such far-reaching practical
consequences from his position as he did: the rejection of all
dependencies, material as well as spiritual, on people and on
ideas; this was complete anarchy, complete individualism.

2. *Opposition to Moral Norms*. If there is nothing outside
me, then there are no norms for me, no commands, no oughts, and
no tasks that I must fulfill. No moral laws have any foundation, especially the command that I must act disinterestedly
and deny myself. Neither is love a command for me; if I love
people, it is not because I should, but because it is my nature
that love makes me happy. Man is not "called" to anything; he
has no special purposes, just as plants or animals do not have
special tasks. His fate is like that of a bird, which flies
and sings in order to discharge its energy in flight and song,
nothing more.

Because there are no norms, the expressions "good" and
"bad" have no sense. Hence, I have the right to do everything
that I wish to and am able to do. The state should be replaced
by an association of egoists, each of whom is free to do as he
wishes. Because there is nothing outside me, then I am the one
(whence the first half of the title of Stirner's book). In
fact: people and things do exist outside me, but I do not have
to consider them. I can live as if I were the only individual
in the world. I can make use of them as much as possible and
consider them my property (whence the second part of the book's
title).

Stirner's doctrine went farther than that of Protagoras:
not man is the measure of truth, but only I myself. This seems
similar to Fichte's view, but the difference between them is
essential. The "I" of which Stirner spoke was not the Fichtian
metaphysical self, unchanging, creating the world, but a real
human self, changeable and transient. Because the changeable
and transient self was Stirner's criterion, the consequence to
his philosophy was not absolutism, as with the idealists, but
relativism.

Summary

Philosophical theories have always dictated that life
should be made subordinate, if not to God, then to people; they

taught that life should be standardized, if not to good, then to truth: Stirner alone rejected all norms; his doctrine was complete egoism, individualism, anomism; it was metaphysical anarchism. Perhaps such a view was necessary in order, by contrast, to accentuate the nature and assumptions of all other human views. It has remained a paradox, a mad intellectual experiment.

Followers

Stirner captivated many people by his boldness, but he had few followers. The anarchists Bakunin and Kropotkin attempted to put similar ideas into practice. Theoretically, Nietzsche was closest to him.

Opposition

For a long time, Stirner's book was unnoticed. Its content was sensational, but its form was chaotic, rambling, and dull. When it finally attracted attention, it was attacked as morally harmful, asocial, and amoral. But it also merited a logical criticism: that the concepts it used were imprecise and its assertions therefore doubtful. In particular, the boundary between what is me and not me is basically fluid; social, moral, and religious phantoms attacked by Stirner are an inseparable part of my own person. And after excluding them from my life, I myself become an abstraction unfit for life; I become a phantom.

CARLYLE

Life

Thomas Carlyle (1795–1881) came from an out-of-the-way village, from a peasant family with no culture; he grew up among hard, brutal, uncivilized people. He was gloomy, detached from the world, inclined to abstract and unreal meditations. His career began inauspiciously. He enrolled in Edinburgh University but did not remain there long; his parents wanted him to study theology, but he studied mathematics, which he never used in later life. He became an elementary teacher, but his pupils were repelled by him. After this, his fortunes took a radical turn for the better. He became acquainted with more intelligent and sociable people; he married a wealthy and cultured woman. He began to write and to read German litera-

ture, partly because he wished to be original, for at that time
no one in England was thinking about Germany, and partly because of the affinity he felt for the vague and romantic Germans. He began to correspond with Goethe. The letters he received from the old poet were the first sign of distinction to
come to him. With an extremism that was peculiar to him, he
suddenly passed from depression to self-complacency and self-
confidence. Desiring a fuller life, he moved to London, where
he quickly made a career for himself. He discovered effective
themes, which gained readers for him and made him well-known.
From literary themes he passed to historical ones, from poetical to political ones; later he preferred to study Frederick
the Great rather than Goethe. He was successful, though his
views suited neither the English taste nor the spirit of the
times. He gained fame, though as an essayist he had no literary taste, as a historian he never used the archives, and as a
thinker he was capricious and inconsistent. But he had a gift
for words and an imaginative mind. As the years passed and as
his success grew he changed from a daydreamer, weaving his
thoughts far from people and life, to a sage, teaching people
how they were to live. Unexpectedly, he became a moral authority, although he had an unbearable character, egoistical, inconsiderate, arrogant, and despotic, acidly criticizing everyone and everything. But, in fact, he was unusual—as he was
described, "sublime, wild, and chaotic." The internal turmoil
that never left him made him a dramatic figure. He considered
himself better than others (I am like no one else, I am above
all of this, I am with the stars), and others believed him. A
legend grew up about his wisdom and depth. Although he lived
for a long time, this legend outlived him.

Writings

His literary activity covers 50 years. From a study on
Faust (1822) to the historical studies of 1872 there are no
strictly philosophical writings among his works. One might consider the story *Sartor Resartus* (1834) and the treatise *On Heroes and Hero-Worship, and the Heroic in History* (1841) philosophical. But in accordance with his thesis that there is no
history without philosophy of history, each of his works contains philosophical ideas expressing his conception of life.
He did not pursue theoretical philosophy; he cultivated a philosophy of the interpretation and evaluation of human life.

Sources

In philosophy he was self-taught and had little philosophical erudition and culture. He profitted least from the philosophy of his own country: English philosophy, the schools of
common sense and empiricism, did not appeal to his mystical
mind. But the German romantics did appeal to him. Materialism,
expounded in *The Bible of Materialism* though it did not suit
him, at first seemed irrefutable. But when the writings of
Kant convinced him that this was not so, he felt free to follow
the romantics: Schelling in the philosophy of nature and Fichte
in the philosophy of history. Moreover, he knew them only superficially, primarily second-hand and only from popular writings; thoroughness in studies was not his specialty. However,
this also had positive sides, for in the end he posed philosophical problems independently and originally.

Views

1. *Natural Supernaturalism.* Carlyle was convinced that
the true nature of things is hidden. For him everything had
two aspects: the material, accessible to everyone but superficial, and the ideal, hidden to the majority but deep and authentic. For common logic, he said, man is a two-legged omnivorous
creature who wears pants; yet for the superior intellect he is
something completely different—a soul, a divine phenomenon.

Carlyle regarded the body as only the external side of man,
a side that hid the secret self. Here, Kant's view that the
world we perceive is only a phenomenon appealed to him. But
this was Kant's only view that he could accept. Contrary to
Kant, he was convinced that he knew what was concealed beneath
phenomena, namely, that they are manifestations of God. In
this he was closer to the mystics than to Kant. He admitted
that here there can be no appeal to reason; rather, one should
appeal to introspection and intuition. His view of the world
was transcendental, irrational, mystical-intuitive, theophan-
istic. He did not verify this view; he had neither the desire
nor the ability. He accepted it dogmatically. But he derived
practical consequences from it. In part, they were very peculiar: for example, during his youth, when machines began to be
introduced in industry, he came out against them because they
were not a creation of God.

He did not attempt to construct metaphysical theories: he
considered them incompetent attempts to define what transcended
all designation, as efforts to measure what was immeasurable.
Together with the German romantics, he only asserted that the

world is an organic creation, constructed to function harmoniously. For the philosophical eye, he said, everything is a window looking out on infinity. Through nature the world looks supernatural. This was the cornerstone of his position, which he called "natural supernaturalism": it stated that nature is only a manifestation, a symbol, or as he preferred to say, the "clothing" of the divine spirit. This spirit appears in nature, in man, and in human history, especially in the history of great people. They are the most powerful symbols of God on the earth.

In his youth, Carlyle first worked out this general transcendental view on the world of nature; only later, however, did he construct his special view of the human world, to which he devoted exclusive attention for the rest of his life.

2. *The Cult of Heroes*. In Carlyle's view of the world, people, especially great people, were incontestably the most important. God was everything for him only in theory; in practice man was everything for him. Basically, his philosophy of history and ethics were temporal: the divine world was a decoration, and only people were on the stage.

No philosophy of history or ethics devoted less attention to material matters. Indeed, only spirit was real for Carlyle; he believed that exclusive attention should be devoted to it. He opposed all kinds of utilitarianism and hedonism: his position was thoroughly moralistic. The *leitmotif* of his literary works was that only moral people can write well; however, he understood morality in the Fichtean sense, as activity and energy.

Activity, not reflection, characterizes great people and great periods. The healthy organism lives and acts; only the sick organism begins to reflect upon itself. Reflection, concentrating attention on one's self, increasing self-knowledge, he considered harmful (anti-selfconsciousness theory). His philosophy was totally anti-intellectualistic. On the other hand, he valued faith highly. The struggle of faith with disbelief he viewed as the most important event in history.

He defined history as the sum of biographies. He saw its base in individual people not in the masses. The masses are dependent on individuals, and not the individuals on the masses, as a popular view of the nineteenth century claimed. Carlyle's philosophy of history was the most extreme form of individualism. To be sure, not every individual creates history, but only an outstanding one, the "hero." Carlyle introduced the concept of hero and the cult of heroes into philosophy of history and ethics. However, he defined heroes as the most active people: they are the most gifted by nature, and, therefore, they are the most perfect manifestations and symbols of the divinity.

By nature people are unequal: Carlyle was a decided opponent of egalitarianism. From this he derived the consequence that people have unequal rights. The better have the right to everything, for they can make the best use of it. The more active people are the better, and those who are stronger are the more active. Hence, the stronger are the better. The weaker, being inferior, should yield to them. Weaker nations should even give their land to stronger ones when the latter demand it, for only in great hands do great things originate. Land, nature, and material things have no value in and of themselves; they acquire value only when instruments of human activity.

Carlyle was convinced that the better have greater rights, that greater success and prosperity come to them. He viewed this as a manifestation of justice. Otherwise, history made no sense. By nature the better are victorious. He was convinced that in the long run justice and rightness always prevail, because they impart a feeling of strength. Later he did not even wait for this "long run"; he asserted that rightness always prevails. And he even reversed this assertion to whoever is victorious is right. From victory, success, and strength Carlyle made inferences about rightness. As Calvin had introduced the principle that success is a sign of rightness to religious ethics, so Carlyle introduced this same principle to secular ethics and philosophy of history. If someone gained an advantage over others, he must have right and justice on his side, God had destined him for this. For him the partitions of Poland were an act of "divine justice." Whatever happened in history, even the subterfuges of Frederick, was right and just. And finally, for Carlyle there was no difference between what was and what should be, between strength and rightness, between history and ethics. According to his view, morality and justice in man were equated with strength; Carlyle stated that he prized only moral value, but he identified this value with strength and, finally, valued only strength.

Summary

Romantic metaphysics, the world as a symbol of God, seeing from the finite into the infinite world—this was the more remote background of Carlyle's philosophy. However, its direct content was the cult of heroes, individualism, elitism, moralism, and opposition to utilitarianism. Carlyle's slogans were "strength is law" and "success is rightness."

Some say that the German philosophers were the source of his views. Of course, there is an analogy, but the sources were closer and more simple: in the cult of strength, success,

and hero worship Carlyle only returned to the primitive views
of the society in which he grew up, a society that was still
essentially medieval. These primitive views, introduced by
Carlyle into the culture of the nineteenth century, seemed novel and were received enthusiastically, especially by the
stronger and inconsiderate nations, to whom they were useful
and convenient.

Influence

Unknown to anyone in his youth, Carlyle became a popular
figure in his maturity and an authority in history, philosophy,
and morality in his old age. Although his scholarship was
questionable, both Oxford and Cambridge conferred honorary doc-
torates on him, and youth gave him proof of its recognition,
when it elected him rector of the University of Edinburgh in
1865.

His popularity stemmed from the fact that he opposed empiricism and the philosophy of common sense, the most popular
views in England. Everyone who disliked these views espoused
his philosophy; and every anti-empirical trend in English
thought of the nineteenth century found support in him. John
Ruskin (1819-1900) initiated the trend of a spiritual conception of the world expressed by Carlyle, although he changed it
radically, giving it an aesthetic rather than a moralistic interpretation.

Carlyle also had influence beyond England. The American
philosopher Ralph Waldo Emerson considered himself a pupil of
Carlyle. However, he remained closest to Carlyle's earlier
ideas: he was the kind of thinker that Carlyle would probably
have been had he retained his original, abstract spiritualism
and not begun to moralize and reform the world.

Being more of an artist and man of action than a thinker,
Carlyle stimulated people to action rather than thought. His
theses were more accepted in politics than in philosophy, especially the thesis that strength is right, and success is a
proof of legitimacy. The assertion that he bears part of the
responsibility for the great wars of the twentieth century is
not without foundation; he excited German ambition and drive to
conquest when he represented them as a chosen nation, created
to rule the world.

Stirner, Carlyle, and Marx

It is difficult to imagine greater dissimilarities than
those between Stirner, Carlyle, and Marx. Stirner called for
the independence of the individual from society; Marx indicated

that this is impossible, for every person has characteristics conditioned by the society to which he belongs. Carlyle argued that human history is governed by great men, to whom the masses are subordinate, and that events are dependent on the chance that great people will appear; Marx, however, asserted that history is the struggle between social classes and that it runs its course inexorably. It is a striking fact that the same period, even the same years, produced such opposing theories: Carlyle's *Heroes and Hero-Worship* appeared in 1841, Stirner's *The Individual* in 1845, and *Communist Manifesto* of Marx and Engels in 1848.

THE PHILOSOPHY OF FAITH: NEWMAN AND KIERKEGAARD

The majority of philosophers of the nineteenth century followed Comte, Mill, and Marx; they believed in the power of reason, the objectivity of scientific concepts, and the inviolability of natural laws. But a minority took the directly opposite position. It opposed general truths with personal ones, reason with feeling, general concepts with concrete experiences, knowledge with faith. The most outstanding representatives of this minority were Newman and Kierkegaard. They shared one characteristic with positivism: a disbelief in systems, in rational metaphysics. For the most part, however, everything divided them. Even the problems they emphasized were different: not nature, but man and God. The success of positivism caused them to remain in the shade. The nineteenth century followed positivism, not them. They were not so much representatives of their epoch as precursors of one to come.

NEWMAN

Life

John Henry Newman (1801-1890) was born in London, where his father was a banker. After finishing his studies at Oxford, he remained in the university environment. From his early youth, he devoted his life to religious matters: all of his other works and interests, particularly his philosophical ones, served his religious concerns. In 1824, he became a clergyman, and, in 1831, a university preacher in Oxford. His sermons drew crowds, and the published versions attracted a great number of readers; only Walter Scott was more widely read. Newman's aspiration was to free the Protestant faith from its vagueness and individualism, to strengthen the role of authority and the church in matters of faith. In 1833, he and a num-

ber of Oxford friends began a campaign. From the brochures
(tracts) published by this group the campaign has been called
the "Tractarian Movement" or the "Oxford Movement." But while
Newman was directing this movement, his own views began to
change: he concluded that his religious ideal was better realized in the Roman church than in the Anglican, and he wished to
bring the Anglican church closer to Catholicism. Later, when
his recognition and influence in the Anglican church were at
their zenith, he went even further: judging that the whole
truth was in the Roman church. In 1842, he gave up his eccle-
siastical position and moved to the country. After three years
of isolation spent in studies on the development of Christianity, he became a convert to Catholicism (in 1845). As Gladstone
said, this fact marked an epoch in the history of England. By
his decision, he renounced his entire past and gave up the high
position he occupied; for in the church he entered he was a
subordinate for a long time. He was a simple priest, an orato-
rian. Except for four years, when he was the rector of the
Catholic university in Dublin, he lived in isolation in the
provinces. On the other hand, he wrote a great deal, including
a philosophical book: *An Essay in Aid of Grammar of Assent*
(1870). His position changed fundamentally only after the elec-
tion of Pope Leo XIII in 1879; one of the new pope's first acts
was elevating Newman to the position of cardinal. He was then
nearly 80 years old.

Newman had a variety of talents, among them literary ones;
he was one of the great English prose writers. People said
that there was something unusual, "magnetic" in his personality.
He was characterized by a sober, even skeptical, intellect
joined with a great faith. His faith never vacillated; it was
never subjected to doubt: of religious truths he was more certain than anything else. He had a direct and easy relationship
to divine matters and an effortless, natural holiness. He was
so immersed in religious matters and, therefore, so far from
other people, that in spite of his holiness and gentleness, he
aroused fear in them. Extreme individualism and the need to
exercise authority were intermingled in him: this need drew him
into the Catholic church, which nevertheless mistrusted his individualism for a long time. He also united control with great
abilities; he gave full play to them in doctrinal disputes and
polemics.

Newman held only two things as absolutely certain and
"clear as the light of day": his own existence and the existence of God. "I and my Creator": this was his whole world.
The perceived world was less real for him than the world of ideas. From his childhood, he was attracted by the view that material phenomena are unreal. As he writes, he was often overcome
by the feeling that life is only a dream, people angels, and
the whole material world an illusion. His skeptical mind had

such an ability to strip the simplest and most generally recognized truths of certainty and clarity that they no longer seemed more certain and obvious than the mysteries of faith.

Philosophy was necessary to verify his view of the world. He had no metaphysical curiosity: philosophy served not to supplement the truths of faith but to explain why these truths can be trusted. Therefore, he exclusively cultivated the theory of knowledge not metaphysics.

Views

1. *The Individuality of Things and the Abstractness of Cognition.* Newman observed that people are inclined to consider abstractions as facts and to neglect true facts. However, only the existence of individual beings is a true fact, and everything else around is only the play of shadows.

People, as well as things, are individual. Everything has an individual character and an individual history. No two things can be exactly alike. However, the consequence of their individuality is that the infinite number of things of this world cannot be completely fathomed. There is something incomprehensible in individuality: abstractions are simpler and more comprehensible to the intellect. We understand abstractions, general truths, better than individual things in their immense complexity. In particular, science, which operates with general concepts, does not have the means to apprehend the individuality of things. It is too simple and precise to serve us as the complete measure of things. By this view of the individual nature of things Newman departed from universalism and rationalism, which generally predominate in philosophy and were particularly strong in his times.

People and things can be known in two ways: concretely and abstractly. Newman called the first real and the second conceptual. The first operates solely on the basis of experience, the second, however, uses analysis and generalization. Of course, even conceptual knowledge has its ultimate source in experience, but departs from it to a greater or lesser degree. With this departure, however, it loses sight of the unique and individual in things. For example, when man is conceptualized, he is not a real man; he is a creation of comparison and analysis: when we consider him conceptually, we apprehend not reality but only a verbal definition. We consider man most frequently in this latter way: our most frequent conceptions of people, nations, and societies are primarily abstract and verbal. It is no different with our conceptions of things. Of the immense number of characteristics that each real and individual thing possesses, conceptions retain only a small number; therefore, these conceptions reveal nothing of its reality and individuality. Such a conceptual approach impoverishes things and strips them of their diversity. Hence, it does not apply to reality; it is subjective and arbitrary.

2. *Evidence and Assent*.   The assertions we recognize as genuine also have a double nature: some we recognize because we have evidence for them, others because we have direct "assent" concerning their authenticity. We do not necessarily need proof to assent to something; we may assent even though we have no proof. The reverse also happens: we may be able to cite evidence to support our assertions, yet we fail to assent. Assent without argumentation, without reasoning that has the power of proof, is so common that, if we consider it irrational, we have to admit that human nature is irrational.

Newman's beliefs corresponded to a rather common opposition in philosophy to discursive and intuitive knowledge, an opposition of rational knowledge to irrational. For him, assent not based on evidence was not only a distinct kind of knowledge, but the most important kind. Proved assertions are neither the most important nor the most certain part of our knowledge. Evidence disappoints us in the face of life. To understand concrete truth we need a more subtle, pliant, and diverse approach than verbal argumentation. For this reason, logical knowledge, with its concepts and proofs, operating with abstractions, is of a lower order, whereas assent is derived directly from concrete life. The logical world is our construction no less than the world of poetry. Moreover, even logic appeals to assent: its first principles cannot be proven and, therefore, can only be a matter of assent. This concept of assent became the central point of Newman's theory of knowledge.

3. *The Illative Sense*.   According to Newman, however, direct intuition of reality supplies the material for our assents. In addition to this, we have a particular "illative sense." This is the ability of concrete and individual reasoning, different from the ability of reasoning according to general rules: it is an individual gift, not a method or a rule. It has as many forms as there are objects: for example, Newton had this ability in physics, but lacked it in theology. Newman modeled this concept on the earlier concepts of "sense of beauty" and "moral sense," which played an important role in the philosophy of the eighteenth century but were later rejected as too dogmatic. Newman, however, renewed and expanded these concepts,

asserting that besides the sense of beauty and good, there is
also a sense of truth. He united two seemingly incompatible
characteristics in one concept: inference, or approaching
truth according to rules, and instinct, or the ability to approach it directly, without rules. This concept, called the
"illative sense" or "personal logic," expressed the whole paradoxical nature of ascribing impersonal as well as personal
characteristics to inference.

The illative sense gave Newman's theory of knowledge a
dogmatic feature, in contrast to the general tendency of modern philosophy. In clear opposition to Cartesianism, he wrote
that if he had only had one choice, he would be inclined to assert that men should begin from belief in everything rather
than doubt of everything. Descartes directed us to begin from
doubt, Newman from faith.

This individualistic conception of cognition was not subjective and relative. Newman did not understand "individual"
logic to mean that everyone has his own personal truth, but
rather that, in some mysterious way, truth penetrates the very
depth of human individuality, and only there can be discovered.

Having broken with impersonal conception of knowledge,
Newman countered the modern philosophical traditions of rationalism and empiricism. Nevertheless, he believed that he was a
true empiricist, not Locke and all the others who assumed this
name. He asserted that Locke at most indicated how the mind
should operate, whereas he showed how it really works.

Half of Newman's theory of knowledge was skeptical and
negative; no weakness of the human mind escaped his attention.
He believed that there is no universally valid logic just as
there is no universally valid theory of poetry and politics.
Not without reason Huxley called Newman's book a "handbook of
skepticism." The second half of his theory, however, the theory of assent, was wholly positive. But what was Newman's "assent"? More or less what is generally termed faith. He did
not respect knowledge and committed himself to faith. This was
not the first time in the history of philosophy that a critique
of knowledge had ended in subordinating knowledge to belief.
This was natural for a thinker like Newman, so preoccupied with
religious matters.

Newman's theory was a general theory of knowledge, but it
originated from reflections on the knowledge of God. In such a
case, reason, verification, and logic can play no role. We
have no convincing proof concerning the existence of God. On
the other hand, we do have nonreasoned assent. We do not and
cannot have proof, because every proof must derive its premises
from the world, and the world is unlike God. Moreover, religion is life, and life in its complexity cannot be subjected to
proofs. It is in the nature of reason that it not only does
not substantiate religion but destroys it. No truth, even the

most holy, Newman admitted, can withstand the attack of reason:
because reason always turns in the direction of disbelief and
raises difficulties. If he had no inner conviction, the sight
of the world would have made him an atheist, pantheist, or pol-
ytheist, he said.

Predecessors

Newman had very little philosophical erudition; it ended
with Hume and Butler. He did not know the critical philosophers such as Kant. He was less acquainted with continental
thought than were many Englishmen of the Victorian Age. In
connection with his most important theory, he stated that he
had never devoted himself to studies of what others had said on
the subject. He had no interest in the ideas of contemporary
thinkers. He never studied Kierkegaard, Carlyle, or Ruskin for,
as was stated on one occasion, "prophets do not read one another." He tried to derive his views from early Christianity, as
the most certain source, but he was little acquainted with the
greatest of the Church fathers, Augustine, who was closest to
him.

Nevertheless, his autogenous philosophy belongs to a trend
with a long tradition: Augustinianism. It is related to fide-
istic doctrines, which were quite numerous in the middle ages
and in later times produced Pascal and Malebranche. Newman's
reliance on faith was modern in claiming to be based on a psychological analysis of the mind.

The main event of Catholic philosophy of the nineteenth
century was the renewal of Thomism. Newman's views preceded
this event; they were proclaimed while Catholic thought was
still fluctuating. If Augustine and Thomas are taken as poles,
Newman was nearest to the former in the nineteenth-century
thought.

Summary

The predominance of concrete knowledge over conceptual,
direct assent over proof, personal logic over general logic,
and faith over knowledge: this is Newman's contribution to
nineteenth-century philosophy. He did not argue that such a
predominance was necessary, but that it occurred in reality;
for him it was not something to be desired but a description of
the human mind.

This position opposed the prevailing trends of the nineteenth century, especially those of its second half. It was a
harbinger of trends to come. In particular, Newman was a pre-
cursor of pragmatism, Bergsonism, activism, all irrationalisms,

intuitionisms, personalisms, and radical empiricisms of the twentieth century. Seeing this relationship, one of Newman's enthusiasts asserted that his *Grammar of Assent* will mean the same thing for future generations as the *Summa Theologiae* of St. Thomas and Descartes' *Discourse on Method*.

Influence

Newman had the greatest influence in theology. His desertion shook the Anglican church to its foundations. He also influenced the Catholic church by entering it. He embodied an antithesis to intellectualism, a church tradition from the time of scholasticism; with him, a new wave of Augustinianism entered Catholic philosophy and apologetics. Parallel views also appeared in other countries, especially in France, where they were represented by A. Gratry, L. Laberthonnière, and E. Le Roy.

In England, as Carlyle did, he represented opposition to empirical rationalism and utilitarianism, the dominant trends of the nineteenth century. His opposition was of a different kind, however; Carlyle presented the idea of the independent hero, whereas Newman presented the idea of the universal church, "the communion of saints."

In twentieth-century philosophy, Newman's ideas returned in another, more worldly form through people who sometimes did not even know of Newman. This was more the case on the continent than in England. Those who referred to him directly in philosophy were very few. Henry Bremond, who applied his ideas both in the history of religion and in aesthetics, where he preached an exclusively emotional theory of "pure poetry," was his most faithful follower. In Poland, Stanislaw Brzozowski admired Newman and, as the years passed, was more and more influenced by his ideas.

Newman and Kierkegaard

Kierkegaard was born later and died much earlier than Newman, but the 1840s were climactic in both their lives. Both were exceptions in their epoch. Both were estranged from its intellectualism and universalism; they belonged neither to the waning rationalistic metaphysical trend nor to the rising positivistic one. Both were religious philosophers: their interests began and ended with religious matters, with the relation of man to God. Yet, in spite of these common interests, much separated them. They did not know of each other, although they did not live far apart. But one might assume that, had they known of each other, they would not have agreed. Their religiosity was extremely diverse, one cheerful, the other tragic.

For Newman, the relationship to God was full of confidence; for Kierkegaard, it was full of dread. Both originated in a Protestant milieu, and both abandoned it, but Newman later entered the Catholic church, while Kierkegaard after breaking with his own church joined no church.

Newman strove to explain the nature of cognition. He believed that everything else is quite simple. There is no need to philosophize, one only needs to listen to what "assent" tells each of us, which is that man can trust in God, and then all doubts will vanish.

For Kierkegaard it was just the opposite: faith, religion, the intercourse of man with God, are sources of dread, anxiety, and the tragedy of human existence. This inescapable tragedy, not the question of cognition, is the content of his philosophy.

KIERKEGAARD

Life

Sören Kierkegaard (1813-1855) was a Dane and spent his life in Copenhagen, a city in which scientific and philosophical activity was then overshadowed by literary and theological trends. He was brought up in a somber religious atmosphere and from this background acquired a strong feeling of guilt and dread of divine retribution. "If I had lived in the middle ages," he wrote, "I would have entered a monastery." At the same time, he compared his state with one that was called "acedia" in the middle ages, a state which characterizes recalcitrance to religious practices and longing for the world. From his earliest years, he masked his melancholy with irony and eccentric behavior. For the most part, he lived alone, but one should not imagine him as a sullen hermit. Like Socrates, he stopped people on the street and conversed with them. In his youth he frequented coffee houses and theatres. He used to spend the late evenings alone in his huge Copenhagen apartment, but the suite of rooms had to be lighted *a giorno*. His total immersion in religious matters and his obsession with the dread of existence came later, toward the end of his short life. Among other things, his unusual mind had the quality of exaggerating each thought, of expanding it to supernatural proportions: this explains some features of his philosophy.

Writings

Kierkegaard had short but intensive periods in which he devoted himself to literary work: one lasted from 1843 to 1846, a second from 1849 to his death. In the first period he published *Either/Or* (1843), *Fear and Trembling* (1843), *The Concept of Dread* (1844), and *Stages on Life's Way* (1845). The psychological romance, entitled *Diary of the Seducer*, is part of the book *Either/Or*.

In 1848, he went through a crisis: "God acquired a meaning for me such as I had never assumed." He then thought of becoming a clergyman and settling in a village parish. But he abandoned these plans and returned to literary work. Yet, this second period of activity already had an exclusively religious character. Among his works that are important in philosophy are his *Diaries*, which he kept from 1833 to 1855.

From the beginning, he had philosophical and religious interests, and his talents were both philosophical and literary. Hence, the content of his works fluctuates between philosophy and theology and their form between science and literature.

Predecessors

Kierkegaard's predecessors are difficult to find: he owed more to himself than to others. He knew Hegel's philosophy, which was widespread during his lifetime, but opposed it. In 1841, he went to Berlin specifically to hear Schelling, but afterward became quickly disenchanted. His model was Socrates: he referred not to philosophical tradition but directly to life. Taking little notice of what philosophy had accomplished before him, he created his own concepts, terms, and problems.

In every generation he wrote, two or three people have to be sacrificed for others and consumed by terrible sufferings in order to discover what the others need. "Having sorrowfully discovered that I am destined for this, I understood myself."

If anyone preceded him in this manner of thinking, it was Augustine and Pascal. They had in common with Kierkegaard their exclusive preoccupation with man, and all of them saw that infinity continually opens up before him. The relationship of a finite creature to terrifying infinity was their problem as well as Kierkegaard's.

Views

1. *Existentialist Philosophy*. Kierkegaard's understanding of philosophy had three basic peculiarities.

First, he was exclusively interested in man, mainly in his relationship to God. The problems he posed arose from feelings of anxiety and dread, which he endured, believing that they are inseparable from life: in this he was in agreement with Pascal, but in opposition to Newman, whose faith was without anxiety and dread.

Kierkegaard's was a philosophy of life, but for him the problems of life were exclusively moral and religious. He treated philosophy in a manner similar to Socrates: he did not intend to develop it systematically; rather, he wished, as he said, to "make difficulties" for it.

Second, he was a subjectivistic, programmatic thinker: "I want to find a truth that is the truth for me. And of what use would such a so-called objective truth be for me if it did not have deep meaning for my life?" In this, he was in accord with Newman and in disagreement with the aspirations of his time.

He was also a pluralistic thinker—in clear opposition to contemporary philosophy, striving to systems and unity, he saw multiplicity and alternatives. He saw that life has many forms and that man is faced with an inescapable "either-or," the necessity of choice.

Third, philosophy, as it was usually practiced, with general concepts, seemed too abstract to him. As Newman did, he wanted a philosophy that would penetrate man's concrete existence and his ethical and religious characteristics. He called such a philosophy "existential."

This entire concept of philosophy—humanistic, skeptical, pluralistic, existential—directly countered the prevailing concept among both metaphysicians and positivists in the nineteenth century.

2. Finitude and Infinity in Existence. The basic characteristic of human existence is its temporality. It cannot be contained in a system or formula, for it is always developing, becoming something different without end. It can only be embraced by thought if it is stopped, for one always thinks back but lives forward. Since human existence is becoming, then existential philosophy must also be a philosophy of becoming. It cannot be scholarly and systematic, because its subject is existence with its changeability and anxiety. In the face of continually growing multiplicity and diversity, existence cannot be unity; unity is only the creation of thought. And only thought, not existence, can be contained in a system. The error of idealistic philosophy, particularly the Hegelian, is that it did not see the difference between thought and existence and patterned existence on the model of thought.

Human existence is always temporal, finite, mundane. Despite this, man looks at it from the viewpoint of eternity. In this way, temporality inevitably conflicts with eternity. "Man is a synthesis of finitude and infinity, temporality and infinity, determinateness and freedom." This is the source of the worst contradictions and sufferings in man. He cannot free himself from inevitable contradictions and conflicts between changeable existence and unchanging being, between transience and eternity, in other words between man and God.

Divine being, eternal and unchanging, must seem irrational to finite man; for man, who has such a completely different nature from the divine, it is and always will remain a paradox. The paradoxical nature, the incomprehensibility of God is not the result of the weakness of the human mind but a natural expression of the relationship between man, to whom only transient existence is given, and God, who is eternal.

3. *The Pursuit of Infinity and the Fear of It*. Man escapes from existence to authentic being, from transience to eternity; above all, this is expressed in religion. It is indispensable for man, but it brings him doubts and suffering, for nothing can fill the chasm between it and divine being, eternal and absolute. Every approach to God lowers man and convinces him of his own impotence. It evokes, as Kierkegaard said, "fear and trembling," the natural way in which God appears in human existence.

Kierkegaard differentiated two forms of religion, which he called "religion A" and "religion B." Every religion presents man with infinity, but "religion A" presents it only as a backdrop to human existence. Eternity, even seen from a distance, frightens man; it is a paradox and dream for him: yet, it is relatively accessible to him and does not require a departure from his natural way of existence. On the other hand, "religion B" introduces God's infinity into the very existence of finite man: it defies reason, it even increases the paradox and torment. Christianity is such a religion. For Kierkegaard, the natural relationship to such a religion is fear and trembling. To represent Christianity as consolation, as a religion of joy, is complete falsification. "I sit in my quiet room and know only one danger: religion."

Two opposing aspirations develop in man: on one hand, he strives for infinity, but, on the other hand, he defends his own finite existence against it. And, in defending himself against it, he confines himself to the fortune that fate has given him and convinces himself that it is his own decision, that he is unsuited for eternity. He occupies his consciousness with various interests, fills it with amusements or anything that can take his mind away from thinking about infinity. He tells himself that he will think about it some other time, only not now, that there is still time. And ultimately, he never thinks about it. In this way he creates the forms of his usual, everyday existence; in large part they are forms of escape from eternity.

This duality in the attitude of man is joined to another contradiction: that he strives to know himself but at the same time tries to hide from himself, to hide his aspirations, especially the aspiration to eternity, which unsettles him because it pushes him out of his temporal existence. During the entire course of human existence a battle rages between two aspirations: the aspiration to see into one's own inner depths and the aspiration to retain a superficial, but more comforting, picture of oneself.

Depending on which of these two drives is prevalent in man, various "stages" of life are formed. Two of them are most distinctly opposed: the aesthetic and the ethical-religious.

4. *Stages of Life*. One stage of life is inclined not to realities but to possibilities: man freely plays with them in his imagination; because they are only possibilities, they do not encumber him. He continually changes them, makes new combinations out of them, and transforms life into a kaleidoscope. He hardly touches reality; his life is never stable. Such a stage of life, full of undeniable charm, gives the most material to the artist and poet; therefore, Kierkegaard called it aesthetic.

The ethical stage, however, seeks not possibilities but reality in life. It has seriousness and a feeling of responsibility that are lacking in the aesthetic. The aesthetic stage passes from one experience to another, but the ethical stage, having once found appropriate experiences, clings to them and repeats them: this is its basic characteristic. The ethical stage is endurance, just as the aesthetic is change. However, after endurance comes concentration, a deepening of one's immersion in the self. Whoever escapes into the future, says Kierkegaard, is a coward, whoever escapes into the past a hedonist, and only the one who clings to the present and wishes to repeat it is a true man.

Kierkegaard mentioned the religious stage as a third kind of life, but for him it was little different from the ethical type. He understood ethics religiously, as the relationship of man to God, and religion ethically. The difference was only that ethics has a general character and religion a personal one. But, in the final analysis, they comprise a common attitude, which is opposed to the aesthetic. This opposition is basic: for the ethical-religious stage of life brings God into existence, and the aesthetic does not. In essence, however, God is different from man, and therefore, man must live differently with God than without God.

Religion, by introducing man to eternity, fills him with dread and inflicts suffering upon him. It works in his interests, demanding absolute devotion from him, not giving any secular advantage in exchange. But it gives him something else: tension and depth (deepening awareness). To declare for or against religion is a difficult matter. Man has before him an "either-or": he can decide for finitude or infinity. There is no intermediate solution in this "either-or." There is no compromise; as Kierkegaard said, there is a "leap." And man repeatedly chooses the hard road of religion, for he feels that he is something more than what he can realize in the course of his limited existence, that he is never completely himself in finite form.

5. *Subjectivity of Truth*. Human cognition is always uncertain. Man cannot overcome this uncertainty; he will never attain objective truth; at most, he will acquire a subjective feeling of it. Hence, Kierkegaard said that "truth is subjective." And, turning this sentence around, he also said that "subjectivity is truth." Yet, he did not understand this relatively, that there are as many truths as there are subjects. Nor did he conceive this in the sense of Kant's or Fichte's philosophy: that the subject creates or, at least, conditions truth.

His assertion was more compatible with common sense; it rested on the notion that truth can be verified only in the subjective life. Newman had a similar view. The deeper man's personal life, the more truth there is in him. Therefore, for Kierkegaard and Newman authentic cognition had to be grounded in concrete personal life and could not have an abstract character.

Summary

The opposition of concrete existence and abstract thought, the opposition of finite existence and eternal being, the struggle between finitude and infinity in human existence, the need for eternity and the flight from it, the "either-or" continually confronting man—these were the main motifs of Kierkegaard's philosophy. More than any other lay thinker he pointed to the religious, transcendental factor in temporal existence. More sharply than anyone else he saw the tragedy of this existence, for man must choose either finitude or infinity. If he opts for finitude he chooses nothingness; if he opts for infinity, he chooses torment. Yet, Kierkegaard believed that whoever chose finitude for the sake of peace and comfort deprived him-

self of half of his existence, for man is a "synthesis of finitude and infinity."

Influence

In his own time, Kierkegaard had influenced only in his
own country and in the field of religion rather than philosophy.
The period after his death, in which positivism, scientism, and
mechanism prevailed, really could not understand his ideas.
But his time came in the twentieth century. At first, he was
admired as a psychologist and story-writer of the first rank.
Then, as a theologian, his influence gave rise to the Protestant theology called "dialectic" or the "theology of crisis,"
which saw the seeds of death everywhere in temporal life and
understood religion as both the misfortune of man and his only
salvation. Finally, around 1930, Kierkegaard enjoyed a renaissance as a philosopher: the new "existentialist" philosophy of
Heidegger, Jaspers, Sartre, and others, one of the main trends
of the epoch, took from Kierkegaard not only its problem and
name but also its basic motifs. In 1948 a "Kierkegaard Society"
was founded in Copenhagen, and a "Kierkegaard prize" was established for works that developed his problems.

The Second Phase: 1860-1880

Around 1860 a change took place in philosophy. This
change did not come from the formulation of new ideas, for
there were really fewer new ideas in this period than earlier.
Rather, a selection was made from among earlier views. Many
views that had been developed by the previous generation became
secondary as positivism captured the imagination.

This view had already been expressed in the works of Mill
and Comte, but these thinkers were not really representative of
their times. Before 1860, Carlyle had perhaps more supporters
than Mill, and Newman more than Comte. Although the spirit of
positivism had already appeared, romanticism was still vigorous.
But, in any event, the main feature of the preceding period was
the variety and multiplicity of its forms. Now this multiplicity began to be replaced by uniformity. The ideas of Hegel,
the romantics, Carlyle, Newman, Kierkegaard, Stirner did not
become extinct, but they receded into the background.

Discoveries in the Natural Sciences

The predominance of positivism resulted from developments
in philosophy, but it owed part of its success to developments
in the natural sciences. A series of scientific discoveries
were far-reaching and important to philosophy. Around 1860,
the most important of these had already been made and knowledge
of them had become fairly widespread.

In physics, the principle of the conservation of energy
was independently discovered in the 1840s by the Englishman
J. P. Joule and the German J. R. von Mayer. It demonstrated
the common nature of similar phenomena, joining them in an indissoluble chain. This evidence strongly supported the thesis
of determinism.

In chemistry, Kekulé von Stradonitz in the 1850s formulated his theory of the constitution of benzene. This began a great number of theoretical syntheses in organic chemistry, which offered a simple explanation of complex phenomena. Shortly after this, in 1869, the Russian chemist Mendeleev made an even more important theoretical discovery: the periodic table of the elements.

In biology, Schwann and Schleiden in 1838 and 1839 discovered that the cell was the single element from which multiplication and diversification of all organisms proceeds. This proved the unity of higher and lower organisms and provided evidence against vitalism and biological mysticism.

In zoology, Darwin's theory in 1859 offered a natural explanation for the variety of species and permitted the construction of a theory of general evolution in which man was included.

In physiology, the theory of sensory energy initiated by the English anatomist Sir Charles Bell (*New Idea of the Anatomy of the Brain*) in 1811 was further developed and popularized by the German physiologist J. Müller from 1838. This provided evidence that emotional qualities were subjective and led to a quantitative and mechanical understanding of all phenomena.

All of these discoveries, as well as many lesser ones, reinforced the tendency to view the universe as (1) completely determined, (2) uniformly constructed, and (3) wholly accessible to human reason and intellect.

At the same time, however, the minimalistic philosophical doctrines formulated in the previous generation, Comte's positivism and Mill's empiricism, had already become widespread. These doctrines complemented the discoveries made in the natural sciences. Together they painted a picture of the world that became the common property of the age. The elements of this view had been singly created by the previous generation but now were combined into a complete view of the world. Positivism had existed earlier, but now its era had come.

A Philosophy That Did Not Believe in Philosophy

No one expressed the prevailing mood better than Joseph Renan. In 1862 he wrote:

> An astonishing fact, an outstanding characteristic of the last thirty years of thought, is the lack of any kind of speculative philosophy. This lethargy will not end soon. I do not see any indications of its end. I see a great future for the historical sciences. I foresee their improvement and rapid development. I see a future for the natural sciences. But I do not foresee a future for philosophy in the earlier form in

which this science was understood. The specialized
sciences have appropriated philosophical thoughts,
which in earlier ages would have been indivisibly
linked to metaphysics. Philosophers have become phi-
lologists, chemists, and physiologists.

The Uniformity of Philosophy

Rarely had an epoch ever been as uniform as this one. The
various theories and currents it produced—positivism and evolutionism, independent psychology and inductive metaphysics—
were only variations of one philosophy. One great minimalistic
current ran off into smaller ones. Such a uniform minimalistic
philosophy had not existed even in the eighteenth century.

If one can ever speak of any philosophy as "ruling" during
a particular period, then it is safe to say it of the minimalistic philosophy of positivism during those years of the nineteenth century. First, the vast majority of thinkers took this
position. Further, a general consensus existed among philosophers and the intelligentsia, such as had seldom been seen in
history, for the intelligentsia does not usually accept the
views of specialists immediately.

Of course, even at this time there were philosophical deviations from the main current. Some thinkers had not yet in-
tellectually matured to positivism, and others had gone beyond
it. Carlyle and Newman were still alive and writing. Herbart's pupils still held chairs in Germany and Austria, and
Cousin's disciples were prominent in France. Even among
younger thinkers, some belonged to other camps. For instance,
in England soon after 1860 Stirling and Green strove to renew
Hegelian philosophy, an opposite view to the prevailing minimalistic philosophy. In Germany, Fechner was spinning metaphysical poetry. In 1874, Brentano announced his psychology, which
was totally different from the prevailing one. Although these
views would later influence the development of thought, now
they were cut off and hardly noticed.

Varieties of Positivism

Despite the uniformity of the positivistic philosophy of
the nineteenth century, distinctive currents and theories made
their appearance. In each of its manifestations positivism developed in a different environment, in opposition to a different prevailing philosophy. In England, it developed in opposition to the philosophy of common sense, in France to eclectic
metaphysics, in Germany to the systems of Hegel and Herbart.
In England, positivistic philosophy accorded with the previous

tradition of that nation, in France it had predecessors in the eighteenth century, in Germany it was a novelty.

In England, it appeared in its simplest, most dogmatic form, without critical debates and without being subjected to epistemological doubts. In France, it assumed the form of skeptical positivism, riddled with doubts. And in Germany, it was a critical current with epistemological emphases, analyzing its own foundations and assertions.

Only in England was positivism a complete philosophical system. Darwin and Spencer developed the idea of evolution and, from this, were able to unite separate philosophical disciplines into a system. English evolutionism was the only complete philosophical system erected on the foundations of positivism. In England positivistic philosophy was, above all, a philosophy of the natural sciences, while in France it was a philosophy of the humanistic sciences. The French created the most typical positivistic theories of art and religion. The work of the positivists in Germany was in still a different vein. Some worked on the further subdivision of philosophy, separating the particular sciences from it, while others worked on the theory of knowledge and the epistemological foundations of positivism. Still others strove to supplement positivism by some sort of "critical," "inductive," "scientific" metaphysics, a kind that could be fitted into the anti-metaphysical framework of the epoch. Poland was most influenced by English positivism, accepting it as a scientific fact beyond dispute and without considering its assumptions and degree of credibility. But, even in Poland, positivism had its own hue. It was more practically inclined, more life-oriented than in England.

Smaller and younger nations, which had a shorter philosophical tradition, did not play as great a role at this time as the larger ones, but even they had outstanding and influential positivists. The Italians produced an uncommon thinker, Roberto Ardigo. The famous Danish philosopher, Höffding, was quite close to the positivists in his careful method of thinking. In Czechoslovakia, the philosopher and politician T. G. Masaryk was a positivist. Many different countries took part in creating the minimalistic philosophy of this epoch.

The Major Interests of the Epoch

Above all, this epoch had theoretical interests. It strove to acquire knowledge of reality rather than a consciousness of what man should do with this knowledge. It was also more concerned with the common features of reality, the general laws governing it, than with the individual features of things and people, their historical development and their distinctness.

Nonetheless, it also took an interest in religious, ethical, and aesthetic affairs, approaching these problems from its own particular point of view.   Toward religion it assumed a basically negative posture: nothing can be contained in philosophy that has not been verified by or is not verifiable by a fact.   However, religion also has facts.   If what people believe in is not a fact, that they do believe is.   Positivists were willing to take this into consideration.   Among them, some even considered faith an important component of the human psyche, purifying and elevating it.   Yet, all positivists believed that it was an error to link faith with knowledge, religion with science.   For this reason, they could not consider such conceptions of religion as those of Newman or Kierkegaard, who saw in religion a source of knowledge and considered it a partner of the sciences.   These views were completely irreconcilable with the spirit of positivism.

The attitude of positivism toward social and political matters was also chiefly negative.   This conception had no place for a mystical and irrational view of power, the state, and law, or for an appeal to tradition or authority.   To be sure, Comte became a devotee of authoritarian politics, but only liberalism was harmonious with the spirit of positivism. Mill had the greatest influence on political views in the second half of the nineteenth century.   Positivism valued freedom and equality above all, it had no use for hierarchical conceptions of society.

Realism marked the aesthetic theory of the positivists. Art stemmed from the same real needs and abilities of people as other aspects of life.   Real life was the most appropriate expression of its essence, in the plastic arts as well as in literature.   In 1855 Courbet proclaimed the slogan of "realism" in painting.   Impressionism was also an attempt to capture in art what is most real to us, our own impressions.   Reality itself, without constructions, without retouching, is in these impressions.   A similar tendency was evident in literature: the "experimental" stories of Zola and the Russian and Scandinavian realists almost eradicated the division between science and art.

Trends and Theories in the Era of Positivism

This epoch was uniform, but it had many shades and hues. To understand its philosophy precisely all of them must be mentioned.

1. Evolutionism, the great system of the epoch, united the findings of science according to the spirit of positivism.

2. Popular positivism, more properly called "scientism" and primarily espoused by specialized scientists and the intelligentsia, placed unqualified faith in the specialized sciences.
3. Positivism attempted to subdivide or parcel out philosophy and distinguish it from the specialized sciences, especially psychology.
4. A theory of knowledge, appearing in the form of empiriocriticism, attempted to create a base for positivism.
5. Positivism attempted to create a "critical" or "inductive metaphysics."
6. Developments in the humanities were in the spirit of positivism.
7. Some positivists arrived at skeptical proposals.

HERBERT SPENCER AND EVOLUTIONISM

Positivistic and empirical philosophy in the nineteenth century profitted from the results of the particular sciences, especially the natural sciences. Herbert Spencer formed the base of an evolutionist system of philosophy from the naturalistic concept of development. Evolutionism became a strong trend in minimalistic philosophy, supplementing positivism and empiricism.

Herbert Spencer (1820-1903) was an engineer by education. In his youth, he was primarily concerned with politics and wrote articles in the spirit of liberalism and individualism. Also among his early interests was the problem of organic and social development. He introduced the evolutionary explanation of phenomena in *Social Statics* (1851). Darwin's *On the Origin of Species*, which appeared in 1859, confirmed his assumption. In 1860 he arrived at the idea of working out a whole system of philosophy from this point of view and immediately published a prospectus for his *The Synthetic Philosophy*. From then on he devoted his life to fulfilling this program. He made few changes, working unhurriedly but ceaselessly for nearly forty years. Included in this system are *First Principles* (1862), as well as the several volumes of *The Principles of Biology* (1864-67), *Principles of Psychology* (1855-72), *The Principles of Sociology* (1876-96), and *The Principles of Ethics* (1892-93).

His system was exceptionally uniform: the diverse material drawn from the various sciences is reduced to one idea in this system. It is perhaps the most complete and most extraordinary achievement of a great ambition known to modern philosophy. Spencer accomplished a work of such great dimensions, despite unfavorable material circumstances and fragile health, thanks to the regularity of his life, isolation, and absolving himself from conventional obligations. To the end of his life, Spencer retained the intellectual characteristics of his youth: he remained an individualist and liberal as well as an engineer for whom mechanism is the only genuine explanation of phenomena. He discussed his life and career in his *Autobiography*, published posthumously in 1904.

Predecessors

Spencer was led to the idea of the evolutionary explanation of phenomena—even before the appearance of Darwin's work—by Lyell's geological investigations, Owen's zoological work, and von Baer's embryological enquiries. Owen taught him that higher organic creatures have greater common dependence than lower organic forms, von Baer that development increases the diversity of organisms. But, strangely, Spencer also benefited from the idea of the metaphysical poet Coleridge that life proceeds in the direction of increasing individualization.

Darwin was co-creator of this evolutionary system. Only with the help of his biological theory could Spencer have carried out his general philosophical conception. Spencer's *Synthetic Philosophy* conformed to the views of Darwin, who greeted him as a "great philosopher." Darwin influenced Spencer's theory, but Spencer also influenced the fortunes of Darwin's theory. It became widespread primarily in the terminology that Spencer gave it: Darwin originally did not use the term "evolution"; it was introduced by Spencer and only later applied to Darwin's theory. Darwin influenced nineteenth-century philosophy indirectly, through Spencer. Spencer was instrumental in shifting philosophical interest from physics to biology. For a time Darwin became for philosophy what Copernicus and Galileo had once been.

On the other hand, Spencer's evolutionism, based on the natural sciences, had little relationship to the Hegelian philosophy of idealistic evolutionism, based on speculation. Only this general idea united them. Beyond that, everything separated them. Spencer's evolutionism had links with earlier views, even those of ancient philosophers, for the general concept of evolution was as old as philosophy itself, having first appeared with the Greek hylozoists; but these views had been only programs. Spencer was the first philosopher to construct a detailed evolutionary philosophy. Moreover, he had only a minimal amount of historical training and was not well-read in philosophy. He said that, if he had read as much as others, he would have known as little as they did. However, he benefited from philosophers, especially in questions of epistemology. He was most impressed by Hamilton's relativism and agnosticism, and through Hamilton he benefited from Kant. Of course, he al-

so knew the most famous English philosopher of his times, J. S.
Mill, and shared a minimalistic position with him.   However,
Spencer represented a very different stance within the minimalistic framework.   Besides Mill, he also knew Comte.   They had
much in common: among the minimalist leaders of the nineteenth
century they were most alike.   One can almost say that Spencer's "synthetic philosophy" is the "positivistic philosophy"
of Comte enriched by the idea of evolution.   More precisely,
half of Spencer's system was dependent on Comte, and the second,
entirely different, was dependent on Kant.

Darwinism

The role of Charles Darwin (1809-1882) in biology was twofold: (1) He introduced empirical proof of the origin of new
species.   Earlier philosophers (such as Empedocles) had specu-
lated on this theme, and earlier scholars (such as Buffon or
Lamarck) had offered individual observations and materials as
proof.   (2) He formulated a hypothesis that explained the origin of new species, basing it on the fact that individual variations appear in each species.   Breeders use these variations
to select desirable characteristics; and Darwin believed that
nature also made selections, that "natural selection" also exists.   Some individuals have characteristics that favor their
continued existence, just as others have characteristics that
the breeder considers desirable.   When a surplus of individuals
exists, a "struggle for existence" (as the English zoologist A.
R. Wallace called it) results.   Only those who are best adapted
to the conditions of life can survive—the survival of the fittest.   Thus, nature keeps alive only those individuals who are
suitably constructed.   Their progeny inherit their characteristics and thus, thanks to insignificant and accidental variations, relatively stable species are formed.   These species are
effective, suited to life, not because everything that is born
is effective, but because ineffective forms have perished in
the struggle for existence.   Darwin was aware that his theory
of "natural selection" gives only a partial explanation of the
evolution of species: he knew that the origin of the life process itself, the growth of organisms, their multiplication, inheritance, and the appearance of variations were not explained.
His theory marked an epoch in both biology and philosophy.
It was important, because it broke an inveterate habit of thinking, common since the time of Aristotle and strengthened by
modern natural scientists, such as Linnaeus and Cuvier.   It
proceeded without theological assumptions and dispensed with
the Platonic-Aristotelian assertion that being has eternal, unchanging forms.   It opened the possibility of a purely causal
understanding of the world.

Darwin himself applied his theory to man (in *The Descent of Man*, 1871). It breached the dualism between man and the rest of the world and represented his nature in a different light. Darwin also laid the foundations for a new theory of knowledge. He explained that the concepts that man uses are also changeable, that they are plastic, that they develop in a natural way and maintain themselves only to the extent that they are suitable to the conditions of life.

Views

1. *Evolutionism*. The leading concept of Spencer's philosophy was evolution, or development. This concept contains three ideas: (1) that matter is subject to development; it is changeable; (2) that its changes take place continually and by stages; and (3) that changes take place in one direction, according to one law.

Here, Spencer took the position that the whole world is subject to development in all of its parts, that development is the universal law of the world. The name evolutionism was applied to this position.

Biology was point of departure of evolutionism. Development is clearest in the world of living creatures, but it is clear only for individuals. Species seem unchanging. But Darwin's theory indicated that species do develop; after him, the organic world in its entirety could be conceived evolutionistically. The qualities of living individuals could be explained not only by their own evolution, but also by the evolution of their species, achieved through generations.

Sciences influence each other many times and in many ways. Darwin's biology was the point of departure for universal evolutionism. But Darwin himself admitted that his model was Malthusian economics, which indicated that only a part of humanity can survive, while the other part perishes in the struggle for existence.

However, for Spencer, only biological development was the point of departure. He considered development as a universal law, governing not only organic creatures but all of nature. He went beyond Darwin, for whom this law was exclusively biological.

He also strove to explain what development was. He asserted that it is, above all, a matter of diverging parts. In a developing structure the parts of the structure become more diverse: this is the first feature of development. But other features are also associated with it: the developing structure enhances its value as well as its distinctness, harmony, and balance. In development, the structure passes from a state of homogeneity to a state of heterogeneity, from a loosely connected to a highly connected state, and from an indefinite and chaotic to a more determined and ordered state.

The term evolutionism, in its widest meaning, applies to all theories of development, and in its narrowest sense, it is specifically applied to Spencer's theory, where development means a differentiation, linking together, and ordering of parts.

According to Spencer, this law is universal and acts everywhere: in the formation of social systems, the creation of chemical bodies, organisms, intellects, societies, and cultures. It appears most clearly in the organic world, but it also takes place in the inorganic and the supraorganic, or social, worlds. As an organism forms itself by imbibing food, so clouds form by soaking up loose vapors, and sand banks by absorbing grains of sand: here, too, the parts pass from less to more highly complicated structures. This linking together, differentiation, and ordering of parts takes place everywhere. For this reason, all fields of science can and should be united in one system and considered according to one law.

Development, differentiation, and linking of structures invests them with ever greater balance and therefore perfects them. Hence, there is progress. However, progress has limits: when a structure arrives at a point of balance, it can no longer progress. It stops and even begins to regress, for every state of balance is unstable; it cannot continuously maintain itself. Therefore, after a period of progress comes a period of regression; what has been formed begins to decompose. For this reason, successive periods of progress and regression appear in history.

Spencer's conception was evolutionary, not revolutionary. His principle was gradual transformation. This was entirely different from Cuvier, for example, who saw the results of violent and catastrophic changes in the world. It has been said that Spencer was inspired by geology and reflections on English history.

Spencer subjected all nature, including man and psychic and social phenomena, to the law of development. Nothing and no one is an exception to this universal law. In particular, he did not believe that cultural laws were different from natural laws. His philosophy was characterized by monism and naturalism. The only law he recognized, derived from the natural sciences, was the law of nature.

Spencer was an engineer, accustomed to the operation of mechanisms: in looking at things he primarily saw the mechanisms that called them to life and operated in them. However, this influenced the character of his theory. He understood the world mechanistically, according to the functions of matter,

movement, and forces. In particular, he understood evolution
in this way. He reinterpreted biology according to the action
of mechanical forces. He believed that the phenomena of life,
the mind, and the social order develop in the same way as mechanical structures do, that they are more complicated phenomena with the same nature. He saw a mechanical process in every
kind of development: this was the most characteristic feature
of the evolutionism he created and passed on to the nineteenth
century.

2. *Evolutionistic Psychology and Theory of Knowledge.* Although biology was the point of departure and mechanics the
model for Spencer's evolutionism, the area in which he most
frequently applied it was psychology and the humanities. For
the most part, his views of evolution in nature were derived
from others, but in the evolution of culture they were original.
He was the first to identify the evolution of culture with the
evolution of nature.

He believed that psychic phenomena represent links in the
development of organic nature. They are as they are because
they were needed by the individual or the species for survival.
The forms of the intellect arose through adaptation to the conditions of life. Hence, they are neither first in order of appearance nor unchanging. Development creates them, development
substitutes others for them. For the mind there are no unchanging forms, about which the rationalists and critical philosophers had argued: all of them develop and change. But neither are these forms accidental: all of them are necessary
creations of development.

Spencer went even further: he believed that even the mind
itself is a creation of development. It was necessary to the
organism for survival and arose for that purpose. If its activity were not biologically useful, it would not have arisen
and maintained itself in the world.

Two main ideas appeared in Spencer's psychology: the idea
that psychic phenomena represent an unbroken continuum from the
lowest creatures to man, and the idea that these phenomena
develop under the influence of the environment, just as the
organism does. Both ideas gained wide currency.

The evolutionist conception of the mind was compatible
with the spirit of empiricism, although it granted the individual innate forms of thinking. These forms are innate only to
the individual, but they are inherited by him and are dependent
on the experience of previous generations: this was a new solution of the old debate between empiricism and apriorism. It
made allowance for apriorism but resolved the debate in favor
of empiricism. It even supplied empiricism with a new argument,

pointing out that we owe to experience even what we ourselves have not experienced. It created a new variant of empiricism.

Spencer's ideas created a peculiar form of relativism in the theory of knowledge. Its most usual form had been psychological, asserting that cognition is dependent on the cognizant mind's psychic processes. However, Spencer initiated biological relativism. He asserted that cognition is dependent on the cognizant organism, on its adaptation to the needs and conditions of life.

3. *Evolutionistic Ethics.* Spencer explained human behavior and thinking through the laws of nature and development: if people acted and thought differently, they would not survive. Similarly, he tried to establish how they should act. He was convinced that the only law is the natural law; hence, the criteria of duty, good, and evil, if they exist, must be found in these laws. "Good" behavior is in accordance with and adapted to nature. Spencer based his biological and evolutionist ethics on this criterion: goodness and morality are only what life and its development demands. This was an extremely naturalistic ethic: moral behavior and natural behavior were one and the same. It was also a completely relativistic ethic, considering no value as eternal, especially moral value. In contrast to the majority of moral philosophers, Spencer believed that moral value is temporary and will cease to be binding when the development of humanity reaches its limits, for then people will be completely adapted and moral norms will be unnecessary.

These foundations of Spencer's ethics were relatively new, but the conclusion was old: they led to the theory of hedonism. Pleasure can be recognized as the measure of every good, for then the organism feels that it is adapted to the conditions of life. Spencer represented an old theory as resulting from naturalistic, biological facts. Earlier hedonists had appealed to its obviousness or to our manner of feeling; now, however, rejuvenated hedonism appeared in the guise of Darwinism, evolutionism, and adaptation to life.

Spencer's hedonism differed from Mill's contemporary hedonism, which was spiritual, almost ascetic. It returned to the hedonism of the eighteenth century. It did not recognize the superiority of spiritual pleasures over physical pleasures, opposing moral asceticism and defending egoism. Man was correct in striving to secure goods and pleasures for himself alone, particularly material goods and physical pleasures; it recognized as a law, even a moral obligation, that one should care for oneself more than for others.

The most general precepts of Spencer's ethics were: life must be differentiated, made as intense and rich as possible.

If something should be done for others, it should be for the elite capable of a rich and intensive life, not for the weak and naturally handicapped.

This belief departed greatly from Christian ethics, based on love and charity. Spencer believed that it stemmed from the assumptions of evolutionism, but one important source was his own individualistic and liberal disposition. However, he did not derive the logical political consequence that weaker individuals should be subordinated to the stronger; freedom he felt, should be given to all.

He explained universally recognized ethical judgments in light of his views: they are founded in the inherited experience of the human race. What was a matter of experience and calculation for our forebears we have inherited as instincts and intuitions. Whence the feeling of necessity and obviousness. In this manner, he reconciled contending positions, just as he had done in the theory of knowledge: as in the latter he had reconciled empiricism with rationalism, here he reconciled utilitarianism with ethical intuitionism to the advantage of utilitarianism.

4. *Agnosticism.* Evolutionism was the most important part of Spencer's philosophy, but it had a second part that was totally independent of the first. Evolutionism dealt with phenomena, while this second part went beyond phenomena. Spencer wished to cultivate a positivistic philosophy, but he also posed nonpositivistic problems. Besides creating a system of knowledge embracing all phenomena, he wished to explain what their ultimate foundation was.

He then assumed that authentic reality exists beyond phenomena. But he also maintained—nonetheless revealing his link with minimalistic trends—that it is unknowable. Hence, he called this authentic reality "the unknowable." For this part of his philosophy he appealed to the philosophers, Hamilton in particular. One of his pupils, Huxley, gave this position the Greek name "agnosticism." This view was similar to Kant's, yet essentially different.

Spencer reasoned rather simply, as Hamilton had, that phenomena are relative. What is relative is not final but points to the existence of something absolute. Hence, he recognized an absolute state of existence, independent of us. He was a realist, an opponent of the subjectivistic conception of the world created by Berkeley and preserved by Mill. He called his realism "transformed," for it departed from naive realism. Idealism maintains that nothing exists above ideas in the consciousness; naive realism asserts that what exists is exactly like ideas, whereas transformed realism maintains that there is only a correspondence between them. What we have in our consciousness is not false, but neither is it a true reproduction of reality.

At first, Spencer believed that everything knowable is in the domain of science, and everything unknowable is in the domain of religion. Later, however, he concluded that both science and religion approach a mysterious, "unknowable" being. No conception really permits the world to be understood rationally: we cannot imagine it as immemorial and uncreated, nor can we imagine its beginning. The same difficulties appear in both science and religion: scientific concepts such as time, space, and matter cannot be conceived as either finite or infinite. In the final analysis, its explanations lead to something inexplicable. Mystery is the final thesis of science, just as it is the first thesis of religion. Spencer wished to satisfy man's scientific and religious needs with his system of "synthetic philosophy."

Summary

On one hand, Spencer's system derived its principles from the natural sciences, especially the principle of development, which Spencer used as an aid in explaining phenomena. On the other hand, however, he was inspired by the philosophers and recognized the existence of a reality beyond phenomena. His system was a peculiar creation of the mind. Through its link with the natural sciences it was close to positivism, but through its system-building ambitions and its recognition of absolute being it was related to metaphysical theories. In one part it had a minimalistic character, in another a maximalistic one. But the minimalistic part predominated, for relative phenomena are knowable, and absolute being is unknowable. Spencer's philosophy was predominantly an evolutionistic, monistic, and naturalistic theory of phenomena.

Opposition

Spencer was attacked from two directions: according to some, his theory, in its agnosticism, was dangerous for philosophy; according to others it was useless for the science of metaphysics. Some combated evolutionism because it asserted more than the facts permitted; others, however, attacked it because it asserted less than they permitted.

Spencer's naturalism, which reduced the laws of culture to the laws of nature, evoked the most criticism. His mechanistic way of considering development was also attacked. Critics charged that biological, psychological, and social phenomena

cannot be described in mechanistic terms, that this is not description but metaphor. Besides, Spencer did not retain his
mechanistic conception consistently: in defining development as
the transition from a less differentiated to a more highly differentiated state, he introduced a qualitative element, a definition that applied better to biology and sociology than to
mechanics.

His opponents found fault with the facts that his system
did not have an epistemological foundation, that it was insufficiently verified, and that it was dogmatic. Spencer did not
disclaim the dogmatism: Basic intuitions, he wrote, were indispensable to the functioning of thought; they had to be accepted
without discussion; verifying them was left to others.

Perhaps the majority of contemporary academic philosophers
reacted negatively to Spencer's "synthetic philosophy." They
considered its creator a "philosopher for the street," although
he based himself on science and pretended to scholarliness.

The Ambiguity of Evolutionism

"Evolution," was an ambiguous term. It means: (1) any
kind of change; (2) gradual change (in this meaning it was opposed to revolution); (3) change in a fixed direction; (4)
change proceeding from a lower to a higher state (here "evolution" becomes synonymous with "progress"); (5) change con-
sisting in structural differentiation. Darwin saw progress in
evolution; Spencer, above all, saw differentiation. These two
meanings are not identical: differentiation is not always progress; in technology as well as culture an opposite process,
simplification (or "involution"), often gives rise to progress.
The conviction that changes in nature lead to progress was natural for Darwin, who saw the action of Providence in nature
and its changes. On the other hand, as Bréhier correctly notes,
this conviction lost its foundation with the positivists and
materialists who took it from Darwin. This ambiguity in basic
concepts was one reason why unending disputes arose over evolution and why it continually assumed new forms in the course of
years.

Influence

Nevertheless, its unity, its completeness, and its link
with the discoveries and slogans of science made Spencer's philosophy unusually attractive. Many natural scientists, especially among the English, agreed with the system of evolutionism. Among these were the well-known physicist John Tyndall
(1820-1893) and the distinguished biologist T. H. Huxley (1825-

1895), who, together with Spencer, stressed the unknowableness of reality and considered metaphysical theories, materialistic no less than spiritual ones, as absurd aspirations to penetrate the final nature of things. The outstanding historian of philosophy G. H. Lewes (1817-1878) also supported Spencer.

Of the independent philosophers, J. S. Mill, who saw this theory as an acceptable addition to and enrichment of empiricism, greeted evolutionism favorably. The evolutionists conducted many debates with the empiricists of Mill's school and the positivists of Comte's school. For the most part, however, these were family quarrels; in most cases, the groups formed a common front. Positivism, which became almost obligatory in the progressive circles of Europe in the second half of the nineteenth century, arose from the union of their doctrines.

The Theory of Evolution and the Conception of Man

The idea of evolution exerted wide influence on the understanding of nature and man. Especially in this area (as the American historian J. H. Randall demonstrated) it resulted in many changes: (1) It shifted inquiries from the purpose of things to their particular causes. (2) It introduced the biological point of view to the social sciences and humanities and excluded the "geometrical spirit" that had predominated in the sciences from the seventeenth century. (3) It directed interest to the diversity of phenomena, to inquiries of people in their diversity rather than of man in general. (4) It introduced a new measure of value: earlier, what was natural, rational, and lasting had seemed most important; now what was new and progressive was most important. (5) It gave rise to the conviction that human affairs can develop in various ways and that they can and should be controlled. (6) In introducing the biological point of view to social phenomena, it involuntarily increased irrationalism; if everything is the result of adaptation to life, then science and its laws must also be an adaptation. In this regard, objective truth and cognition in the old-fashioned meanings of the terms lose their sense, and reason cannot pretend to be the ultimate criterion of truth. Although this was not its intention, this view prepared the ground for relativistic and irrational theories, for all varieties of pragmatism and conventionalism to appear in succeeding generations.

SCIENTISM

The achievements of the specialized sciences and minimalistic philosophies—positivism, empiricism, materialism, evolu-

tionism—created a certain common view for people of this epoch.
It is most frequently called "positivism," in the broad and
popular meaning of this term, although it took rather less from
Comte than from other philosophers. More correct is the term
"scientism" (from Renouvier), for the foundation of this view
was complete confidence in science in its sober and narrow
meaning. This view had thousands of representatives in various
countries. None was particularly outstanding, for originality
was not a concern of science at that time. However, among
these men none was more typical than Karl Pearson.

Representative of the Movement

Karl Pearson (1857-1936), professor of eugenics at the
University of London, director of the Galton Eugenics Laboratory, and for a time professor of mathematics and mechanics,
was an outstanding and universal scholar, competent in such
comprehensive fields as mathematics, probability theory, statistics, anthropology, sociology, history, and eugenics. His
most influential and noted work was *The Grammar of Science*
(1892), a fully developed statement of the version of science
commonly accepted at the end of the nineteenth century. Pearson himself has been called "the most superb, radical, and sin-
gle-minded embodiment of the scientistic view of the world."
Though he arrived at his synthesis rather late, it was
more complete than most others; it took account of the views of
Comte and Mill as well as Mach's theory of knowledge and the
newer Kantians. Scientism developed only in its details
through the absorption of new ideas, while its basic conception
remained unchanged. It lasted at least to the end of the century. Even after 1880, when philosophers began to oppose minimalism, it still remained the faith of the progressive European
intelligentsia.

Predecessors

The English empiricists, especially the Mills, were predecessors of scientism. Their most active successor was Alexander Bain (1818-1903), a link between the Mills and Pearson.
Bain's main works, published in the 1850s, were psychological,
but they contained all the important theses of empiricism such
as the falseness of all metaphysics, the unknowability of the
qualities and even of the existence of the world, the reduction
of all our knowledge to sense impressions, the determinative-
ness of all events and human actions, and the conviction that
morality stems from social pressure and experience, which
teaches that noncompliance with some norms incurs negative con-

sequences, disapproval, and punishment. In Pearson these theses of agnosticism, empiricism, determinism, and utilitarianism returned in modern guise.

Views

1. View of Science. The position of Pearson and many contemporaries who shared his views can be summarized in a few points:

1. Do we have certain knowledge? We have, but only in science.

2. In what kind of science? The natural sciences. Mathematics has only an auxiliary function; the humanities are useful only when they pattern themselves on the natural sciences.

3. What is the function of science? Verifying facts, but only their description not their explanation. Science only asks "how," not "why"; it cannot answer "why."

4. What is the scope of science? Everything that exists. No area is unfit for scientific inquiry.

5. What tools does science have to fulfill its task? Broadly speaking, general concepts and general assertions, or laws. Without these, science could not perform its descriptive function. The descriptions of science are abbreviations, a kind of shorthand necessary for economy of thinking. The concepts of science, in particular such general ones as "atom" or "electron," are not copies of reality; they are creations of the imagination of physicists. They are not absolute and fixed for all time; they are subject to instant challenge when they cease to be useful in describing facts or when more useful ones are created.

6. What is the aim of science? The aim is not pure theory, "science for the sake of science," but important practical tasks: science can help man adjust to his environment and serve as an effective instrument in his struggle for existence. The measure of its worth should be what it does to increase human comfort and raise the standard of living.

7. What is the relationship of science to theology? Absolutely negative. One goal of science is to eliminate all unfounded judgments appealing to faith rather than knowledge. Science also has a negative attitude toward metaphysics and even toward philosophy in general. "Neither Plato, Schopenhauer, Kant, nor Paulsen advanced knowledge in the least," wrote the Polish natural scientist Benedict Dyboski. Philosophy can justify its existence only within the limits of science, but even within these limits it is not independent (in Pearson's classification of the sciences philosophy is not even repre-

sented). If philosophy has scientific importance, it is only as the history of philosophy. Pearson was typical of nine-teenth century philosophers who abandoned philosophy.

8. Has science already reached a state of perfection? No, it must be refined and rid of unnecessary concepts that no longer suit its nature and tasks. Among these are even such generally accepted ones as causality, matter, and force—which are seemingly scientific and indispensable. Experience gives us no grounds for formulating these concepts. Moreover, phy-sics does not and need not know what causality, matter, and force are.

9. What is the nature of the reality described by science? It is not transcendental, absolute, or mysterious; it is direct-ly given to us through sense perception. Such reality contains only sense impressions not things-in-themselves. Beyond sense perceptions nothing exists. What we call things are only con-structions from impressions we have received.

10. How can one determine the value of science? Pearson regarded science as the most valuable human activity, despite his reservations about its earlier and current state, its un-certain results, and its unwillingness to offer explanations or treat causal relationships. He defied science; for him it was an act of faith with a mission for humanity. What Christianity meant to the Middle Ages, art to the Renaissance, unchanging natural law to the seventeenth century, and reason to the eight-eenth century, science became for the nineteenth century.

11. Does science have a religious mission? Yes, to serve the human spirit, the highest form of existence. Scientists are true priests. Just as it had with Comte, humanity and sci-ence became imbued with a kind of religious dignity. As Renan emphatically put it, "Science is religion."

12. Does science have a social, moral, and political mis-sion? Yes, it should serve freedom of thought. Pearson devel-oped this idea in a special work, *The Ethic of Free Thought* (1888). We approach the ideal of morality through the progress of science. Ethics is not a matter of feeling, as had been as-sumed, but of knowledge. Reason and knowledge are the only moral factors. For Pearson the political consequence of this position led to socialism. But socialism would be reached through gradual evolution and progress, not through revolution as Marx had said. In the name of progress Pearson advanced ideas that were new for his time: eugenics, emancipation of women, free love, and freedom of work and thought.

This was the credo of the majority of contemporary scien-tists and intelligentsia. To be sure, laymen did not study the details of positivism or critically analyze its concepts; many refused to believe that science limited itself to sense impres-sions and descriptions. Rather, nonscientists worshipped the natural sciences and deprecated theology and metaphysics, even though they did not know much about them.   Nearly every educated person believed in the mission of science and was sympathetic to scientism.

This position was so uniform and widespread for several reasons: this sober philosophy was a reaction to romanticism and reflected the influence of important new scientific discoveries.   Even more important was the influence of practical inventions and industrialization—the development of steam engines, industry, and mines underlined the importance of material development, and the new science of political economy, which was enthusiastically developed by empiricists, argued that human behavior is governed by unchanging motives and laws quite different from moral and ideal ones.   "The law of supply and demand became gospel, the locomotive a fetish, and Manchester a holy city."   Prophets of this faith were Comte, Mill, and Spencer.

2. *View of the World*.   The following beliefs were most characteristic of this time:

1. Everything in the world is basically intelligible, clear, nonmysterious, and accessible to science and the mind. As Taine said, "Everything is explicable, even existence." This is particularly true of nature, but even man is not a riddle.   He is the sum of his parents and ancestors, the product of time and place, air and climate, light and sound, nourishment and clothing.

2. Everything in the world has one nature, belongs to one universe, and is subject to common laws.   The world is nothing more than a complex of facts.   The pure positivists accepted the results of science without considering their philosophical implications.   Some were even inclined to regard such philosophizing as harmful to the advance of science.

3. *Consequences*.   From this position, philosophers and the intelligentsia derived further views.

1. The relationship of scientism to religion is hostile: because only nature exists, belief in the supernatural is superstition.   Most typical scientists were against religion without exception, while others, following Comte and Feuerbach, kept a kind of "religion of humanity." Still others were influenced by F. A. Lange and regarded any religion, even a false one, as the most important human act.   These men were exceptions among the adherents of scientism, for they left religion to individual faith; religion was theoretically permissible as long as it

was not professed as knowledge. Any other views of religion were anachronistic.

2. The relationship of scientism to social problems was clear: liberalism as formulated by Mill and supplemented by the theory of evolution. This theoretically radical age was cautious and conservative in practical affairs. Freedom and gradual progress were its main slogans. Although Marxism with its stress on struggle and revolution did develop in this epoch, it was atypical because its social program was too radical and revolutionary.

3. Scientism took the following stand on moral questions: reject supernatural slogans and live by nature. Every man is an end in himself. Hence, the ethics of scientism were altruistic. But because only real goals were important, utilitarianism predominated. A secondary trend with origins in Darwin's theory also developed: it emphasized the struggle for existence and the selection of the fittest; its ethic approached elitism.

4. The relationship of scientism to art was realistic; suddenly, polished stories and paintings that had been highly valued only a short time before became anachronistic. Realism became the leading genre in the plastic arts and in literature. This was the time of Courbet and Zola.

As one of its leaders described it, this generation was positivistic, self-assured, realistic, enamored of facts, confident in the certainity of science, and hostile to individualism, lyricism, and autobiographical frankness. Its understanding of nature and the soul was mechanistic. The cult of man was mixed with contempt for him. The literary style of the time was dry, factual, and unadorned.

This generation lived in conditions of peace that no previous generation had enjoyed. Its ideal was science and its social slogan was liberalism. By casting off transcendental and metaphysical superstitions and fears it was confident that it led humanity to its highest stage of development. It enjoyed prosperity, convenience, and comfort. Yet, despite these advantages it was not completely happy. More than any other generation it was plagued by boredom and surfeit. The confidence of this generation in the definitiveness of its view of the world was illusory. After only a few years the world changed so radically that it became unrecognizable.

THE PARCELING OF PHILOSOPHY

The minimalism of the second half of the nineteenth century, composed of positivism, empiricism, evolutionism, and scientism, believed that philosophy itself should be minimalistic. It limited philosophical aspirations. A rather common opinion was that less should be expected of philosophy than be-

fore. The philosopher who disapproved of philosophy became
rather typical.

The short buoyant burst of metaphysics at the beginning of
the century discouraged thinkers from now pursuing it. The
positivists were not interested in absolute being; they no
longer needed metaphysics. Indeed, they even stopped caring
about philosophy in general. To them it seemed that the exact
sciences had advanced so far that any philosophy, not just metaphysics, had become superfluous. Philosophy was a product of
impatient minds; through deduction it tries to anticipate what
science would sooner or later discover empirically. Philosophy,
if it has any role to play, must work in association with the
exact sciences.

There were two possibilities: as with Comte and Spencer
philosophy could become a synthesis of what the sciences had
achieved, a kind of encyclopedia of their results; or, as with
Mill, philosophy could be a methodology of the sciences. Neither of these roles was independent of the sciences, but they
were tasks to be fulfilled. They were even considered superior
to the tasks of the exact sciences. For the most extreme group
of positivists, however, philosophy did not have even these
tasks. The sciences could analyze their own methods and syn-
thesize their own results. And when all areas of inquiry had
been divided up among the positivists, nothing was left for philosophy. Inquiries can only be made using the normal method of
the exact sciences. Any other method is either illusion or bad
practice. To philosophize rather than to inquire scientifically is a theoretical and even moral transgression. Only those
parts of philosophy can survive that are capable of becoming
independent sciences.

If the positivistic philosophers still wished to save philosophy, it was by transforming it into a series of special
disciplines. In 1858 F. A. Lange wrote: "My logic is the arith-
metic of probability, my ethic the statistics of morality, my
psychology physiology. In short, I try to move exclusively
among the exact sciences." Progressive thinkers of this period
did speak of "philosophy" or the "philosophical sciences," but
they had in mind only specialized sciences whose themes corresponded to the interests of traditional philosophy. Part of
the earlier range and scope of philosophical problems was discarded, and the rest was divided among the specialized sciences.

Because the natural sciences had progressed the farthest,
the natural ambition of philosophers was that the "philosophical sciences" should be similar to the natural science. This
was most quickly and successfully achieved in psychology.

PSYCHOLOGY

It may seem strange that psychology had not earlier become a specialized science. There were probably two reasons for this. First and foremost, the mind is naturally directed to external phenomena, and it is much more difficult for it to concentrate on internal ones; besides, it has difficulty understanding how elusive and complicated these phenomena are. Secondly, psychology deals with important life matters, and man tends to treat such matters in an a priori fashion, not routinely by gradually pushing scientific inquiries forward; such matters are too important to postpone until suitable methods for their solution are discovered.

Nevertheless, the foundations of scientific psychology had been laid long ago: the ancients had known basic laws of psychic life, and the scholastics were able to identify particular psychic functions. The art of introspection was advanced greatly by the French and English in the eighteenth century, but these observations were scattered and unsystematic. Despite these advances, "rational" psychology still predominated; its a priori constructions seemed more certain than empirical observations.

"The book I should most like to write," said F. A. Lange, "would be a critique of psychology, showing that the greater part of this 'science' is prattle and self-deception. After Kant's *Critique of Pure Reason* it would be the next great step forward." Though he did not write this book, psychology changed during Lange's lifetime. The new psychologists of the second half of the nineteenth century regarded it as an empirical science similar to the natural sciences. Some of them thought of it as one of the natural sciences, because the physiological phenomena on which psychic behavior is founded are part of nature. But they all agreed that psychology is not a philosophical science and that it should be a "psychology without a soul." They meant that psychology is not a speculative science of spiritual substances but an empirical science of psychic phenomena.

English Introspective Psychology

The English tradition of empirical investigations in psychology was the strongest. This tradition originated with Locke, whose work was really descriptive psychology. In the eighteenth century Hume, Hartley, and Priestley developed an introspective psychology of cognition; Hutcheson, Hume, and Smith introduced an introspective psychology of moral experiences; and Hume and Burke developed an introspective psychology of aesthetic experiences. This psychology was empirical not

experimental. Its foundation was the rich variety of life experience rather than the laboratory. It was descriptive, genetic, and empirical, deriving all psychic phenomena from sensations and associations. At the beginning of the nineteenth
century this psychology produced James Mill's famous treatise.
In the second half of the nineteenth century English psychology
turned to Mill and this entire tradition while continental philosophy, which had no such tradition, began to explore new
paths. At this time England's main psychologist was Alexander
Bain, author of *The Senses and the Intellect* (1855) and *The
Emotions and the Will* (1859). Bain introduced much new material and detailed observations, but essentially he remained
true to the introspective method and empiricist-associationist
theory of earlier English psychology. Bain's psychology helped
Spencer, who introduced a new motif to English psychology—evolutionism.

German Experimental Psychology

Psychology on the continent had greater ambitions—to become an experimental science, not just an empirical one. Introspection and internal experience gave way to specially designed
experiments. This psychology did not verify ordinary facts; it
authenticated facts that had been observed under laboratory conditions and subjected to precise control and measurement on
special apparatuses.

William James organized psychological experiments in the
United States. In Europe the physicist and physiologist H. von
Helmholtz began to admit psychologists to his physiological
laboratory in Berlin. Finally, in 1879 Wilhelm Wundt established the first special university psychological laboratory.
He was quickly recognized and acclaimed as a pioneer. In the
years 1880-1900 experimental psychology became the greatest
novelty of science and Wundt's laboratory a Mecca for students.
Grandiose expectations were joined with this endeavor—it was
expected to investigate and measure mental processes in the
most precise scientific manner. But these mental operations
were narrowly conceived. In Leipzig and other centers it was
believed that only sense impressions readily lend themselves to
experimental investigation, and experiments were generally limited to these. Of course, these experimentors did believe that
sense impressions are the real foundation of psychic life and
that if we only know them we shall know all of psychic life.
Experimental investigations did not go beyond these elementary
processes, and for the most part they were monotonous and not
very productive. Of these German works William James once said
that no other nation could have endured such boredom.

Physiological Psychology

About the time that psychology was making the transition to the experimental method there was a partial shift from psychic phenomena to their somatic counterparts. In the previous century Harvey and Cabanis had hoped to develop such a psychology, but they were exceptions. Now nearly everyone demanded a "physiological" psychology whose task would be to investigate the anatomical and physiological conditions behind psychic phenomena. These inquiries bordered on physiology. They were a kind of physiology of the senses and the brain but sometimes went beyond these limits.

In principle, physiological psychology was supposed to be an auxiliary discipline of psychology, but because of its objectivity, its similarity to the natural sciences, and the possibility it afforded to carry out experiments and make exact measurements it seemed at that time the most important branch of psychology. Its development left other areas of psychology behind, especially general psychology, which investigated psychic phenomena themselves and not the conditions under which they developed. From 1865 the physicist and physiologist von Helmholtz made advances in the psychophysiology of sight and hearing that shed light on the workings of the ear and eye. He showed how the eye perceives distance and space and how many-colored vision arises from the perception of a few colors. These investigations advanced so rapidly that by 1874 Wundt was able to systematize them in a two-volume work, *Physiological Psychology*. The larger part of this work dealt with purely anatomical and physiological analyses and described the apparatuses used in psychological experiments; the psychological part of the work rarely went beyond an analysis of sense impressions.

The original purpose of physiological psychology was to explain the somatic origins of psychic phenomena, but most of its adherents believed that these origins were the real cause of psychic phenomena. Hence, they were convinced that the psychology they were developing was the most important area of this science.

Psychophysics

The psychological investigations of this time were concerned not only with the relationship between psychic and physiological phenomena, but also with the relationship between these two and the external phenomena that stimulated them.

The physiologist E. H. Weber discovered one complex aspect of the relationship between perceptions and stimuli. A stimulus must increase proportionally to that of an already acting stimulus if there is to be any perceptible increase in perception. If stimuli increase in a geometric ratio, perceptions increase arithmetically. G. T. Fechner considered Weber's law a fundamental principle of psychic life and began systematic investigations of the relationship between stimulus and perception. This area of inquiry he called "psychophysics." In 1860 he published *Elements of Psychophysics*. He thought that by measuring the relationship between stimulus and perception the relationship between the physical and psychic worlds would be presented in precise figures, thus resolving the old metaphysical problem of the soul-body relationship. Though replete with illusory ambitions, Fechner's work did contribute to the quantification of psychological studies and initiated the future science of psychometrics.

Social Psychology

Experimental investigations dealt with nothing beyond the lower forms of psychic life. Wundt even thought it completely impossible to investigate more complex psychic phenomena directly, either through experiment or through introspection: they could only be approached indirectly by investigating external, social products. Wundt therefore considered social psychology or "ethnopsychology" as a necessary supplement to individual psychology. His opinion was that only language, art, religion, law, and other cultural creations could shed light on the higher psychic forms; only these complicated social products could indicate the ability of the human mind. The first systematic studies to follow this line were made in the mid-nineteenth century by two pupils of Herbart, Lazarus and Steinthal. In 1900 Wundt began to compile a vast synthesis of results, *Völkerpsychologie*, which contained the psychology of speech, myth, religion, society, law, civilization, and history.

French Psychopathology

French psychology was first influenced by English, then by German psychology. But it was distinct because it used a great deal of psychiatric material to explain normal psychology. The great neurologist J. M. Charcot had started this trend. It was then applied by his pupil Pierre Janet (1859-1947) and by T. Ribot (1830-1916) whose book on contemporary English psychology in 1870 inspired the French to separate psychology from philosophy. The psychiatric method overturned the belief in the "unity of the soul" and led to an awareness of the similarity between the normal and the sick psyche.

But of all these kinds of psychology, the most typical
were German psychophysiology and psychophysics. Because they
believed that psychic phenomena themselves could not be treated
precisely and objectively, German psychologists studied them
indirectly by investigating their physical determinants. One
reason for the strength of this belief was that psychology was
almost exclusively the province of natural scientists. Fechner
had started as a professor of physics, and Wundt had been
trained as a physiologist; von Helmholtz was both. Donders,
who did influential work in physiological psychology, was also
a physiologist. Lotze had studied medicine as well as philosophy. At that time only somatic and quantitative psychology
were regarded as really scientific by progressive scientific
circles. Brentano's psychology, which was empirical but not
experimental and showed little interest in physiology, was considered backward.

English Individual Psychology

Psychology of another type originated simultaneously in
England. This psychology was isolated; it was not typical of
the thinking and predilections of the time. The leader of this
trend was Francis Galton (1822-1911). Though only an amateur
scientist, he had a wide range of interests that he developed
with great ingenuity. His model of psychology was biology, not
physics as with the Germans. He investigated man in relation
to his environment, not in isolation from it. He was enthusiastic about eugenics, and in adjusting psychology to its purposes he gave it a more practical and life-oriented character.
Galton initiated the biographical method, which consisted of
the psychological history of families, psychological studies of
the likenesses of twins, and the comparative psychology of
races. While the Germans (especially Wundt and his school)
were interested in the common features of the human psyche,
Galton started the psychology of individual differences. He
tried to find ways of measuring individual abilities and developed the testing method. He also used statistics and question-
naires, applying the latter in his famous investigations of
graphic thinking, which delineated a great variety of psychic
types. While the Germans were mostly interested in the separate elements of psychic life, Galton used a holistic approach
in his studies of the psyche and discovered problems and methods that later became very important.
Psychology, especially the dominant German physiological
psychology, avoided any relationship with philosophy. But it
was impossible to dissolve links with philosophy. Psychology
could not avoid taking a position on the relationship between
psychic and physical phenomena. Debate developed between par-

allelists and interactionists. Nor could psychology avoid taking a position on the nature of consciousness, and it became an arena for the debate between the substantialists and the actualists. However, the sympathies of the epoch were clear enough: the parallelists were a majority in asserting that the mutual operation of the soul on the body and the body on the soul is impossible. The actualists, who stated that the concept of substance is inapplicable in psychology, were also dominant. Finally, the intellectualists had a clear initiative in placing ideas first and will second in the sequence of thought (though Wundt was a voluntarist). Generally speaking, the majority regarded the mind as passive: the mind is capable only of passive perception, not of independent and active "apperception." The advantage belonged to those psychologists who confined the object of psychology to the content of consciousness, those who believed that psychic acts could not be discovered through introspection.

The importance of psychology for contemporary philosophy was twofold. First, psychology was to be a separate and independent science modeled on the natural sciences and free of philosophical positions, systems, and old debates. Psychology was to realize the scientific ideal from which traditional philosophy was so distant. Second, psychology hoped to replace traditional philosophy, hoped that logic, ethics, and aesthetics could be reduced to psychology. Contemporary philosophers, especially those most representative of the period, argued that logical, ethical, and aesthetic problems were basically psychological.

LOGIC

In the second half of the nineteenth century various interpretations of logic were represented: the grammatical, derived from Aristotle; the transcendental, derived from Kant; and the metaphysical, derived from Hegel. Mathematical logic was an innovative side trend with few supporters. Its popularity would come later. Psychological logic was the typical, recognized logic of the times; it seemed to be an empirical discipline, hence genuinely scientific.

The line of argument was as follows. Logic deals with judgments and inferences which are psychological functions. Logic is the science of correct thinking or the science of the laws of thinking—and thinking and its laws belong to psychology. Mill wrote that logic, to the extent that it was a science, was only a branch of psychology, differing from psychology as art from science. Logic owed its foundations entirely to psychology. The German logician Sigwart thought that logical laws were only "forms of our moving thought," and the German psychologist Lipps said that "logic is a psychological discipline, for cognition appears only in the psyche."

Some thinkers understood logic as a "physics of thinking," others as an "ethics of thinking." In other words, some regarded it as a body of laws, others as norms of thinking; however, these norms and laws were derived from processes of thinking studied by psychology. In this way logic was relativized. Sigwart stipulated that logic concerns only "our" thinking, others that logic evolves along with our thinking. These philosophers were convinced that they were basing their theories on facts, that they were making logic truly scientific and empirical. The reduction of logic to psychology was later called psychologism.

As a general rule contemporary scientists did not value formal logic itself and did not attempt to further develop it. For the most part they shared the Kantian view that logic is a formula and closed science with few avenues for further development. Nevertheless, they did try to give it both a foundation, the theory of knowledge, and a superstructure, methodology. This ambition was in keeping with the spirit of the times. "Logic" continued to be studied, but it was really the theory of knowledge or methodology. Interest in logical principles was not for their own sake but for thought processes they might reveal or for their potential applicability in the scientific method. Mill, the most highly esteemed contemporary logician, in his *System of Logic* treated both the theory of knowledge and the methodology of the sciences. Sigwart, the most famous German logician, was really a methodologist.

ETHICS

To make a psychological or even empirical science of ethics was most difficult, for ethics investigates what should be, and one can empirically investigate only what is. To reach this goal the problem of ethics had to be changed from "what is duty?" to "what do people consider duty?" Ethics began to study not what good is but what people consider good to be. Such a study can be empirical, because it is essentially psychological. Special efforts were made to discover how primitive people had viewed these matters before their simple view had been distorted by later reflections. Ethnologists now began to play a decisive role in ethics. Typical books on primitive morality such as those by Letourneau, Westermarck, and Swiętochowski (in Poland) were widely read. Though these investigations were empirical, they were not concerned with ethical questions. The problems they posed were from a different science, one that Ochrowicz said should be called "ethology" not ethics.

Nonetheless, some still attempted to make ethics a science. Philosophers admitted that ethics establishes norms of what should be and not facts about what is. Yet, they believed that although ethical norms are not facts, they have their justification in psychological facts. This was ethical psychology. The human mind creates norms that are like the mind that created them, and the mind is a psychological fact. Beneke stated that human nature creates moral laws just as surely as a cherry tree bears cherries and an apple tree apples. Mill said that good is what corresponds to human desires; therefore, it is a psychological fact.

The argument went even deeper: psychological facts themselves, the source of judgments and norms, have their own source in biological facts. We desire what we need for life and what gives strength in the struggle for existence. Once we analyze our moral norms, we become convinced that they contain exactly what life demands. This same spirit is present in Spencer, Nietszche, and Guyau.

Norms were also derived from social facts: a norm is what the community to which an individual belongs demands of him. Without society there would be no norms or duties; there would not even be the concept of norm or duty. Everyone has some kind of ideal by which to guide and judge his life, but such ideals are a creation of the social conditions in which people live. These conditions are the ultimate facts from which duties, norms, ideals, and values are derived.

Such theories—later called "ethical naturalism" because they derived norms from nature rather than opposing norms to nature—were typical of the second half of the nineteenth century. Not until the turn of the century was there opposition to these theories: their falsity resides in the fact that one cannot imply what should be from what is. Just because people value a characteristic does not mean that it should be valued. Neither does the fact that a particular characteristic appeared in a higher stage of development imply that it is morally superior. But these theories, especially pure ethical psychology, were an expression of the times. They were a transition from the earlier view that ethics creates norms to a newer one that ethics investigates norms. And this led to the even more novel view that the task of ethics is only to investigate the meaning of the concepts of obligations, goals, values, and ideals.

AESTHETICS

In the eighteenth century (especially in England) aesthetics was already psychological and empirical. In the nineteenth century (especially in Germany, where it was most highly developed) aesthetics became enmeshed in general, a priori, specula-

tive philosophical investigations. It strayed from facts and
contemplated the ideal of abstract beauty. In the second half
of the nineteenth century when minimalistic trends predominated
there was a reaction to this state of affairs. The most general expression of this was Fechner's determination to oppose
speculative, metaphysical aesthetics "from above" with a scientific, empirical aesthetics "from below." Different people
from various countries simultaneously began to develop an aesthetics from below in two forms: they investigated either art
itself or aesthetic feeling, that is, external or internal aesthetic facts.

Investigations of art tried to show how art had originated
and how the great variety of its forms had developed. In England this problem was approached biologically. Darwin represented art as a factor of sexual selection, Spencer as a kind
of game necessary in the struggle for existence, which sharp-
ened the efficiency of the senses. James Sully in 1876 and
Grant Allen in 1877 developed a distinct evolution-based aesthetics. In France Taine explained that art had assumed various forms in different times and places as a function of the
environment and historical moment. And in Germany Gottfried
Semper applied a technical argument: he explained the forms of
art by the requirements of the materials and instruments that
were used.

A second trend of aesthetic investigations that took feeling for its subject was developed in empirical and experimental
forms by Fechner. In *Introduction to Aesthetics* (1876), he
described new methodological aesthetic experiments. Aesthetics
was based on psychological principles—for example, the "principle of threshold" (that only sensations of sufficient
strength act affectively), the "principle of aesthetic relief"
(that in combining many sources of pleasure art gives a greater
satisfaction than the sum of these satisfactions taken singly),
the "principle of homogeneous union of diversities" (that unity,
diversity, and change are all necessary for aesthetic enjoyment,
for without them there is monotony, barrenness, and meagerness),
or the "principle of association" (that in the aesthetic pleasure we receive when looking at things the ideas associated with
these things often have a stronger influence than the things
themselves).

The experiments by Fechner and his first successors
treated simple matters, components of what we like rather than
the pleasure-evoking elements of the things themselves. They
dealt with simple colors and geometrical figures, squares and
circles; they tried to establish which of these were pleasing
and when. Through his experiments Fechner hoped to determine
which colors and figures were beautiful. He believed that true
beauty could be discovered in the laboratory by statistical
methods.

But soon these ambitions of experimental aesthetics had to be limited: it was realized that statistics and apparatuses do not help to determine what is beautiful. However, they can establish something else: what happens in the consciousness of a person who experiences aesthetic sensations. Experimental aesthetics then changed its original objective goal to a subjective one: Fechner's experiments bore fruit in psychological aesthetics. The Pole Jacob Segal, in the twentieth century, was one of the first scholars to carry out experiments in such a spirit.

Psychological aesthetics tried to formulate a general theory of aesthetic experiences. There were many such theories, mostly German: a hedonistic one—that aesthetic experiences are simply the feeling of pleasure; a formalistic one—that aesthetic pleasure is evoked only by the formal characteristics of objects (the school of Herbart: R. von Zimmermann and E. Hanslick); a functionalistic one—that aesthetic experiences are pleasure produced by the functioning of the mind (K. Groos); an illusionistic one—that aesthetic experience is conscious submission to illusion (K. Lange) or experience of superficial feelings (E. von Hartmann); or that aesthetic experience depends on contemplation (H. Siebeck, W. Wundt, O. Külpe), on detachment from one's own individuality (H. Münsterberg); or, contrariwise, that aesthetic experience is a projection of one's own feelings into things (F. T. Vischer, T. Lipps).

Hence, there were many theories. Each was based on observations and experiments; each contained a partial truth; each tried to universalize this truth. But these theories were quite incompatible with one another. There was no one aesthetic; there were as many aesthetics as there were different theories. These theories did take account of facts, and to this extent at least they were progressive in comparison with the speculative aesthetics of the early nineteenth century. Nonetheless, these theories were backward compared with the purely observational aesthetics of the eighteenth century. Though it detached itself from philosophy and took a psychological, empirical, and experimental approach, aesthetics was not successful in its efforts to become a model science. Neither were logic and ethics successful in this regard.

THE THEORY OF KNOWLEDGE IN GERMANY: NEO-KANTIANISM AND EMPIRIOCRITICISM

The problem of knowledge assumed prime importance in Germany at this time. Philosophy became exclusively epistemology. It asserted that any philosophy not *beginning* with an analysis of cognition is uncritical, for nothing judicious can be said about a phenomenon unless one first defines what knowledge is

and determines how it is acquired. An even narrower assertion
was: any philosophy that does not *end* with this problem is uncritical; the problems of being are of quite a different kind,
and the theory of knowledge shows that being is subjectively
conditioned and cannot really be known.

NEO-KANTIANISM

Kant's position in the theory of knowledge remained predominant. Other positions making greater or lesser claims
seemed uncritical. Rarely had any philosophical view been so
authoritative in academic circles as Kantianism was in Germany between 1860 and 1900. From Germany it passed to other
countries, because German philosophy had never before enjoyed
such prestige. The Kantian position seemed the ultimate in the
development of philosophy. Other philosophers (especially Hegel and Comte) had said the same thing about their philosophies,
but the Kantians thought that only Kantianism had found a genuine middle ground between the overly great ambitions of Hegel
and the much too modest assertions of Comte. The Kantians were
convinced that human knowledge develops and will never be finished, but this development goes in one continuous direction,
the direction Kant had indicated. This position was called
criticism, Kantianism, or more frequently neo-Kantianism, to
suggest Kantianism in modernized and improved form.

The return to this position in Germany was the result of
historical forces. It was a reaction to Hegelian metaphysics,
which now became repellent, especially in the form given it by
Hegel's imitators—dry, pedantic, and without Hegel's imagination. The first reaction to Hegelian metaphysics had been materialism, started by natural scientists with no philosophical
preparation. From the natural sciences premature consequences
were deduced that repelled the philosophically sophisticated,
who wished to accept neither the materialism of the natural
scientists nor the idealism of the metaphysicians. These philosophers thought that both idealism and materialism had made
the same mistake; they had constructed a theory of being without first prefacing this by a critique of knowledge. In such a
critique they saw the first and most important task of philosophy.

In Germany's philosophical history only Kant had devoted
himself to this problem. It is therefore understandable that
these newer German philosophers should have based themselves on
him. Kant's solution was also attractive because it was more
broadly conceived than empiricism. It recognized both intellectual factors and sense data, both a priori and empirical
elements. The Kantian movement began about 1860, attracted

those who sought improvements in philosophy, and brought about real changes.

The initiators of the movement were academic philosophers, mainly specialists who held university positions. But the movement itself sprang from diverse sources: almost simultaneously it was initiated by natural scientists, historians, and philosophers. The outstanding representative natural scientist was von Helmholtz, the historian Fischer, the philosopher Liebmann. Already in 1855 the great German physiologist and physicist Hermann von Helmholtz (1821-1894) began to base himself on Kant: he was drawn to Kant's position by his investigations on the physiology of the senses and by his reflections on geometrical axioms and the assumptions of physics. Von Helmholtz believed that his investigations supported Kant's teachings on the a priori factors in knowledge. He provided impetus to the Kantian movement and sustained it by his great scientific authority. (Among his writings the most philosophical was *Facts of Perception*, 1876.) Kuno Fischer, professor at Heidelberg and one of the most famous historians of philosophy of the nineteenth century, author of the great *History of Modern Philosophy*, published his work on Kant in 1860. This work also helped to win recognition and acknowledgment for the Kantian position. Among the philosophers, Otto Liebmann (1840-1912) coined the phrase "return to Kant" in his youthful and temperamental book *Kant and the Epigones* (1865). In this work he successfully criticized every philosophical trend of the nineteenth century and ended every criticism with the conclusion: "and hence we should return to Kant."

But the most typical representative of early, relatively unsophisticated Kantianism was Friedrich Albert Lange (1828-1875), who in his last years held a chair at Marburg. In character and spirit similar to Mill, Lange was an attractive figure, an ardent campaigner for honesty in thought and action. His short life was spent in intensive work: he worked in Switzerland and Germany as a gymnasium teacher, political activist, and publicist. In 1872 he received simultaneous offers of a bank directorship and a chair of philosophy. He elected to take the chair, though he was already fatally ill and held this new position for only a short time. His main work was *History of Materialism* (1866), a theme far removed from Kant but written in his style and spirit. This work tried to base philosophy on experience and the specialized sciences.

At the beginning of the 1860s the Kantian movement had already established itself at many universities, especially in Marburg where H. Cohen succeeded to Lange's chair and in Heidelberg where W. Windelband followed Fischer.

Views

1. General Characteristics of Kantianism. To be a Kantian
meant to believe first, that philosophy should begin with a
critique of knowledge (in contrast to all philosophical dogmas
and authorities); second, that in view of the subjective foundations of knowledge the theory of being should be abandoned (in
contrast to metaphysical, particularly materialistic, philosophers); third, that knowledge cannot go beyond the limits of
experience (in contrast to constructive, idealistic, particularly the Hegelian, philosophers); fourth, that experience is
not a simple collection of facts but a complicated creation of
the mind conditioned by its a priori forms (in contrast to the
empiricists and positivists). Kantianism combined empiricism
and apriorism.
    At least at the beginning, to be a Kantian also meant to
be a realist. The mind in the cognitive process impresses
a priori forms of space and time, causality and substance, on
the object of cognition; therefore, the mind changes this object and sees things not as they really are but as they appear
to the mind. Nonetheless, things that appear in the mind some-
how exist independently from it in reality. This reality is
inaccessible to the mind, but it does exist. Every sense impression that the mind receives from outside gives evidence of
this. This reality is even of a dual nature, just as external
and internal experience is dual. One part of this reality
gives evidence of the existence of the material world, the second of the existence of the self. Of course, we do not experience the self directly; it, too, we know only in phenomenal
form. As Lange wrote, "The transcendental base of our own organization is just as unknown to us as the things that act on
it. Only the joint product of these two elements—things and
our organization—is always before us."
    To be a Kantian also meant to be a dualist. The monistic
view seemed incompatible with Kant's teaching, which postulated
two worlds: a world of phenomena and a world of things. Even
if phenomena are omitted there are still two worlds in Kantianism: a material world, evidenced through external experience,
and a spiritual world, evidenced through internal experience.
    Finally, to be a Kantian meant to be a formalist, to recog-
nize knowledge only within the limits of what the mind itself
creates: connections, relationships, and forms. We know causal
relationships better than the components of these relationships;
we know the forms better than what has formed them. Because of
its formality our knowledge is universal and necessary, but it
is also incomplete and limited.

The result of these assumptions was that the basic concepts of Kantianism were different from those of common opinion and traditional philosophy. "Knowledge" could not be a reflection of objects, only their formation by the mind; "experience" was not opposite to apriorism, because experience contained a priori elements; the "object of knowledge" was not opposed to the subject, because this object was a creation of cognition; "verification of truth" could not mean correspondence of thought with things, for things are not directly accessible to thought and cannot therefore be compared with thoughts. For this reason, only the internal agreement of phenomena and their agreement with the requirements of the mind can determine "truth" and provide verification. "Philosophy" cannot be a science of being that is impossible to know; it can only be a science of knowledge. The set of problems in the theory of knowledge now changed: these problems were no longer a description of the process of cognition or an analysis of its genesis (as it had been with Aristotle and Locke); now the problems were to analyze how knowledge was possible and what its conditions and assumptions were.

2. *Minimalistic Understanding of Kantianism.* Kant's philosophy contained some minimalistic motifs: one of these was phenomenalism, which stated that our picture of the world is subjective and phenomenological. A motif of a different kind was apriorism, which expressed the belief that we possess universal and necessary knowledge. Kant had indicated that things-in-themselves cannot be grasped through theoretical investigations, but he did arouse the hope that they could be grasped by appealing to the demands of life. Hence, like the minimalists he criticized all metaphysics up to his time, but like the maximalists he also seemed to proclaim a new metaphysics.

To be sure, the interpretation that Kant's supporters gave his views was extremely minimalistic. This was especially true of the interpretation of Lange and von Helmholtz.

According to them, Kant's real contribution lay not in apriorism, but in phenomenalism and subjectivism. To them subjectivism meant something quite simple: the mind grasps everything in its own way. Such an interpretation of Kant's doctrine differed little from Locke's view on the subjectivism of perceived qualities: in general this interpretation stated that thought is just as subjective as perception and, like them, introduces the element of subjectivity to knowledge. This was a psychological, even physiological interpretation of Kantianism: the forms of thought are dependent not only on man's intellectual organization, but also on his physical constitution. "The sensual world," wrote Lange, "is a creation of our organiza-

tion." In his optical and acoustical investigations von Helmholtz had shown that the organs of sight and hearing transform
their stimuli, and this he took to be the essence of Kantianism;
he thought that physiology verified Kant's theory. Lange and
many before him accepted this physiological interpretation.

But from all appearances Kant's intention was more complicated; it was not psychological or physiological but epistemological: in a priori forms Kant saw not the qualities of the
human mind, but the conditions under which any kind of mind
acquires knowledge of objects; if the human mind did not fulfill these conditions, then human knowledge would not be distinct—it would be completely impossible. Kant therefore understood the matter far less subjectively and relatively. The
later neo-Kantians returned to Kant, but in the period around
1860 the more subjective interpretation was popular.

3. *Things-in-Themselves*. Things for Kant were unknowable;
only the self was knowable. Here neo-Kantians saw an error:
they thought that the self, too, was unknowable. We know only
phenomena of self. Our knowledge is like an equation with two
unknowns: one is the self; the other is things. If one of
these were known to us, then we could make inferences about the
other. But we have no such knowledge; therefore, the equation
is unsolvable.

For the Kantians the essential problem was the relationship between phenomena and things-in-themselves. They started
from the realistic view that things exist, for there must be
something to evoke phenomena. But shortly they took the position that because we know nothing about things, perhaps they
are only creations of the mind and do not exist at all. Perhaps the very opposition of phenomena and things is conditioned
by our way of thinking. Things are only a "conceptual limit"
(*Grenzbegriff*) that marks the limit of phenomena and knowledge.
We are like a fish that swims in a bowl and butts against the
walls: what we call things-in-themselves is the same thing as
the walls of the bowl for the fish.

Lange postulated that human knowledge had passed through
four phases: in the first phase man relied on the naive faith
that the world is as we know it through the senses: for example,
we hear sounds simply because things make sounds; in the second
phase science modified this belief by stating that sounds are
only vibrations in the air that evoke sounds in our ears; in
the third phase even this view was altered by critical philosophy, which opposed things to phenomena and asserted that vibrations of air are only phenomena and constructions of the mind;
in the fourth phase the idea appeared that the very opposition
of things and phenomena can be a creation of the mind. Lange

thought that Kant had not seen this possibility, which was the
logical conclusion of his assumptions. Lange himself saw this
rather late and had to modify his ideas.

   4. *Theory of Value for the Kantians*. One outcome of neo-
Kantianism was that philosophy must give up the theory of being.
What remained was the theory of knowledge and the theory of
value. The former is theoretical, the latter practical, philosophy. In practical philosophy the neo-Kantians diverged
from Kant more than in theoretical philosophy: they took the
position that the theory of value cannot be a subject of science. They did have ethical beliefs, but these were strictly
personal and without scientific value. In ethics, Kant had
already operated with postulates rather than assertions, and
Lange regarded postulates as fictions. These fictions may be
necessary in life, but they have no basis in reality. They
concern ideals, not realities. This led to the following: the
objects of our knowledge are phenomena; the objects of our morality are fictions.
   Ethics became more life poetry than science. Lange
treated aesthetics and theology in similar fashion: these also
use fictions. But in no sense did Lange reject these fictions.
On the contrary, he regarded them as the most important creations of the human spirit. His interpretation of theoretical
philosophy was like that of the positivists, but in practical
philosophy he followed another approach. He did not favor
holding to facts as the positivistic utilitarianism would have
required (positivists had wished to treat practical life scientifically). Lange thought that the scientific methodology
and point of view loses sense when applied to practical life,
norms, and action. Practical problems cannot be resolved by a
simple appeal to facts; here one must appeal to ideals. A positivistic theory of science with an idealistic superstructure,
facts supplemented by ideals, was his view of the world. The
minimalism of the positivists consisted in reducing culture to
science, the ultimate authority, whereas Lange's minimalism
limited science by asserting that the moral, artistic, and
religious culture of man is outside scientific jurisdiction.

Varieties of Neo-Kantianism

   Kantianism remained the leading philosophy in Germany until the end of the century. The periodical *Kantstudien* established by his followers (1898) became the most important German
philosophical publication, and the Kantgesellschaft remained
the leading philosophical organization in Germany until Nation-

al Socialism. At the beginning of the twentieth century Kantians were still in the vanguard of the philosophical movement,
but they had split into many camps and deviated significantly
from the original variety of neo-Kantianism: some of them
retained the psychological view, while others formed an epistemological interpretation of a priori forms. Some denied the
knowability of things-in-themselves, others denied even their
existence. Some Kantians crossed the metaphysical boundary and
became idealists or realists; others moved further from metaphysics and approached positivism. The most important Kantian
schools were the Marburg school (Cohen and Natorp) and the Baden school (Windelband and Rickert), but in time both of these
schools arrived at positions that were significantly different
from original neo-Kantianism.

Some Kantians of the nineteenth century wished to revital-
ize, defend, popularize, and faithfully interpret Kant, and others wished to develop and improve his teachings. They could be
divided into historians and systematizers, but the division between these two groups was fluid. F. Paulsen attempted a simple, psychological interpretation of Kant based on common sense
while simultaneously advancing his own philosophy, which became
quite popular. F. Adickes, arguing that Kant's position left
room for metaphysics, developed a realistic metaphysics.

Agnosticism is the position most frequently found among
the views of the neo-Kantians. This view became popular outside philosophical circles. It also attracted many natural scientists, for whom it became a leading philosophical tenet. The
outstanding spokesman for this view was the Berlin physiologist
Emil du Bois-Reymond. In his lecture "On the Limits of Natural
Cognition," presented at a conference of German natural scientists and physicians in 1872, he asserted that the scientist
encounters two absolute limits to his understanding of the
world—the essence of matter and the origin of consciousness.
Before these problems the scientist is helpless: he must say
not only *ignoramus* (we are ignorant), but also *ignorabimus* (we
will be ignorant); our ignorance is not temporary, but definitive.

Du Bois-Reymond returned to this problem ten years later
in his work *Seven World-Riddles* (1882), which marked the limits
of knowledge even more clearly. Four problems were definitely
unsolvable: the essence of matter and force, the beginning of
movement, the origin of consciousness, and freedom of will.
For three others there was no solution presently in sight: the
beginning of life, the purpose of nature, and the origin of
rational thought.

The agnosticism of contemporary thinkers was not an isolated trend: it had appeared earlier in England with Spencer
and Huxley (from 1869). Contemporary minimalism had two ways
of skirting ultimate issues: it either admitted that there were

unsolvable problems, or it stated that unsolvable problems are only poorly formulated, and deal with transcendental forms that do not exist. Kantianism took the first approach, positivism the second.

Neo-Kantianism and Positivism

In the 1870s and 1880s the main rivals of the German neo-Kantians in the theory of knowledge were the positivists, but even in academic circles they were a minority. The earliest were G. Göring (1874) and E. Laas (1879), but they did not play a great role. Those who gained fame and followers, Mach in Austria and Avenarius in Switzerland, wrote in German but worked outside Germany.

The essential difference between the positivists and the neo-Kantians was in their relationship to a priori elements of knowledge: the former denied them, the latter defended them. But both groups held some common minimalistic beliefs. The Kantians defended apriorism, but their interpretation was close to the position of the positivists. More than one contemporary philosopher could be placed in either group. As an example, it was debated whether the views of the physicist Heinrich Hertz made him a Kantian or a positivist.

In the spirit of the age both groups outdid each other in cautiousness. Unknowable things exist, said some. No, said others, such things do not exist. There is nothing beyond knowable facts. Some said that knowledge is extensive but subjective. Others said, it is not subjective, but it is limited; it does not go beyond facts.

In Germany especially the positivism of those times was distinct in that its main area of inquiry was the theory of knowledge. The original Comtian positivism had asserted that science should investigate facts without attempting to determine their knowability, but the newer positivism hoped to find epistemological reasons why it should investigate facts alone. One can call this the "second positivism" or "epistemological positivism." This term can even be extended to include "empiriocriticism," the name Avenarius used for his philosophy.

EMPIRIOCRITICISM

There were several varieties of epistemological positivism: the most original was derived from Richard Avenarius and takes the name "empiriocriticism" from him. Nearly identical to this theory of knowledge was one developed simultaneously by the Viennese physicist Ernst Mach. The year 1877, in which Avenarius founded the periodical *Vierteljahresschrift für wissenschaft-*

liche Philosophie, marks the intensification of the positivistic trend in Germany.

Initiators

Richard Avenarius (1843-1896) was born in Paris, but did his most important writings as a professor at Zürich. His philosophical position was expressed briefly and simply in his thesis, *Philosophy as Thinking of the World According to the Principle of the Smallest Energy Measure* (1876). His later presentation in *Critique of Pure Experience* (1888-1890) was complex, difficult, dry, and replete with strange terminology.

Ernest Mach (1838-1916) was a professor of physics at Vienna from 1867, and a professor of philosophy from 1875. For the most part his writings are detailed studies of specialized subjects on the borderline between the natural sciences and the theory of knowledge. They were published collectively in the volumes *Contribution to an Analysis of Feeling* (1886) and *Understanding and Error* (1905). In contrast to the works of Avenarius these were popularizations and played an important role in spreading the new positivism. Avenarius was the most independent thinker, but Mach was the most influential writer of the "second" positivism.

As critical philosophy was derived from Kant, empiriocriticism and epistemological positivism were derived from Hume. Mach in particular referred to Hume as his predecessor.

Views

1. *Introjection*. The most common epistemological position is: physical things exist in the external world, and psychic reflections in consciousness correspond to these things; only these images are given, and it is only through these images that we know something about things.

Such a view seems quite natural, but there is a basic difficulty in it: if only images are given, how can we break away from them and get at things? This difficulty would be insurmountable if the view is correct that only images are given.

Avenarius concluded that this view was wrong. The error lies in what he called "introjection" (or projection within). When color or form exist we assume that their forms must be in the mind of everyone who looks at them. Thus, in a sense we project their images within people. There is, however, no basis in experience for doing this: we only have experience of things, which is itself divided into images and things. We as-

sume that things cannot be in the mind, and from this we infer
that they must exist beyond the mind. But the mind contains
only reflections of things. The duality of things and images
is our creation. We know nothing about this from experience.
There are no physical or psychological phenomena separate from
them; there are only phenomena, which can be grasped in one of
two ways. For example, when we consider color in relation to
light, we understand color as a physical phenomenon; when we
consider it in relation to the eye, we understand it as a psychological phenomenon. Such an explanation supported positivism, which limited itself to the concept of fact from the very
beginning and did not oppose things to thoughts or being to phenomena. Here positivism was already distinct from Kantianism.

2. *Pure Experience*. Avenarius, Mach, and this entire
group of positivists wished to base their theories on "pure" experience; for them anything foreign to such experience was
metaphysics.

The mind has a tendency to include interpolations and additions supplied by itself as part of its experience. Science
removes these additions. This distinguishes "pure" scientific
experience from the naive, common variety. First, science removes "timatological" interpolations (as Avenarius called them),
that is, all kinds of judgments, ethical as well as aesthetic.
Second, science removes "anthropomorphic" interpolations, those
ascribing to things characteristics that we ourselves possess.
There are many such interpolations in the common mind and even
more in philosophy. Science corrects these errors.

Science itself is not perfect. Avenarius and Mach found
metaphysics (going beyond pure experience) in philosophical systems, in psychology, and in the natural sciences. Such concepts as "things-in-themselves" or "absolute" in philosophy,
"self" or "psychic faculties" in psychology, and "atom,"
"force," and "cause" in the natural sciences were metaphysical.
In this regard even the sciences needed correction. Mach and
Avenarius distinguished between contemporary metaphysical science and the science of the future based on pure experience.
Such a criticism of science was not new: Locke and Hume had already shown the nonempirical nature of such concepts as substance, force, and causality and the difficulties to which
they lead. But Mach and Avenarius were more radical than their
predecessors and demanded a complete removal of these metaphysical concepts in the name of pure experience.

The paradox of positivism was that it began as a cult of
science and ended as a severe critic of science. To an extent
positivism rehabilitated the natural, nonscientific view of the
world, because with its generalizations, laws, hypotheses, and

abstractions science goes even further from pure experience than the natural attitude of the world.

Scientific knowledge is not higher than other forms of knowledge. There is nothing in science that could not be discovered without it. The only distinctive feature of science is that it discovers things more quickly. Mach's opinion was a reaction to the one-sided cult of science. Although the scientism of the twentieth century profitted from some of Mach's ideas, Mach himself had already started the reaction to scientism.

3. Science as the Economic Description of Facts. Another feature of the new positivism was its opposition to the widespread view that science's task is to explain phenomena. Explanation means to give causes, and cause is a metaphysical concept with no foundation in experience. The task of science, therefore, can only be descriptive. Some scientists shared this view of the positivists: the position had been originally stated by the English physicist J. C. Maxwell; in his works, G. R. Kirchoff spoke of physics as a description of facts; J. R. von Mayer stated that the task of science is finished when it had made a fact known in all its aspects. Theories are only indirect descriptions, and scientific laws are basically descriptive.

Positivism stated that scientific description differs from common description only by being more economical: it contains the most facts in the simplest formula and helps us to understand them with the least effort. In reality every fact appears only once and is different from every other fact, but when we compare them with one another we form general laws to relieve the burden on our memories. We must remember that these laws are only a shorthand report of facts and that the virtue of such laws is their economy. Mach presented a paper on the "principle of the economy of thinking" to the Viennese Academy of Sciences in 1882. At just about the same time Avenarius also developed this principle.

Avenarius argued in the following manner. Our powers are not unlimited; therefore, we must be economical. The body and the mind must perform their functions efficiently by adhering to the principle of least effort. Even more important is the basic principle of thinking: thinking is apperception or the grasping of new impressions with the help of those we already possess. Powers are stored up when apperception becomes automatic or when the ideas we possess are ordered, put into a system, and arranged in the form of general concepts. Sciences use concepts and laws to describe phenomena in abbreviated form: every concept takes the place of many ideas, and every law the

place of many individual assertions. In this way we save effort. Philosophy in particular does this, for its concepts are
the most general and the most abbreviated: philosophy encom-
passes not just part of experience but the whole world. Philosophy represents the aspiration to understand the world scientifically according to the principle of least effort.

But by no means does such activity represent ability of a
higher order: this ability has no other task but that of antic-
ipating experience. Forms that seem most perfect are only the
most economical; necessities are only habit; reputed explanations are only the reduction of new ideas to old ones.

4. *The Scientific Picture of the World*. The natural sciences represent the world as a collection of bodies and forces.
The philosophy of pure experience questioned this: experience
has no knowledge of "forces"; such a term is only a shorthand
description or a subjective phrase for describing continual
links between phenomena. Such concepts as "matter" and "atom"
are also subjective creations of our mind. For this reason
such concepts should be eliminated from science. But if these
concepts are eliminated what will remain in experience? Only
particular colors, sounds, spatial and temporal structures.
Only "impressions" will remain, or what Mach preferred to call
"elements." What we call the world is a collections of element
and nothing more.

These collections of elements change, but some of them are
more lasting than others. These we call bodies. Also relatively more lasting are certain combinations of memories, moods,
and feelings. These we call the self. Selves and bodies are
only names for relatively durable combinations of elements.
But even this durability is imperfect. Changes are slow and
continual. To retain the self as an immutable substance is impossible. The view of self as substance leads to insurmountable difficulties and superficial problems unless it is understood that there is no real individual, that self is only a
concept introduced for practical purposes as a more convenient,
economic description of experience.

Mach reduced the world to "elements," but he had no clear
conception of what elements were. Sometimes he thought of them
as reality discovered by the mind, but at other times he called
them "impressions" and viewed them in a Berkeleyan fashion, as
subjective and idealistic. Avenarius did likewise. Both denied the duality of things and impressions, but they were unde-
cided as to whether reality was composed of things alone or of
impressions as well. Therefore, among thinkers who were dependent on Avenarius and Mach, some saw the world as a combination

of things, and others viewed it as a combination of impressions. The latter were in the majority.

Summary

What separated Mach and Avenarius from traditional philosophy? Just about everything. What made them different from the Kantians? They were separate from even the most minimalistic Kantians in their denial of the a priori elements of knowledge. What separated them from the earlier positivists? At least two things: (1) the effort to substantiate their position epistemologically (the concept of "introjection"); and (2) a radicalization of views (expressed in such slogans as "pure experience," "pure description," and "science free from metaphysics").

VARIETIES OF POSITIVISM

The slogans "pure experience" and "pure description" were controversial, yet they were understandable. But to regard "elements" as reality conflicted with ordinary habits of thinking and was also unclear. If the sensual image is the only reality existing beyond us, two interpretations are possible: the sensual image is what reality is normally understood to be, or reality is normally understood as a sensual image. The first interpretation was realistic, the second idealistic. Mach thought that his concept of "elements" had resolved the duality of realism and idealism by introducing a third, neutral position. But his solution did not decide the debate between idealism and realism. Avenarius began from idealism but later changed to realism. Other positivists went in two opposite directions: some like the immanentists, moved toward idealism, while others, like Riehl, moved toward realism. This split spawned many doctrines. Another factor influencing the formation of these doctrines was their relationship to Kantianism. In one way or another everyone associated positivism with Kantianism.

Immanent Philosophy

Immanent philosophy stemmed from the assumption that transcendental being cannot be imagined and is therefore absurd. This doctrine passed from Berkeley to Kant and then to Fichte. Those who shared this view thought that if one analyzed the "external world," one would be convinced that it is composed of nothing but states of consciousness. Between consciousness and

object, between self and world, there is an indissoluble tie:
no object is not an object of consciousness, just as no form
of consciousness is not consciousness of an object.

Idealists have always been attacked on the grounds that
their position leads to solipsism: only I exist, and the whole
world is my idea. Unlike other idealists, the immanentists did
not defend themselves against this criticism. They admitted
solipsism. However, they qualified this position by stating
that their solipsism was epistemological not metaphysical.
This meant that although the world is really my idea, it is not
a dream to which nothing in reality corresponds: my ideas are
as real as I am.

This was called "immanent" philosophy in contrast to transcendental philosophy, which recognized a form of being beyond
consciousness. Some also called this philosophy "critical idealism." The main representatives were Wilhelm Schuppe (1836-
1913) and Richard von Schubert-Soldern. Greifswald, where
Schuppe was a professor, was the main center of the movement.
The immanent philosophers stressed their close relationship to
Kantianism, and they thought of Lange as the initiator of their
movement. But above all they formed an alliance with Avenarius
and Mach, even though this did not signify complete agreement.
They did not even agree among themselves: Schubert-Soldern
thought that if everything is composed of states of consciousness, then the self and external objects must also be states
of consciousness; Schuppe denied this.

Riehl and Realism

Alois Riehl (1844-1924) advanced his theories as early as
1870, and in 1876 he published his main work, *Philosophical
Criticism*. He was born in Austria and from 1878 was a professor at Graz. In 1906 he was called to Berlin, but by then his
philosophical creativity was exhausted. Riehl began from the
same assumptions as the immanentists—that subject and object
are mutually dependent on one another—but he arrived at the opposite conclusion: he was a realist, and the immanentists were
idealists. This realism was new and intermediate; it recognized the existence of real things beyond the self but not beyond consciousness.

Neither the subject nor the object can be the starting
point for philosophy: to treat self as the original form of being is just as dogmatic as to regard matter as original. Kant
took this error from Descartes. Where, then, should we begin?
With consciousness. Consciousness is not identical with self:
it comprises a whole of which self is a part; consciousness is
a uniform process with a subjective and an objective aspect.
From this process emerges the subject on the one hand and the

object on the other; the emotional elements form the self, and the sensual elements form the object.

Impressions are the link between consciousness and objects; therefore, one should base the theory of knowledge not on *cogito* (I think) but on *sentio* (I feel). One can then say not only *sentio ergo sum* (I feel therefore I am), but *sentio ergo sum et est* (I feel therefore I am and it is). Causal reasoning is not needed to prove the existence of external objects ("I receive sense impressions; therefore, something must cause them"). Impressions themselves point to the existence of objects, because impressions are objective. Furthermore, impressions indicate the existence of the external world but tell us nothing about its essence. Hence, we have knowledge of objects, but our knowledge is only phenomenal.

Riehl admitted that knowledge also contains conceptual, rational, and a priori elements. These elements are indispensable; they unite and order impressions. Without these elements the external world would be chaos. But they also introduce a concomitant subjective factor to knowledge: these elements are indispensable but harmful.

The mutual dependency of subject and object, which was Riehl's starting point, was the main theme of the new positivism. Riehl was considered a Kantian, but in his philosophy Kantian motifs were subordinate to positivistic ones. From Kant it might be possible to derive mutual dependency of subject and object, realism, and the subjectivistic understanding of cognition, but it would be impossible to derive the epistemological primacy of sense impressions and a belief in the direct knowledge of reality.

Simmel and Relativism

Georg Simmel (1858-1918), a bold and active thinker, was particularly creative in the philosophy of culture and history and had the knack for selecting unusual topics and arriving at surprising conclusions. He was the author of *Problems of the Philosophy of History* (1892) and *The Philosophy of Money* (1900). For a long time he was a private tutor in Berlin, then later a professor at Strasburg. He began from the Kantian position but gave this position a completely positivistic form.

He combined Kantian apriorism with a biological and sociological emphasis derived from positivism. He thought that no conscious being could look at the world impartially. Each of us brings his own aprioris with him. A person's way of looking at the world depends on biological factors, psychophysical construction, and especially the construction of the senses: the world must be different for man than for a fly. One's picture of the world results from a selection of impressions, and each species carries out this selection differently.

The a priori also depends on social conditions. The givens for an individual are not only the characteristics of his species, but also the characteristics of his social group. A man's mind contains both personal and social elements. Laws of logic, moral commands, everything to which the individual must submit, things that seem objective, necessary, a priori—all of this is of biological or social origin, even though the individual might not be aware of it.

Nor are these objective and a priori things unchanging: they are products of history and are dependent on it. The apriorism that Kant had used to support universality, necessity, and nonrelativity in knowledge was interpreted by Simmel and related thinkers most relativistically. Their apriorism was totally different from Kant's. They combined Kantianism with positivism to the advantage of the latter.

The originality of Simmel's thinking was in his application of apriorism to history; he broke with the realism of historians who regarded their science as simple recording of the past. For Simmel history, like nature, was a subjective creation of the spirit modeled on its own a priori forms. Just as Kant had once pointed to the role of the human mind in the apprehension of nature, now Simmel applied this notion to our understanding of history. The historian knows only fragments of events, which he combines with the assistance of a priori categories and then uses to create history. Out of chaotic material he forms a continuous chain of development. He deceives himself if he thinks that his ideas and judgments are objective. In general, these judgments tell us more about the historian than about the past. As a historian Simmel was a relativistic apriorist.

His philosophical writings were also symptomatic of the times. He did not see the task of philosophy as that of reproducing reality; such a reproduction of reality would be accomplished by the specialized sciences. Philosophy has another task: to express the internal world. Philosophical theories are of no value as pictures of the world, but they are of value as pictures of the philosopher. Each theory is the expression of a human type.

Vaihinger and Fictionalism

Hans Vaihinger (1852-1933), professor at Halle, has always been regarded as a leading Kantian: he established the Kant Society and edited a Kantian journal. He was one of the greatest experts on Kant. His commentary on the *Critique of Pure Reason* was so detailed that the remarks on the preface and introduc-

tions took up a few volumes. After he lost his eyesight in
later life he published his systematic work, *The Philosophy
of "As If"* . . . (1911), written 30 years earlier during the
first period of neo-Kantianism and positivism. After this work
appeared it became apparent that Vaihinger had few Kantian
traits and many positivistic ones. The foundation of his entire philosophy was the concept of fiction, which he had inherited from Lange. For this reason Vaihinger's philosophy has
been called fictionalism. He himself preferred the term "positivistic criticism."

A fiction is everything in the mind that (1) does not correspond to reality, and yet (2) is practically necessary.
There are many such fictions in philosophy and science: nearly
all general concepts and theories, all artificial classifications and definitions, all schemata and models, all conceptions
and abstractions, all personifications and hypotheses (such as
"soul" or "force"), concepts in mathematics and mechanics (such
as absolute time and space), various legal definitions (*fic-
tiones iuris*), statistical terms (such as "average man"), naturalistic concepts ("atom" and "ether"), psychological concepts
(like intellectual faculties), economic and ethical concepts
(like the idea of freedom), and innumerable other concepts and
philosophical theories. The statue of which Condillac wrote,
Adam Smith's reduction of all economic matters to egoism, Bentham's derivation of all governmental arrangements from interest, Galileo's concept of the isolated body, Newton's concept
of gravity, Plato's concept of ideas, and Kant's things-in-
themselves—all of these things are fictions.

Not only do these fictions fail to correspond to reality,
but some contradict it. Examples of such contradiction are infinity, independent matter, the absolute, the atom, absolute
time and space, a point without extension, a line without thick-
ness. For Vaihinger these were contradictory fictions in the
most precise meaning of the term.

Though they are unreal, these fictions are nevertheless
efficient, useful, and necessary. We know that they are only
fictions, but we cannot avoid them. Yet even the most useful
are not unchanging. All of them are temporal: when they no
longer fulfill their tasks, they are rejected. The superiority of some is relative: Copernicus' theory is no more true
than Ptolemy's; it is only newer and better. Vaihinger became
as relativistic as Mach and Simmel.

Truth and reality are full of fictions, hence relative and
even false. "What we generally call truth, namely, the world
of ideas, which corresponds to the external world, is only an
efficient error." "Our entire understanding of what we perceive is subjective; what is subjective is fictional; what is
fictional is untrue; and what is untrue is an error." "The
boundary between truth and falsity is fluid."

What we call reality is full of fictions: it could not exist in contradictory form. What will remain if we eliminate fictions? Only impressions. Vaihinger agreed with Mach and Avenarius.

What, then, is the task of cognition, to reflect reality? No, this would only be repeated experience. To understand reality? No, for "To wish to understand the world is not only unfeasible but senseless." Purely theoretical aims are cognitively impracticable. Only practical aims remain. In joining fictionalism with practicalism Vaihinger expressed the belief that the task of science is strictly practical. Its only aim is to widen the possibilities for life and action. More precisely, science tries to predict later effects and to organize life accordingly. To demand more from knowledge, to wish to find the causes or the essence of reality leads only to impractical solutions of senseless questions.

Vaihinger was not alone in his aspirations. During the 1880s when he was developing his ideas many others thought in a like manner. In 1876 Avenarius developed his biological view of cognition, seeing it as a life function; in 1878 C. S. Peirce began to develop the pragmatic theory of knowledge; at the same time Wundt formulated his voluntaristic conception of man and Nietzsche his conception of truth as necessary falsehoods.

Fictionalism made a strong impression when it was proclaimed in the twentieth century. It developed one of the leading themes of positivism in a paradoxical, radical, and effective manner. It did not create a school, but it did become an important element of many philosophical doctrines.

Hans Cornelius

Hans Cornelius (1863-1947) further developed and deepened idealistic positivism by retaining some Kantian motifs. He began as a private scholar, then lectured at the universities of Munich and Frankfurt. His aim was to analyze direct knowledge that was free from signs and symbols. This knowledge was composed solely of perceptions linked together to make up the stream of consciousness. This linkage of perceptions he called "transcendental regularity." Like direct evidence itself this is the final and irreducible fact. The thesis that the link between the elements of consciousness and the elements themselves made their appearance at the same time was a Kantian element in the positivism of Cornelius. Perceptions and their relationship are all that is given directly. Neither the self nor external things are given: here we must already use inferences. On this point Cornelius retained Hume's position.

Nevertheless, Cornelius tried to eliminate from positivism the dualism that Hume had given it. Indictive generalizations from facts (for example, that gold is different from silver) are no less certain than analytic ones (such as two times two is four) and are no less important for science.

Cornelius was younger and active longer than the other positivists of the "second positivism" led by Mach and Avenarius. In some respects he was already a link between them and a "third" positivism that developed in the twentieth century in the Vienna Circle.

Relationship to Materialism

This new theory of knowledge was hostile to earlier philosophical views, especially to speculative and idealistic metaphysics. But it also regarded materialism in the same light as metaphysics. The earliest and most powerful attacks against materialism were made in Germany by the philosopher Lange (1866) and the natural scientist Du Bois-Reymond (1872). The latter criticized materialists for deriving consciousness from matter, for the relationship of matter and consciousness is inconceivable. Lange based his criticism on the theory of knowledge, which says just the opposite: the concept of matter is a pure creation of the mind. The immanent philosophers saw the materialism of the natural scientists as their greatest enemy. The natural scientist-philosophers such as von Helmholtz, Mach, and Verworn were influenced by epistemology and asserted that we only know the material world as the content of our consciousness. One quarter century after the statement of Du Bois-Reymond the chemist W. Ostwald at a conference of natural scientists in Lübeck in 1895 again announced that materialism had been defeated by science itself.

The relationship to materialism in England was similar, not only among philosophers, but also among scientists. In his famous speech at Belfast in 1874 the physicist Tyndall said that the concept of matter, an invention of Democritus, must be transformed in the name of evolution. Huxley wrote that materialism went beyond its powers, because it is only a hypothesis and yet lays claim to philosophical truth: matter is really only a name for particular states of consciousness.

Meanwhile, materialism was not inactive; it even began to use new arguments derived from scientific advances—the principle of the conservation of energy and the evolution of species. At the end of the century the zoologist E. H. Haeckel revived materialism under the name "monism," materialism coupled with evolutionism. He called his book *Riddles of the World* (1899), an allusion to Du Bois-Reymond's agnosticism. Haeckel argued that there are no riddles in the world, because monism solves

them all. One need only apply a broad conception of matter:
sensitivity and will must be attributed to matter. Even earlier (1876) he had combined forces with acts of will and had
asserted that there are forces in atoms. Atoms are therefore
spiritual. Without this "ensouled atom" it is impossible to
explain even the simplest phenomena of chemistry.

There was nearly universal opposition to this position.
Epistemologists in particular regarded Haeckel as an anachronistic thinker. The natural scientists themselves also attacked him. The Russian physicist Chwolson said that Haeckel
sinned against the "twelfth commandment": he wrote about something he did not understand. The energism of W. Ostwald (from
1888, particularly in *Overcoming Materialism in Natural Science*, 1895) asserted that—contrary to materialism—the
basic concept of the new natural sciences was no longer matter
but energy: the concept of energy can explain all phenomena,
and the concept of matter becomes superfluous. We know the
world only through the senses, and they tell us about energy
not matter: the senses work when there is a change in the
stress of energy. But energism failed to satisfy epistemologists, for it also treated consciousness as a form of energy.
Finally, energism encountered the same difficulties as materialism.

The objections of the philosophers and scientists did not
prevent Haeckel from achieving considerable success. His *Riddles of the World* went through many editions and translations
in ten years. Under Haeckel's leadership the German Monists'
League (Monistenbund) was established in 1906. As frequently
happens, a philosophy was popularized after it had been abandoned by professionals. When the league met for its first congress in 1911 it already had 358 branches. The rallying cry
was "naturalistic monism": recognize only natural, temporal
existence and fight against dualism, religious beliefs, and
supernatural forces. The monists regarded the developing notion that the humanistic sciences are distinct from the natural sciences as an anachronism, a relic from those times when
the humanistic sciences had not yet matured in their scientific approach. The monists posited the unity of the sciences
in a naive fashion by stating that all sciences are constructions of the human brain, but they were immediately opposed.
The Kepler Society, expressing a directly opposite tendency,
was established as a counterweight to the monists.

Two Solutions, Materialistic and Idealistic

Philosophers and natural scientists who philosophized—
from von Helmholtz to Mach—had no sympathy for materialism.
They saw it is outdated, a relic of backward thought. But

among the average natural scientists, those who had little use
for philosophy, perhaps the majority were materialists, though
they were probably not as dogmatic, naive, or aggressive as
Haeckel. The majority of natural scientists had no respect
for philosophers, even for those like Mach who had a background
in the natural sciences. Helmholtz and Mach contributed to philosophy, but the average natural scientists of those times
avoided it: this was natural during a time when the specialized
sciences had become a cult. But the materialism of these natural scientists was materialism in its earlier meaning. They
did not know the new dialectical materialism of Marx and Engels,
just as the opponents of materialism did not know it.

Materialism was only one philosophical solution of the
time. Another one, particularly popular among philosophers,
was its opposite, subjective idealism. Thinkers took up extreme positions—materialism on the one hand and subjective
idealism on the other. For the latter what we call the world
is only an invention, the content of our consciousness. This
is the final conclusion of science and philosophy. Compara-
tively speaking, there had never been so many subjective idealists. To some extent the rather numerous agnostic realists
(influenced by Kant and Spencer) shared a common front with the
idealists: for the realists, reality existed independently of
man but was not accessible to him. The realist philosophy also
implied that man lives among his ideas and is never free from
them. The proclamation of this view passed for a great achievement in those times, evidence that a critical attitude had finally been achieved. In this particular sense one can describe
the ideas of the epoch as idealistic, just as one could call
them materialistic on the basis of other facts. Philosophical
problems were solved in extreme and mutually contradictory ways.
But these opposite positions had something in common: both of
them were monistic and opposed dualism. This was the main characteristic of the times.

Relationship to the Mechanistic Conception of the World

Mechanism had continued to develop for three centuries and
made significant advances in the natural sciences in the nineteenth century. It was regarded as the final word of science.
This was also true in philosophy: especially among the philoso-
pher-natural scientists the belief grew that mechanism revealed
the true nature of things, that as the physicist Boltzmann
stated in 1897 "mechanism is the picture of reality."

The Kantians even admitted that science must be mechanistic, because mechanism would correspond to a priori forms of
cognition. They made one reservation—that this belief does

not prejudge reality: reality can be governed by nonmechanistic laws.

The positivists were more extreme in their opposition to mechanism. Mach stated that the essence of the mechanistic view is that all impressions of the world are replaced by tactile sensations: this is an economic approach—a shortened form that fits into the scientific framework—but it does not pretend to reflect reality. Here mechanism was combined with atomism, but when positivists doubted atomism (believing that the concept of atom has only instrumental value) mechanism was still further undermined. If mechanism claims to be more than methodology, then it is metaphysics; if it pretends to mirror reality, then it is unfounded as well as unnecessary.

Opposition

Kantianism, the moderate philosophical view at the end of the nineteenth century, was reputed to be scientific and critical. But empiriocriticism and related views of knowledge and science, the so-called left wing of contemporary epistemology, were frequently opposed to one another. The opposition of Kantians, natural scientists, and surviving traditional philosophers charged that empiriocriticism oversimplified science by unjustly making it relative and subjective, omitting the fixed and objective elements in science. The most extreme criticism of Avenarius and Mach was made by dialectical materialism in Lenin's work, which stressed the weakest points of empiriocriticism. But this work appeared in the twentieth century, 1909.

In general, however, opposition declined in the twentieth century: people had become used to positivistic extremes. The philosophical situation now reversed itself: the positivists retained at least some of their supporters, whereas Kantianism, until recently the leading view, was almost completely abandoned. New trends such as realism, phenomenology, intuitionism could not be reconciled with Kantian apriorism, subjectivism, and rationalism.

But a peculiar thing happened. When it first started, positivism seemed the credo of the natural scientists against philosophers. However, in the twentieth century some philosophers accepted it, while the natural scientists began to give it up. This change took place concomitantly with new discoveries in physics. At a Congress of Scientific Philosophy in 1936 Niels Bohr charged that Mach had harmed science because his struggle against atomism was sustained by anti-metaphysical motives.

Development

Epistemological inquiries were well developed in the last third of the nineteenth century, and new ideas in this field quickly followed one another. This development went in two directions:

1. Kantianism, the leading trend, gradually lost ground before positivistic opposition. It continued to defend intellectual elements in cognition, but it no longer held that these were a priori. Rather, it called intellectual elements hypothetical and treated them as subjectively, biologically, or sociologically conditioned. Characteristic is the change in the view of von Helmholtz himself: at first he thought that the law of causality was a priori, that proof is neither possible nor necessary, for experience establishes it from the outset; this law is a further guarantee of the reality of the external world, whereas impressions by themselves only permit us to make inferences about their objective cause. Later (as his posthumously published notes indicate) he concluded that the regularity of nature and the consistency we see in its causal relationships are only hypothetical.

2. Kantianism also developed from a psychological to an epistemological understanding of the a priori elements of cognition. These elements now lost their subjective character, opening the way for a new metaphysics. The outstanding expression of this development was the Marburg school of philosophers.

METAPHYSICS IN THE TIME OF POSITIVISM

In this time of minimalism there was still a vital need to create a view of the world and to understand the essence of being. Even now there were metaphysicians. But metaphysics had to be based on experience and the specialized sciences. It could only be their extension and final conclusion. Examples of such a metaphysics are the philosophies of Wundt in Germany and Renouvier in France.

WUNDT AND THE GERMAN METAPHYSICIANS

Life

Wilhelm Wundt(1832-1920) studied medicine at Berlin and Heidelberg. He graduated at Heidelberg in physiology, but his interest changed to psychology and then to philosophy. He was appointed to the chair of philosophy at Leipzig, and his name is generally associated with this university. There he founded

the first psychological laboratory, which became famous. His
scholarly activity lasted nearly 60 years.

He went through four periods of development: in the first
period he worked on physiology; in the second period he pursued
psychology, won fame, and became a world authority in this subject; in the third period he passed to general philosophy and
developed logic, ethics, and a philosophical system; in the
fourth period he returned to psychology, social psychology in
particular. His views developed in a continuous manner; in the
1880s they were already completely formed.

Wundt's knowledge was more extensive than that of any of
his contemporaries. His was the most encyclopedic mind of the
nineteenth century. Often he has been compared with Aristotle
and Leibniz. Wundt was thoroughly familiar with nearly all of
the specialized sciences, but with the exception of physiology
he did not actively cultivate them.

Works

His works are titanic. He had a real ability to synthe-
size broad areas of inquiry. In 1873-74 he published a great
two-volume compendium, *Physiological Psychology*, the first such
work to consider experimental investigations. Later he wrote a
three-volume *Logic* (1880), a three-volume *Ethics* (1886), and
ten volumes on ethnopsychology (*Völkerpsychologie*, 1900-20).
His most general philosophical views are contained in *System of
Philosophy* (1889).

Views

1. Psychology. Wundt owed the greater part of his fame in
psychology to the fact that he gave it an experimental and physiological character. Both Europe and America learned the laboratory method from him, but his general psychological views
were not shared by all his followers.

His position was that psychic reality is continuous in nature. The soul is not a substance. Wundt claimed that the
soul must be understood in connection with events that current-
ly affect it. Neither the materialists nor the spiritualists
had understood this: both of them had regarded the soul as a
substance. Wundt thought that this was a manifestation of the
materialistic way of thinking in which even the spiritualists
were unconsciously entangled.

The life of the psyche does not develop mechanically. New
contents of consciousness arise in combination with its old

elements. A continual "creative synthesis" takes place that is governed by the principle that energy increases rather than being conserved.

Psychic life cannot be explained by the laws of association alone. Rather, one must appeal to apperception. Wundt rehabilitated this old concept of the metaphysical psychologists Leibniz and Herbart and argued that this was verified by experience. Here he expressed the belief that psychic life is not passive; its course of development depends not only on stimuli that impinge on the psyche, but also on the psyche itself. The characteristics of the self are a product of its history; therefore, its experiences are dependent not only on the time in which they occurred, but also on the totality of its life. This basic idea of the Wundtian theory of apperception created a breach in the empiricistic understanding of psychic phenomena.

Hence, the will occupied a leading place in Wundt's psychology. For him it was the most typical expression of the psychic process, for the will is active and directly influences the psyche. Wundt's voluntaristic psychology was directly opposed to the intellectualistic view prevalent in his times. Nonetheless, this voluntaristic psychology did not include the will among the elements of the psyche; these elements were solely impressions and feelings.

Wundt understood the relationship between physical and psychological phenomena as psychophysical parallelism. He thought that cause and result are always identical. Thus, a psychic phenomenon could not cause a physical one or vice versa. Therefore the theory of their mutual interconnectedness is rejected, leaving the theory of parallelism. Wundt thought of this idea only as a working hypothesis. To regard it as anything else would be metaphysics, and he opposed metaphysics in psychology. He never treated parallelism materialistically, as did many of his contemporaries. He held that psychic phenomena are concomitant with physical phenomena, but they are not simply a manifestation or product. Wundt believed that parallelism takes place only in impressions and sensations, not in the totality of consciousness. He campaigned on two fronts: against materialistic and spiritualistic psychology.

This indicates that the views of Wundt, the founder of experimental psychology, were not identical with those regarded as typical of experimental psychology. Wundt's model of psychology was neither passive, mechanical, not intellectualistic like that of the positivists. He did not include psychology among the natural sciences. In his classification it belonged to the third division of the humanities, next to philosophy and history.

Wundt was influential in liberating psychology from philosophy. He felt that, when separated from philosophy, psychology gives more to philosophy than it takes from it. Above all, psychology teaches that experience depends on our perceptual forms and ideas; therefore, it supports idealistic philosophy. It is all too apparent, however, that this psychology had many problems, difficulties, and philosophical assumptions.

   2. *Theory of Knowledge.* For Wundt the main task of the theory of knowledge is to determine the boundary between what is given to the mind and what the mind introduces to cognition. Man tends toward naive realism, the view that everything one is aware of is directly given. He abandons this view only when it is argued. He retreats gradually from this position as he recognizes the various elements of cognition as creations of the mind. From total realism man slowly passes to partial realism, from naive realism to critical realism. This is the only genuine direction of development and progress in knowledge.

   Extreme positions have contended with one another for centuries in the theory of knowledge: empiricism with apriorism, realism with idealism. In Wundt's opinion all of these views are wrong, pure empiricism as well as pure apriorism, for we never deal with pure experience. Experience is already shaped by thought. Nor do we deal with pure thought, for the material of thinking is provided by experience.

   Wundt had the same opinion of realism and idealism: both of these extreme positions are wrong. What we perceive is neither a form of being independent of us nor an exclusive creation of our thought: it combines features of being and thought. The correct position is monism: it takes neither being nor thought but their indissoluble unity as its point of departure. Everyone recognizes this unity in practice but denies it as soon as he begins to construct a theory. One can and should differentiate between being and thought, but it is wrong to consider them independently. Many philosophers, including Kant, had committed this error.

   3. *Metaphysics.* Wundt defined philosophy as a view of the world that satisfies the needs of the mind. This was not a very precise definition, especially because Wundt did not indicate whether philosophy should also satisfy emotional needs or whether intellectual needs could also be satisfied by means other than philosophy. Of course, such a conception of philosophy could not be limited to the theory of knowledge. Wundt divided philosophy into the science of knowledge and the science of principles. In part, the science of principles is general metaphysics, particularly the philosophy of nature and the

philosophy of the soul. To the philosophy of the soul belong ethics, aesthetics, and religious philosophy.

The mind inevitably passes through three stages in its efforts to know the world: in the first stage it operates with concrete perceptions; in the second it replaces these with general concepts; in the third it tries to embrace the world in its totality and goes beyond experience. This is a necessity that no skepticism or empiricism can avert; therefore, metaphysics is a necessity for the mind.

This process has already begun in the specialized sciences with principles and hypotheses: these principles and hypotheses are necessary to join empirical facts together, but the principles themselves are not subject to proof. Hence, the principles must be metaphysical. Every final hypothesis is metaphysical, just as every metaphysics is hypothetical. There is no sharp division between the specialized sciences and metaphysics, because metaphysics already appears in the specialized sciences. The natural scientist, psychologist, and historian are metaphysicians when they encounter problems that they cannot solve empirically. To a large extent Wundt's conclusion resulted from the ambiguity of his definition of metaphysics: on the one hand, its object was supposed to be transcendental and, on the other, nonfactual, hypothetical.

Wundt derived his main metaphysical view—that the world is a complex of beings endowed with will—from psychology. His view was spiritualistic, personalistic, and voluntaristic. But he resolutely opposed materialism in metaphysics, a view to which he might have been inclined by his original physiological investigations and by the principle of psychophysical parallelism. In experience we are given psychophysical facts that are as spiritual as they are physical. These facts give us no grounds for believing that body came before spirit.

The thesis that philosophy is hypothetical was an expression of the epoch, based on premises typical of the times: first, that there can be no philosophy beyond science; second, that the world is not completely knowable for science. Wundt saw philosophy neither as conceptual poetry (as Lange did) nor as a summation of the results of the sciences (as the materialists did). He did not reject philosophy (as the extreme positivists had): he regarded it as a hypothetical supplement to the specialized sciences. The method of philosophy is no different than the scientific method. Therefore he believed that he was developing a "scientific" and "inductive" philosophy, one in keeping with the ambitions of the times.

4. *Ethics*. If the vast ethics of Wundt introduced anything noteworthy, it was in sociology. One of Wundt's typical

theses was that there are no isolated individuals; therefore, history cannot be the sum of individual actions. History shapes individuals rather than the reverse. Hence, Wundt rejected the individualistic conception of culture held by Taine and many other positivists. But he was as inclined to compromise in ethics as in other areas, and he finally tried to reconcile individualism with universalism.

The most outstanding feature of Wundt's ethics was what he called the heterogeneity of ends. This meant that human actions generally have results different from the ends they are supposed to serve. These unpredictable results create new impulses and ends of actions. The origination of new ends is a basic law in the development of culture. It is even important for ethics. It explains why there are not and cannot be fixed ends of actions: all ends are temporal. This evolutionistic motif in Wundt's ethics was typical of the epoch.

Criticism

Wundt was full of enthusiasm but, like the majority of his contemporaries, had little ability for constructing general philosophical theories. Initially the positivists thought of him as an ally, but they later disavowed him. Even in his own country and in psychology his dominance was not complete: the university of Berlin appointed Carl Stumpf, a pupil of Brentano, not Wundt, to a chair. Wundt's fame was great, but scientific opinion was not favorable to him in every detail. The famous American psychologist William James described Wundt as a typical German professor from the time of Wolff, and this was not meant as a compliment. What offended James was that Wundt's philosophy tried to mask inner uncertainties with excessive external slickness; it borrowed its style from predecessors, including their superficial resolution of all doubts and the definitiveness of their theses.

Influence

Wundt's laboratory in Leipzig was the first great psychological laboratory. It attracted students and scientists from all over the world. The English psychologist J. Ward and the American psychologist E. B. Titchener (who both remained faithful to Wundt) worked there. Among Poles, Mahrburg, Massonius, Twardowski, Kobylecki, and Witwicki attended his lectures.

The two most important psychologies in the second half of the nineteenth century were the German experimental (whose greatest authority was Wundt) and the British descriptive. Methods were adopted from the Germans, theories from the Brit-

ish. Wundt's methodological ideas, his experimental apparatuses, and his laboratory techniques created a school, but his
theories had no such influence. The development of psychology
did not follow his approach: the spirit of positivism rejected
Wundtian "apperception" and "creative synthesis" and either
held to English associationism or shifted to another psychological extreme, as with Brentano.

In philosophy itself this most popular thinker of the
times also left few traces: some of his ideas had influence,
but his general method of philosophizing did not. Everyone
knew him, but few followed him.

Summary

Wundt's views contained motifs characteristic of the minimalistic epoch in which he lived: an aspiration to "view the
world on scientific foundations," a conception of philosophy as
hypothesis, efforts to make psychology an independent science,
an evolutionistic and relativistic understanding of ethics,
anti-substantialism in psychology, treatment of psychophysical
parallelism as a working hypothesis, a struggle against extreme
philosophical doctrines—idealism and realism, subjectivism and
objectivism, apriorism and pure empiricism.

What was most original in Wundt went against the mainstream: his belief in the active nature of the mind, his notion
of creative synthesis, his voluntarism, and his metaphysics.
He lived a long and normal life: in youth he carried out specialized investigations like the positivists; later he passed
to an analysis of cognition like the critical philosophers;
finally he tried to create a world view, which inevitably was
dogmatic.

Predecessors

In psychology Wundt was a pupil of physiologists. During
his youth he came into contact with the most famous German
scholars of the nineteenth century: in Berlin he worked in the
laboratory of the aged J. Müller, whose name is associated with
the principle of sensory energy, and in Heidelberg he assisted
von Helmholtz. He learned the experimental method from them
and applied it to psychology.

In philosophy he was self-taught, and, as frequently happens, he learned a little of everything. Eduard von Hartmann
maintained that Wundt took the theory that conceptual cognition
is superior to sensual cognition from Leibniz, the concept of
apperception from Kant, the activist interpretation of being
from Heraclitus and Fichte, opposition to the substantialist

understanding of the soul from Lange, voluntarism from Schopenhauer, the possibility of the necessary truth of cognition from
various dogmatic philosophers, and psychophysical parallelism
from Fechner. Von Hartmann added that Wundt was unfortunate,
for he took views from each of these philosophers that more
developed philosopers had rejected. In any event, Wundt belonged to two completely different lines of development in philosophy: one led from Kant and the German idealists, the other
from the natural scientists who thought empirically and natural-
istically.

Other German Metaphysicians

Wundt was the most popular and most representative philosopher of the time in Germany, but in metaphysics several others
had equal or greater success.

1. Fechner. Gustav Theodor Fechner (1801-1887) was a professor at Leipzig but resigned his chair rather early in his
career because of an eye disease. By training a physicist, he
initiated psychophysics (*Elements of Psychophysics*, 1860) and
experimental aesthetics (*Introduction to Aesthetics*, 1876). Opposed to the apriorism of Kant and the idealists, he was an empirical investigator who thought that even the relationship between the soul and the body could be measured empirically, but
beyond the empirical sciences he saw the need for and the possibility of metaphysics. Unlike the majority of his contemporaries he did not make the same demands on metaphysics as on science. Science must be mechanistic, but metaphysics does not
have to imitate science. The arguments of metaphysics lead to
panpsychism. The understanding of the specialized sciences
tend to deprive phenomena of life, but metaphysics gives life
back to them. The former give a kind of "nocturnal" picture of
the world, the latter a "diurnal" one. Science has an obligation to be precise, but even in its style the metaphysics of
Fechner was more like a fantastic story (*Nanna, or Concerning
the Spiritual Life of Plants,* 1848; *The Sight of Day as Opposed
to the Sight of Night,* 1879).

2. Lotze. Rudolf Lotze (1817-1881), professor at Halle,
was a physician who contributed to empirical psychology (*Medical Psychology, or the Physiology of the Mind*, 1852), but his
universal and independent mind led him to believe that the
world view of the mechanistic sciences was as unsatisfying as

that of speculative idealism. He thought that this problem would be solved by empirical metaphysics: such a metaphysics is possible because the mind comes into contact with being. Lotze held that mechanism is a scientific requirement not only in physics, but also in biology and psychology. But mechanism can be reconciled with the purposefulness of the world and the existence of values: machines also serve goals. Neither does mechanism imply materialism: souls can also communicate with the help of mechanical devices. Lotze leaned toward spiritualism. To be sure, the influence of bodies and souls on one another is a secret, but no less a secret than the influence of one body on another (*Microcosm*, 1856; *System of Philosophy*, 1874-79).

Later generations showed little interest in Lotze's system, but they did value and develop some of his particular ideas: for example, a psychic act must be distinguished from its content; values do not exist, but acts "have value" (*Geltung*); science is based on faith in the existence of truth and the ability of the mind to know it.

3. *Von Hartmann.* Eduard von Hartmann (1842-1906), one of the most important German philosophers, was not an academic and first prepared himself for a military career, but an illness crippled him and he became a philosopher. He combined Hegel with Schelling and Schopenhauer, rationalism with irrationalism. He interpreted all phenomena spiritually and, rather unfortunately, called this spiritual base "unconscious." He published *The Philosophy of the Unconscious* in 1869. Von Hartmann developed his philosophy broadly, systematically, and with great learning in *The Phenomenology of Moral Knowledge* (1879), *Aesthetics* (1887), *The Science of Categories* (1896), *The Science of Metaphysics* (1899-1900). He always relied on his detailed knowledge of the natural sciences in his metaphysical arguments, and this led him to believe that his results approached a "naturalistic inductive method." His conclusions were pessimistic: the world is evil and will always remain so, though it is the best of all possible worlds. After Schopenhauer he was the greatest classic pessimist. Perhaps this was the reason for the short but wide popularity of his philosophy.

Despite differences, the metaphysicians in this nonmetaphysical epoch had many features in common: they shared a cult of science, the natural sciences, mechanistic theories, the inductive method; at the same time they believed that by one method or another they could prove the reality of the soul, the purposefulness of life, the freedom of man, and the nonrelativity of ethical norms. They fought against Hegelianism, but having been raised in its atmosphere were dependent on it. Fechner and Lotze had already begun their work in the first

half of the nineteenth century, though they reached the peak of
their creativity in the second half. They made a case for
spiritualistic metaphysics in a time of universal sympathy for
the exact sciences, where they also made successful contributions. One doubts whether they advanced the cause of metaphysics, but they were symptomatic figures of their country and
their times.

RENOUVIER AND FRENCH METAPHYSICS

Life

Charles Renouvier (1815-1903) was a philosopher who worked
outside the university and the prevailing philosophical mainstream. He never associated himself with a school or founded
one. He gave no lectures but wrote profusely. At first he was
a political activist, a republican socialist and typical man of
1848. During the Second Empire, however, he became discouraged
with politics and devoted himself to scholarly work. He was
then nearly forty years old but devoted the next half-century
to philosophical activity. His work began with *Essays on General Criticism* (1854-64) and ended with *Personalism* (1903). Between these works he published a whole series of others: *Science and Morality* (1869), *Sketch of a Systematic Classification
of Philosophical Doctrine*, (1885-86), and *The New Monadology*
(1899). In the later part of his life (from 1896) he was primarily concerned with the problems of the humanities, and his
views became very personalistic. He always strove to reconcile
his position scientifically and critically with the postulates
of religion and morality.

Predecessors

Renouvier called his doctrine neocriticism to emphasize
the connection of his philosophy with Kant's. This was only
fitting: first, he limited knowledge to phenomena; second, he
saw the main task of philosophy as the establishment of the
main categories of thought. But this Kantianism was simplistic:
there were no noumena and antinomies. Renouvier's conception
of phenomena related him to Kant but even more to Hume; his
philosophy had roots in criticism as well as positivism. It
is quite understandable, then, that he should oppose the spiritualistic metaphysics prevalent in France. Renouvier also
developed a metaphysics, but it was very different.

Views

1. *Phenomenism*. Philosophy and science must begin with
phenomena, for phenomena are the only things we can know directly. This view was rather common—but Renouvier did not understand phenomena in an ordinary way. Like many philosophers
of his time, particularly the Kantians, he believed that phenomena are something more than subjective reflections of things
and that, at the same time, they cannot exist beyond us. Indeed, one cannot determine whether they exist only in us or only beyond us. Rather, the basic opposition of objective things
and subjective images in consciousness is spurious. Experience
is uniform and does not know such a duality. But experience
has two aspects—subjective and objective—for every experience
is experienced *by* someone and is an experience *of* something.
It is common but wrong to make two independent worlds of these
two aspects of experience. Such an interpretation leads to the
controversy between idealism and realism. It forces us to
choose between them when they are both wrong: realism causes us
falsely to assume that objects are abstracted from the ideas we
have of them, whereas idealism leads us to assume that ideas
could exist even if there were no objects. Kant in particular
was wrong when he assumed the existence of "things-in-themselves" beyond phenomena and created a situation in which the
knowable became unreal and the real became unknowable.
     "Phenomenalism" generally means that we know only phenom-
ena and cannot know real being. This was not Renouvier's view.
Only phenomena exist; there is no other form of being beyond
them. For this reason he gave his belief a somewhat different
name—"phenomenism." This was not an agnostic view: because
there is nothing beyond phenomena, nothing is unknowable. This
view approached Avenarius' theory of "introjection" and Mach's
theory of "elements."

2. *Through Postulates of Faith to Metaphysics*. Knowledge
of phenomena is not flawless. Only introspective knowledge of
ourselves is free from these errors, because it is wholly direct. Therefore, the task of philosophy is to criticize knowledge of phenomena and to differentiate between the objective
and the subjective.
     We grasp phenomena with the help of nine categories: rela-
tionship, number, extension, duration, quality, becoming, causality, purposefulness, and personality. All of these categories are more or less subjective; they do not give absolute
knowledge; they are always relative.

Polar opposites that are difficult to resolve arise in great philosophical problems. Renouvier reduced these polarities to six: thing and idea, finitude and infinity, freedom and necessity, development and creation, happiness and duty, evidence and faith.

But Renouvier saw two ways to absolute knowledge: one through the principle of contradiction, another through faith. The principle of contradiction—which one must accept, for thinking would be impossible without it—permits us to deduce far-reaching consequences. Above all, from this principle Renouvier deduced that the world is finite in time and space and that it is composed of a finite number of elements or "monads" as he called them (like Leibniz). He thought that his new metaphysical criticism could solve metaphysical problems that had been insoluble for Kantian criticism.

Renouvier asserted that even more positive results for the knowledge of being are afforded by faith. Faith is an act of will, because the recognition of truth is not forced upon us. If we do not recognize it, it is only through a free act. Nothing prevents us from accepting it. We see truth in the world of phenomena, not in the world of noumena where Kant had placed truth: new beginnings and discontinuities are continually arising in the world of phenomena. Moreover, it is impossible to know freedom in the strict sense of the word. One can only believe in freedom, but we have the right to believe because belief is a demand in our life.

Through his appeal to the principle of contradiction Renouvier came to recognize the finitude of the world, and his appeal to faith led him to recognize freedom. He also acknowledged the existence of God and the immortality of the soul: these are also needs of man and postulates of his faith.

In resolving metaphysical problems by appealing to faith, needs, and postulates Renouvier followed Kant. He went even further: he ascribed a greater power to postulates and faith as evidence than Kant had. This method made it possible to regard his metaphysics as critical and at least partially in keeping with the minimalism of the epoch.

Summary

The theory of phenomena, the theory of the finitude of the world, and the theory of freedom are the main theses of Renouvier's philosophy. He started with a critique of knowledge and ended with metaphysics. In metaphysics he reached rather ordinary conclusions: the existence of God, the immortality of the soul, and freedom of will. But he did not arrive at these conclusions through the usual arguments. His arguments—

voluntarism, practicality, faith—are unusual motifs in the intellectualistic and scientific nineteenth century.

Influence

Renouvier did not lecture in any school and had no direct
pupils. Nevertheless, the leading philosophers of France were
influenced by him: O. Hamelin and the historians V. Brochard
and V. Delbos. He also had enthusiastic readers abroad. Read-
ing Renouvier made a philosopher of William James. From
Renouvier he accepted the concept of phenomena and the method
of establishing metaphysical truths by appealing to practical
postulates. He constructed the theory of "pure experience"
from this concept of phenomena, and the method of practical
postulates led to "pragmatism." Through James Renouvier's
thought influenced even those who had never heard of him.

Other French Metaphysicians

Among Renouvier's contemporaries three philosophers played
the greatest role:

1. *Fouillée*. Alfred Fouillée (1838-1912), professor at
Bordeaux and Paris, was a prolific and original writer who followed his own path. As he said, he tried to "bring the ideas
of Plato from heaven to earth" and in this way to reconcile
idealism and materialism. He thought that he could do this by
giving idealism a practical turn. Thoughts are indeed forces
that influence our lives. For example, the very idea of freedom breeds determination in us, and these resolutions give us
strength. The thought of freedom acts in this way regardless
of whether indeterminism is true. This doctrine of "idea-
forces" (idées-forces) led to a voluntaristic, anti-intellectualistic of idealism. Like the metaphysics of Renouvier it
was hardly symptomatic of the epoch. Rather, it was a harbinger of the one to come.

With his contemporaries Fouillée noted that in metaphysics
results can only be hypothetical. Yet, contrary to most of
them he did not believe that this view made it necessary to
give up metaphysics. There are many possibilities for metaphysical systems. Fouillée stated that metaphysical systems lead
to a "struggle for existence" among themselves, and the system
is best that most agrees with science. The advance of science
will leave less and less place for systems, but there will always be some place for them.

2. *Guyau*.   Marie Jean Guyau (1854-1888), a stepson and pupil of Fouillée, was tubercular from early youth and had a
short life but managed to develop a synthetic philosophical
system.   His basic concept was that of life and its fullness.
This has been alleged to reflect the contemporary flowering of
biology.   Guyau developed his view in ethics (*Contemporary
English Ethics*, 1879; *Outline of a Morality with Neither Obligation Nor Sanction*, 1885), aesthetics (*Problems of Contemporary Aesthetics*, 1884; *Art from a Sociological Point of View*,
1889), and religion (*The Irreligion of the Future*, 1887).

Guyau asserted that the most primitive drive of man—and
every living creature—is the drive to activity, expansion, and
intensification of life.   We strive toward this goal in a natural and instinctive way.   Ethics cannot and need not formulate
any goal but this.   The task of ethics is only to show the
means that further this goal.   Thus, the basis of ethics is
biological.   The leading precept is to live to the fullest.
This implies leading a social life, for this is the fullest
life.   Though man is bound by no obligations, he should create
obligations and subordinate his life to them because they are
the best outlet for his drives.

In art we search for a richer life.   It is incorrect to
interpret aesthetic experiences as disinterested.   Art and aesthetic experiences flow from the fullness of life and have value only to the extent that they serve life.   This is also the
case with everything else, including society and religion.

Guyau was an even more independent and isolated thinker
than Fouillée.   His views were grounded in the scientific discoveries of his time, but their philosophical tendency was
rather remote from the spirit of these discoveries.

3. *Lachelier*.   Jules Lachelier (1832-1918) was little
known to the general public, but he was the philosopher most
admired by the socialists.   He opposed the two leading philosophical trends in contemporary France: he opposed positivism
because it did not touch the essential problems of philosophy,
and he opposed the official idealism of Cousin because it was
mostly verbal.   He did not regard himself as an original
thinker.   He continued the tradition of Maine de Biran and
Ravaisson and reflected the French philosophical tradition to a
far greater extent than either Fouillée or Guyau.   His philosophy was "spiritual realism where all being is force and all
force thought."   But he accepted the thesis of universal determinism.   Without such determinism nature would hardly be comprehensible.   However, Lachelier tried to prove that determinism is only a superficial aspect of being and that life, spirit,
and freedom are deeper.   In addition to determinism another

principle is necessary: causal chains are mutually incompatible
and reveal an accidental and chaotic world, but the world is
uniform and harmonious. By seeing this harmony and beauty we
penetrate further into its nature than through knowing its laws.

Lachelier made a great effort to think precisely, but his
metaphysical conceptions were imprecise. This is probably
why he wrote so little during his long life. In philosophy he
sought a view of the world but wrote treatises on specialized
topics. His temperament was that of a metaphysician, but his
main occupation was logic. This kind of compromise with the
times aspired to other things and held different convictions.
He successfully continued the spiritualistic tradition in its
most difficult days and transmitted his philosophy of the soul,
freedom, and love to Bergson.

TAINE AND THE HUMANITIES IN THE TIME OF POSITIVISM

Though they valued the natural sciences most highly, the
positivists also paid considerable attention to the humanities,
especially history. The contemporary views in this field were
most clearly formulated in France by Taine.

Life

Hippolyte Taine (1828-1893) was born in the provinces but
studied in Paris at the Ecole Normale. His talent was quickly
recognized, but there was no common language between him and
his professors, who belonged to the old spiritualist school.
Taine failed the final examination and was appointed a school
teacher in the provinces. He soon rebelled, giving up teaching,
returned to the capital, and began a literary career. His success was almost immediate. Though he had philosophical training and interests, he placed little stress on pure philosophy.
He concentrated on literary criticism and history, which he
treated philosophically. In a short time he reached a wide au-
dience and became influential in these fields. From 1864 he
was a professor of art history at the Paris School of Fine Arts.
Outside of some slight difficulties in his youth his life was
uncomplicated. Particularly in his last years he enjoyed peace,
happiness, and fame. Taine was a progressive throughout his
life. His character was complicated: he was a positivist, but
he admired the abstract and transcendental Spinoza; he was an
esthete and art historian who inquired into the beauty of
things, but the austere Stoic Marcus Aurelius was his favorite
author. This complicated nature was also reflected in his
views.

Writings

Taine began his philosophical career with a criticism of the eclectic spiritualistic philosophy that had predominated in France from the time of Cousin (*Classical Philosophers of the Nineteenth Century in France*, 1857). Taine was one of the writers most instrumental in defeating this philosophy. Later he wrote more specialized works in aesthetics, psychology, and history. His main work in aesthetics was *The Philosophy of Art*, published in several volumes beginning in 1865. His main psychological work was *The Theory of Intelligence* (1870). The war of 1871 influenced him and caused him to return to ethics and history. The fruit of these studies was the great work *The Origins of Contemporary France* (11 volumes, 1875-93). His works are only partially philosophical in the strict sense, but he had always been attracted to philosophy or to holistic deliberations and the basis of things (*l'ensemble et le fond des choses*). His talents and interests were primarily in the humanities, but as he said his experiences "were the experiences of an artist rather than a writer." As a result his philosophy is different in tone from that of the majority of positivists, who primarily emphasized the natural sciences.

Predecessors

For a Frenchman of the nineteenth century Taine had many intellectual ties with philosophers of other nations. He admired Spinoza, Schelling, and Hegel. As late as 1870 he and Renan exhorted the French to contribute to a monument in Berlin for the "great" Hegel. It has been claimed that he was dependent on these thinkers. The truth is that from them he adopted only one motif, determinism, the belief in the universal regularity and necessity of events. But this was only one element of his philosophy, just as it was only one component of the philosophy of Spinoza or Hegel. The major elements of their philosophy were foreign to him.

Taine became a positivist after he had read the works of Mill. In 1863 he devoted a special book to Mill, *English Positivism*. He then wrote, "The only original and vital philosophy today is in England, and Bain, Spencer, and Mill in particular are its leading representatives." His philosophical works were written under the influence of these English philosophers and Condillac, not Spinoza and Hegel. He did not become familiar with Comte until 1860. Taine had reservations about Comte's philosophy and charged him with dogmatism, though he did believe that part of Comte's philosophy was irrefutable and that (as he wrote in 1864) it had conquered Europe.

Taine had many original ideas, but his real talent was in discovering and spreading the ideas of others. He himself said of his historiosophy that "it has been lying on the ground since the time of Montesquieu, and I did nothing more than pick it up."

Views

1. *Methodology*. Taine was a positivist and valued only facts, but his interpretation of their value was quite special. The privileged place of minute facts in his methodology was a kind of reaction to the grandiose ideas of metaphysics. He thought that all science, from the natural sciences to history, is based on facts. Not cataclysms and great deeds but everyday events form culture and influence history. His "microhistory" and his contributions in the humanities have been compared with the work of Pasteur, who also examined microstructures. "Minute facts, essential and carefully selected, are today the only material of knowledge." Beyond these facts there is only falsehood and illusion. On the other hand, it is helpful for students to see these details in magnified form. In this form, however, facts approach pathology. For this reason Taine based normal psychology on psychopathology and became a pioneer in this distinct development of French science in the nineteenth century.

Taine belonged to a rare group of thinkers who faithfully reported observations that conflicted with their views. In science he stressed facts but, well before others had criticized the concept of scientific fact, he indicated that this concept was not as simple as the more gullible positivists had thought. He stated that what we call a fact is "an arbitrary crosscut of reality, an artificial grouping that separates things which are united and unites things which are separated." He went even further. He wrote that "properly speaking, facts, these tiny isolated shreds, do not exist: they only exist for our eyes." And he asserted that general laws, though they seem abstractions to us, are more real than facts.

2. *Psychology*. The facts and laws Taine discovered were essentially psychological. He himself said that he had never done anything that was not grounded in psychology. This was not pure psychology but was applied to the explanation of history.

The leading concept of Taine's psychology saw the mind as "a stream of impressions and impulses." There was no place in this psychology for either a substantial soul or a permanent self. It was consciously atomistic and shattered psychic life into impressions and impulses. This was a characteristic view of the times, but in keeping with an external world where Taine saw multiplicity, discontinuity, fluidity, and *l'écoulement universel*. For him the world was "a series of meteors that ignite only to immediately die."

Taine accordingly developed a theory of psychological atomism and variability, but he also pointed to phenomena that argued against it. He argued that every idea in the mind tries to dominate the mind. If this is so, then the mind is not a collection of atoms mutually independent of one another. Every person has a "leading quality" (*qualité maîtresse*) that represents his entire nature and creates a bond between the various elements of the mind, assuring its unity. In general psychology Taine stressed the atomistic and mechanistic construction of the mind, but in his applied psychology he developed the theory of "leading qualities." This latter interpretation was the more influential.

3. *Theory of Culture.* Taine is known for having explained cultural forms as a product of the "environment." It would then appear that he took the sociological position. However, this was not the case: for him the social group was nothing more than individuals and what was in them. His opinion was that the individual, not society, is the agent of culture and events. "Everything takes place through the individual." "In essence there is neither mythology nor language. There are only people who construct words and images. Language, law, religion are only abstractions: total reality is physical, acting, and visible man." Taine's individualistic position left little place for sociology. He still had no feeling for the distinctness of sociological interpretations. Individual facts are often similar. People speak alike, believe alike, and regard the same things as good. Taine thought that these were the only grounds for speaking of "social" facts. He took no account of the fact that many things seem to happen "over the heads" of individuals. Though he studied society, it was not from a distinct social point of view: he thought that groups formed according to psychological not social laws.

At this time Marx, not Taine, took the social point of view. Marx was still alone, but Taine was in the mainstream. He was the expression of an epoch that had begun to develop sociology but knew only its psychological laws.

Taine's theory of history and culture was individualistic but not in the same way as Carlyle's: it was not the exceptional individuals who created history but numerous, ordinary, and average individuals: "The most creative mind really does not create anything; its ideas are the ideas of the epoch, and what genius either changes or adds is insignificant."

4. *History*. Taine devoted most of his attention to history. First, he interpreted history psychologically, not sociologically. He wrote, "History at base is a psychological problem." Second, history was not evolutionary: there was no continuity, continual development, or progress. Rather, Taine thought that history moves in leaps. "At rare moments in time the human mind was renewed, and generations without parents appeared as after an earthquake, after which the mind, like nature, began to repeat its works and live by imitating itself." This was a view close to one called "catastrophism" in the twentieth century. Third, Taine's understanding of history was naturalistic. Time played a very minor role; therefore, in his opinion human history approached "natural history." In nature things have a fixed structure independent of the time in which they appear, and Taine thought that this was also true in history. He wrote, "Events must be arranged according to their laws, not their dates." Against this background he arrived at a special conception of "general facts" (*faits généraux*), facts that express general laws and have a supratemporal character. The special task of history was to discover such laws. Thus, it is not surprising that he wished to apply the method and concepts of the natural sciences (especially biology) to history. The idea that history could be a different sort of science with different tasks was still foreign to him.

Therefore, for Taine the leading concepts of history were the same as those of biology. These were the concepts of time, species, and class, for he thought that the task of history was to array facts and combine them in groups. The inquiries of both the historian and the natural scientist always consist in classifying phenomena and isolating the types contained therein. Taine's conception of science was morphological and typological. Because the task of science is to establish types, he had to stress the common form of phenomena. "The form is the essential thing for me," he wrote.

To a large extent Taine's conception of history was in harmony with new trends. Typical of the times were psychological and naturalistic conceptions that tried to bring history close to the natural sciences. However, Taine's nonevolutionary, noncontinuous view of history was incompatible with the ideas of Darwin and Spencer. Rather, it was closer to the

ideas of the twentieth century. This was also true of his
typological and morphological interpretation: it was in the
Aristotelian tradition and more compatible with twentieth-century views than with those popular among positivists.

   5. *Theory of Art*. The most well-known part of Taine's
doctrine was his theory of art. Its most characteristic feature was a kind of dual naturalism. The artist does not produce works in a manner different from nature: arts cannot be
opposed to nature but must be understood as analogous to the
works of nature. This means that they must be understood as
products of necessity (as determinism teaches). "Here, as everywhere, one exclusively encounters a problem of mechanics.
The final result is wholly determined by the strength and direction of the forces that have produced it."
   The art of various times, countries, and artists has different features because of three factors: race, environment,
and moment. These three factors, perhaps the most popular of
Taine's views, were very broadly conceived. The concept of
"race" included all of the internal forces bearing on the artist, "environment" all the external forces acting on him, and
"moment" the impetus already given by events or the influence
of everything that has been on what exists now. Such a broad
interpretation of these developmental factors left no place for
any others. To be sure, Taine also said that the characteristics of art also depend on the "administrative abilities" of
the artist, but these also are determined by race, environment,
and moment.
   Another facet of Taine's naturalism was that he held the
activity of the artist to be a reproduction of nature, though
he conceived this old aesthetic doctrine very broadly, almost
as broadly as Aristotle. The artist reproduced the essential
qualities of nature. Taine further stated that should nature
reveal these features insufficiently, then art should heighten
them. However, the value of art depends on what these works
reproduce as well as how they reproduce—fleeting or lasting
values, superficial or profound ones.

Influence

   Taine wrote profusely and effectively on exciting topics
and had the "gift of dramatizing abstractions." His readers
extended well beyond academic circles, and because of this he
exerted tremendous influence. From France his influence spread
throughout the world and reached its peak around 1860. From
this time forward he was recognized as a theoretician of the

"young art." He was the focus of universal interest. The luminaries of the time wrote about him, philosophers such as Mill, Ravaisson, Renan, Vacherot, and Fouillée, historians such as Sorel and Seignobos, sociologists such as Durkheim, economists such as Leroy-Beaulieu, politicians such as Maurras, jurists such as Lombroso, historians of literature such as Brandes, Brunetière, and G. Paris, critics such as Sainte-Beuve and Lemaître, artists such as Viollet-le-Duc, and literary figures such as Gautier, Zola, Bourget, France, the Goncourts, and Barrès. In France he influenced the most famous historians, literary critics (Brunetière and Lemaître), historians of art (Fromentin), and psychologists (Janet). Taine directed specialists to philosophy and philosophers to specialization and scholarship.

His influence was not limited to the theory of art and literature; it extended to art and literature themselves. The beginning of realism with the debuts of Courbet in painting and Dumas *fils* in literature was a stimulus to Taine's theory, but later his theory intensified realism in art and literature still further.

Zola applied Taine's most radical ideas in his stories between 1871 and 1891: he tried to depict authentic man and show how his characteristics were determined by the environment. Zola wrote, "When I was about twenty-five I read Taine, who aroused my sympathies for the positivistic theory." He even exaggerated and misinterpreted Taine's ideas: he wanted to write "experimental" stories, basing art on experiments like those performed in laboratories, which had produced facts and general laws; he wanted to play the role of scientist not artist. This elimination of the boundary between fiction and science characterized the entire period and its philosophical assumptions. Zola was not alone. The Goncourts (in stories from 1884) also tried to present "documents" of life without any retouching, and Bourget in his romances assigned a leading role to the discovery of the influence of race, environment, and moment. English, Scandinavian, Russian, and Polish stories, which played such a great role in the culture of the period and were perhaps as important an expression of its views as philosophical doctrines, also followed Taine.

Opposition

Taine often contradicted his own views. He oscillated between an objective and a subjective attitude. He combined adoration of Spinoza with a cult of Mill; he argued for a sociological approach to phenomena, but he only considered individuals; he treated mental phenomena as aggregates of atoms at the same time as he asserted that they were organic wholes; he was interested only in man, but he considered man a fragment of nature; he was as he wrote, "a lover of moral zoology." None of his ideas were developed in depth. Rather, he was a synopsis of the diverse ideas of his age. Some features of his philosophy were criticized by the positivists, others by the opponents of positivism.

Summary

Taine thought that man and culture were subject to the same laws as nature. "Vice and virtue are the same kinds of creations as sulfuric acid or sugar." Likewise with art: it is a product of race, environment, and moment. For Taine culture was a psychological problem and psychology a naturalistic one. Taine helped to spread the false notion that history or art and literary criticism should employ the same methods as the natural sciences, that they could arrive at a synthesis of intellectual and social life just as chemistry creates a synthesis of physical life.

These views of Taine were essentially positivistic and broadened the influence of positivism. But other elements in his philosophy, such as the nonevolutionary view of history and the typological conception of science, were not a part of positivism.

The probable reasons why Taine's views do not correspond to the general conception of positivism are: (1) The majority of positivists were natural scientists, whereas Taine was a humanist. (2) As a creator of positivism he had already matured before it reached its peak; he retained some of the characteristics of the earlier positivism, whereas the most typical positivists were born in a time when the movement was at its height and did not know any other position. (3) As an original and creative thinker he had many ideas, not all of which fit the simple formula of positivism. Positivism had many shades and hues. Taine belonged to the same period and basically to the same camp as Comte and Mill, Spencer and Pearson, Lange and Mach, but many features of his philosophy were distinct and emphasized other minimalistic possibilities. This was also the case with Renan.

RENAN AND SKEPTICISM IN POSITIVISM

The sole faith of the positivists was science, and if this failed there was only skepticism. This was the fate of some positivists, especially Renan, one of the leading humanists of the period.

Predecessors

Skeptical humanism had been known in France for centuries.
It had three main theses: skepticism, pessimism, and hedonism.
(1) We know nothing and can know nothing about the world; therefore, it is a waste of time to pursue such knowledge.   (2) Only
studies of man are worthwhile; however, we know little about
him, and what we do know about him and his fortunes is not aus-
picious.   (3) Hence, the only thing left to us, without going
into deeper truths and wider perspectives of existence, is to
enjoy the fleeting moments of existence.
     During the Renaissance in the sixteenth century skepticism
and hedonism were most apparent.   This was particularly so with
Montaigne, the initiator of the movement.   In the seventeenth
and eighteenth centuries pessimism took their place: this was
expressed in the seventeenth century by La Rochefoucauld and in
the eighteenth by Voltaire.   The pessimism of the former was
directed toward human nature, its weaknesses egoism, and shal-
lowness.   The pessimism of the latter emphasized human events
in which injustice and misfortune prevailed.   In the nineteenth
century, this trend of skeptical humanism appeared in the time
of positivism with Renan.   He stressed the first thesis, skepticism, and the third thesis, hedonism.

Life

     Ernest Renan (1823-1892) began his studies in a seminary
but left before completing the course.   He devoted himself to
history, especially to investigations of the origins of Christianity.   Scholarly works in this field won him wide popularity
and fame, mixed with scandal.   His *Life of Jesus* (1863) por-
trayed Christ as the most perfect of men but human.   Renan's
scholarly achievements made him director of the Collège de
France in Paris during the Third Republic.   A personal religious crisis and the general political letdown in France after
1871 further intensified his skepticism and pessimism.   To many
contemporaries Renan's skeptical and pessimistic but good-hu-
mored and ironic attitude seemed the wisest and most dignified
attitude that man could take toward life.   Renan was admired
by scholars as well as in the salons.   His skepticism was all
the more impressive, being professed by a famous scholar in
brilliant literary form.
     Renan's eight-volume *History of the Origins of Christian-
ity* (1863-83) and his five-volume *History of the Jewish People*
(1887-93), despite many risky hypotheses, were and are regarded
as the most brilliant synthetic works of French humanities.
Renan was a historian and philologist.   His originality lay in
his ability to resolve difficult historical problems (especial-

ly in the history of religion) through philological analysis. Philosophy for him was a relaxation from specialized studies and a personal examination of conscience. This philosophy did not give positive results. It was an expression of a distrustful age and a suspicious mind.

Development

The thought of Renan passed through several stages. His first beliefs were far from skeptical. In his youth he wrote, "Absolute truth and good do exist. One should believe in the first and practice the second." At this time he interpreted absolute truth and good religiously. When he left the seminary he was already without religious faith, but he was still enthusiastic and optimistic about science. He expressed this attitude in the years 1848-49 in the work *The Future of Science* (published in 1890). Then he was a typical positivist. His new faith was a most common one in the time of positivism. But even this faith could not for long retain its hold on his suspicious mind. With others he overthrew the old faith, but he sensed illusions even in the new faith of the times. After he lost faith in science he had no faith left at all, only an ironic and contemptuous attitude toward the world. In this period he produced his *Philosophical Dialogues* (written in 1871, published in 1876) and *Philosophical Dramas* (1878-86). In 1888, toward the end of his life, he wrote a kind of philosophical testament, *Examination of a Philosophical Conscience*. In this work he even became skeptical of skepticism. If one is to be truly careful, one should not simply doubt; one should vacillate between doubt and faith. But now his irony was more subdued. Contrary to his own theories, he admitted that some things are more valuable and important than others: love, religion, poetry, and virtue.

Renan's social beliefs also changed during the course of his life: from faith in democratic ideals to faith in an elite and finally to complete discouragement and loss of any desire to organize humanity.

Views

1. *Sources of Skepticism.* Renan's skepticism stemmed from a disenchantment with science, history (which Renan knew well from his own investigations), and philosophy. His studies had taught him how many unavoidable errors, illusions, and fictions there are in history. They also taught him that in history and

nature everything is in the process of becoming and eternal
change. Renan said that this belief became the basis for his
view of the world.

French spiritual philosophy, which was then in a period
of eclectic and dogmatic stagnation, caused Renan to lose his
respect for philosophy. Its proofs for the existence of God
and the soul were still largely derived from Descartes and were
obviously insufficient. Naturalistic philosophy seemed no more
certain to Renan, even though it correctly asserted that all
phenomena are part of one natural order and that nothing in the
world is supernatural and absolute. Spiritualism and naturalism are the only philosophies that give a view of the world.
Renan therefore said, "We are only living in the shadow of a
shadow; with what will the people who come after us live?"

Moreover, Renan did not try to find arguments to support
skepticism as the ancient Pyrrhonists had done. He was so certain of the uncertainty of everything else that for him it required no proof. On the contrary, Renan thought that the burden of proof rested on anyone who asserted that we have certain
knowledge. But no one can give such proof. The problem for
Renan was not the uncertainty of knowledge but the consequences for life that stem from this uncertainty. How should
one live in face of this? For him that was the real problem of
philosophy.

2. To Be Only a Spectator. Renan thought there was only
one solution: not to attempt to decide questions and intervene
in events but to take a passive attitude and be only a spectator.

> The first obligation of the honest man is not to in-
> fluence his own views but to allow nature to be re-
> flected in him as in a camera and to take part only
> as a spectator in the internal struggles that rage in
> the depths of consciousness.

He also stated that correct behavior is permitting thoughts and
feelings to parade before the eyes as in a kaleidoscope.

Man cannot know the truth, but he can avoid falsehood and
escape illusion. If he seeks the essence of being, he may find
a void; therefore, it is better not to search. Things man
takes seriously can turn out to be a "cruel joke"; hence, it is
better not to take them seriously. Because every assertion is
a risk, it is better not to assert anything. In the final
analysis, one can take this risk oneself, but one must be careful about the assertions of others. The most careful person is
prepared for everything (*ad utrumque paratus*), even for the

fact that the world is a serious matter and not to be taken
lightly. We encounter infinity everywhere, and nothing is impossible in the face of infinity. Hence, the most correct attitude is not even to decide on doubt; one must avoid deciding
both between various faiths and between doubt and faith themselves. Man must consider the uncertainty and imperfection in
which he lives, but he must not rebel against them. Renan had
the same opinions as Schopenhauer, but the rebellious pessimism
of the latter seemed naive to him. Irony is a more authentic
attitude toward life than rebellion.

   3. Amoralism and Hedonism.   There is no evidence that one
goal is better than another; therefore, everyone has the right
to select whichever goal suits him. There is nothing to justify making sacrifices for any goal. Virtue or morality is no
exception. "Virtue is personal satisfaction, but who would be
so bold as to recommend it to others?" This position expressed
doubt about the very difference between good and evil, not
about any moral doctrine in particular.
   Renan thought that such a theory does not undermine morality in practice

> for nothing more surely gives rise to goodness than
> discouragement and an awareness that nothing in this
> world is to be taken seriously, that nothing has
> deeper foundations. In such an absolute ruin what
> remains? Anger? It is hardly worth the trouble.

This led to hedonism. If there is no other good, then the
pleasures of life itself always remain. Renan in Epicurean
fashion valued the passive pleasures most highly, the pleasures
of a spectator. The greatest pleasure is to enjoy the pageant
that life presents without attempting to penetrate its essence
or intervening in its development. "Enjoy the world as it is,"
he wrote. The attitude of the spectator magnifies pleasure in
a special way:

> We delight in the universe with a kind of general
> feeling that causes us to be sad in a sad place and
> happy in a happy place; we enjoy the worldliness of
> the urbane as well as the holiness of the virtuous,
> the meditations of the scholar as well as the auster-
> ity of the ascetic.

Finally, life can be pleasant, and we can even regret that we
have so little of it. "What is more cruel than the unavoidable
incompleteness of every life? Oh why do I have only one life?

Why can I not embrace everything?" Renan tested the efficacy
of his life attitude on himself. He noted in his memoirs: "I
do not believe that there have been many creatures as happy as
I."

4. *The Organization of Humanity*. Despite his skepticism
Renan continually returned to this question: after all, is
there no goal in life that could give it sense and that would
be worthwhile serving? The answers he found failed to satisfy
him, and he discarded them one after another. Initially, he
saw this goal in the welfare of the people at large. He later
abandoned this democratic faith and began to think of the rule
of reason as a goal worth pursuing. And it was only a small
elite, those "upper ten thousand" (as Renan asserted) who could
serve this goal. The mass is only the soil from which the
elite springs. If this elite is to develop, then the masses
must unfortunately be neglected, for when they come to power
the rationality of life declines. But in the last years of his
life Renan rejected even this theory. In general he lost all
interest in the "future organization of humanity."

5. *Relationship to Religion*. Many skeptics who abandoned
knowledge found relief in faith. This was not so with Renan:
his skepticism was directed at faith in religion even more than
at faith in knowledge. He personified the nineteenth century
spirit of irreligiosity. Up to this time the attitude had been
either great reverence for religion or unqualified condemnation,
either the attitude of a believing Christian or Voltaire's position, either religion as a divine matter or as an affair of
the vulgar masses. Renan, however, retained his respect for
religion even after he had lost faith in it.
     Like the philosophers of the eighteenth century he stated
that religion was strictly a human affair, and he tried to demonstrate this scientifically in history and philosophy. There
is no place for religion in the scientific picture of the world:
either the laws of nature are true or those of revelation. Religion can be explained psychologically without reference to
supernatural factors, and this is the most powerful argument
against it.
     But religion is not a simple matter of interest, an inven-
tion of priests. God is a "category of the ideal," religion "a
beautiful moral order" and a gratification of humanity's moral
instinct. Religion satisfies this instinct better than philosophy: philosophical idealism touches only a few, but religious
idealism touches all. Religion is the most noble human affair.

Though no religion is genuine, every religion is valuable if it is really understood. Renan combated religion no less vigorously than Voltaire, but he also opposed Voltaire's hatred for religion. He increased the range of understanding, tolerance, and peace. Many contemporary philosophers took a similar position (F. A. Lange, for example). Already in the eighteenth century, the time of Voltaire, Hume had taken a similar position in his deliberations of "natural" religion.

Summary

A common expression of the times was: "The great event of our generation was the transition from the absolute to the relative." Renan was a leader of this movement, stressing the relativity of all norms. His main idea was continual experimentation: how to live amid universal relativity. He advanced the following solution: one can live well in this relative world providing one treats it skeptically and does not become engaged, that is, if one is a spectator. Such an attitude is most consonant with human dignity and simultaneously affords the greatest pleasure. Yet, he did not apply this attitude to himself. His life was not the life of a spectator, but the active and devoted life of a scholar.

Influence

In downgrading the role of knowledge Renan increased the importance of feeling. Though he was outside the Church, he influenced a movement toward modernism within the Church itself. His slighting of knowledge and toleration of imprecise and inconsistent thinking also influenced the attitude of succeeding generations. The denigration of knowledge caused him to value life all the more: here again he influenced future generations to turn to a "philosophy of life."

Renan's philosophy, which made no pretensions to scholarliness, played a lesser role in the history of philosophy as a science, but a greater one in the history of philosophy as a life attitude. The intelligentsia of future generations followed his lead.

Nihilism

What is called "nihilism" sprang from the same sources as Renan's philosophy: nothing is certain; there is no absolute good on which life can be based. The term nihilism is derived from Turgenev. In 1863 he wrote, "We had the Hegelians, now there are the nihilists; we shall see how you can exist in nothingness and a vacuum of emptiness." There were nihilists not only in Russia, but also in the West; both philosophy and fiction pictured a life "without dogmas."

Opposition

Renan's era, skeptical, nihilistic, and iconoclastic, did not last long. Even before the end of the century other trends gained ascendancy. Skepticism encountered opposition from the very outset, above all in religious circles, for whom Renan was a most dangerous enemy. But philosophers also opposed relativism and a skeptical attitude toward life. The opposition stressed the fact that Renan took his position to avoid risks, but every position is a risk. Renouvier added that doubt and vacillation are the least productive of facts by which life can be lived correctly and pleasantly. The greatest errors are made when one is afraid of making errors, and this was Renan's fate. The most telling criticism was Renan's inconsistency: he spoke of the uncertainty of everything but admitted finally that there is nothing beyond the temporal world; theoretically, he avoided debate on basic questions, but in practice he resolved these questions in favor of naturalism and finitude.

Successors

A philosophy such as Renan's could not be fitted into a scientific rubric. Consequently, he expressed some of his ideas in dialogues and dramas. He had fewer followers among professional philosophers than among men of letters. Renan was principally concerned with formulating a conception of life, and this could perhaps be better expressed in narrative than in a scholarly treatise. Three French novelists developed Renan's ideas. As Zola and the Goncourts had expressed naturalistic positivism, now France, Barrès, and Gide expressed skeptical humanism. From Renan France took irony, Barrès egoism, Gide the attitude of spectator: for France nothing in life has value, for Barrès only our own person, for Gide only the pageant of life.

1. France. Anatole France (1844-1924) regarded man as mechanism: in the actions of man, in his enthusiasms and beliefs is as much freedom as in the movements of a puppet. All human judgments are subjective; there is no objective good or evil. No paradise awaits man in the after life. Even life itself is no paradise, because it is a mechanism without purpose and therefore without sense. However, in the final analysis one can find pleasure in life by maintaining an attitude of indifference, distance, and irony. France increased the negative elements of Renan's philosophy; no one had a more nihilistic view of the world than he.

2. *Barrès.* August Maurice Barrès (1862-1923) started with the idea that the only important and valuable thing in the world is our own emotions. To strengthen these we must cultivate our self, and this is our real life task. Later (and in a rather odd way) Barrès widened the concept of self to family and race: from them, self derives its energy and culture. Here he deviated from Renan's individualism and indifference to become a supporter of nationalism.

3. *Gide.* André Gide (1869-1951) also emphasized the quantity and intensity of experiences. To increase and intensify experience one must first free oneself from mechanism and habit; one must continually create oneself anew and not lose a single moment of life. "Each moment of life is irreplacable; therefore, try to concentrate exclusively on the moment." Do not stabilize the self, do not make final decisions, do not consolidate anything. This view resulted in moral atomism, the shattering of life into individual moments, the very opposite of what the vast majority of moralists had wished. This also led to hedonism: "The pleasure I receive from any action is an indication to me that I should have done it."

These three writers were read by millions and became the representative thinkers of their time. The zenith of France's success came in the first decade of the twentieth century, Barrès' in the second, and Gide's in the third. None of these writers limited himself to the spirit of Renan's theory. France was initially a proponent of political indifference and later turned to socialism; Barrès became a devotee of nationalism; Gide for a time gravitated toward communism.

"The Bankruptcy of Science"

During the last years of Renan's life this slogan gained wide currency. Paul Bourget, a French prose writer and critic, originated it in 1888, but others also adopted it. There was a superficial similarity between this idea and Renan's philosophy. Bourget saw the bankruptcy of science in the fact that science gives only knowledge of phenomena not the final metaphysical essence of things. For Renan, however, metaphysics was unimportant (he was too much of a positivist for this); the important thing was that no clear life norms could be derived from scientific facts. Moreover, Bourget emphasized the deficiencies of science to convince people that man must seek support in metaphysics or religion. Bourget did not end in skepticism. On the contrary, he was inclined to be dogmatic. Despite external similarity between them, Bourget's views were a harbinger of an age quite different from the epoch of positivism that had produced Renan.

The Third Phase: 1880-1900

The general philosophical attitude did not change after
1880. As before, minimalism, positivism, and scientism were
dominant. Taine, Renan, Avenarius, Mach, Riehl, Wundt, Spencer,
and Pearson were still alive and writing. The number of their
supporters and the number of publications written in their
spirit was increasing. Although in the earlier part of the
century minimalistic doctrines faced opposition, now this opposition was completely overcome. In short, the reigning doctrine had not changed. The only difference was that, in addition to this doctrine, opposition movements began to appear.

The new ideas opposing the majority view and foreshadowing
the new philosophical era appeared first and most clearly in
narrative prose. The leading tendency among progressive writers of the time was naturalism. Naturalism in literature had
its own philosophical position, its own conception of the world
and man, but this position was the same as scientism in scientific philosophy. However, even before 1880 a shift to radically different views in literature had begun. Ibsen, Dostoevski, Tolstoy, and Maeterlinck signaled a turn from literary and
scientific naturalism.

Ibsen's dramas emphasized the tragic moral problems of
man. Dostoevski's novels depicted the metaphysical struggle
between good and evil in the existence of man. But, above all,
the plays and essays of M. Maeterlinck (1862-1949) expressed a
view of man different from that of naturalism. He had translated Ruysbroeck (a fourteenth-century Flemish mystic and theologian) and adored the mystics. His view of the world was irrationalistic and supernaturalistic. The world for him was incomprehensible and full of miracles; individual things were not
true reality but its symbol. He treated them as many earlier
mystical thinkers had, but he added something contemporary:
that forces enter into daily life through these invisible symbols, and that frightening depths of existence are revealed in
the most insignificant phenomena. For this reason, beauty,

greatness, and happiness also depend on insignificant, everyday
things. One need only transfer life's point of gravity to the
center of the soul to "live a deep life." Neither knowledge
nor science (on which scientism had based itself) but wisdom,
or looking at fate from the depths and heights of the soul, is
necessary for this. Wisdom is not just understanding; even
more important is instinct. Wisdom is not a simple matter of
consciousness; even more vital is the unconscious, the internal
sources of the soul. Presentiments are no less important than
experience, "unclear truths" no less vital than the clearest
ones.

All of this was radically different from the majority view
at the end of the nineteenth century. This new attitude at
first appeared unintelligible, even in poetry. This view had
been common before, but for those times it was remote. Nonetheless, poetry played its role. Though it was not philosophy,
it did lay the groundwork for new philosophical trends.

Among the most widely accepted truths of the positivistic
period are the following: (1) in facts and scientific laws we
possess unfailing truth; (2) this truth is particularly evident
in the natural sciences on which every true science must pattern itself; (3) this truth is composed of individual facts,
and laws are only a generalization of them; (4) the object of
truth is nature, beyond which nothing exists; (5) modern culture, which science has created, is the highest attainment of
man.

All of these universally accepted theses were criticized
after 1880. In a point by point refutation: (1) Facts and scientific truths are not certain; both are essentially conventions. The French philosophers and natural scientists such as
Boutroux and Poincaré espoused this view. (2) Humanistic knowledge is not and cannot be the same as knowledge in the natural
sciences. This second objection was advanced by the German
philosophers Dilthey, Windelband, and Rickert. (3) Our knowledge is not supported by facts alone, for we grasp general
truths directly from the evidence as a whole. This was the objection of the Austrian thinker Brentano. (4) Nature is not
the only nor even the most primal form of existence. This was
the view of English and American idealists. (5) Not only is
modern culture not perfect, but it is quite frankly bad and
should be overturned and changed. Tolstoy brought out this objection to culture in literature that served a somewhat Rous-
seauian purpose, and Nietzsche developed it in a new philosophical position.

Some of these opposition views were new, especially the
views emphasizing the conventionality of science and the distinctness of the humanities. Other views went back much further: idealism to views quite recently discredited, Brentano's
ideas as far back as scholasticism or even Aristotle. All of

these views played an important role in the history of philosophy. They appeared at the end of the nineteenth century, but
their consequences were not felt until the twentieth. This
period, regarded as a time of "decline," was not only the decline of one era but the rise of another.

In philosophy of this time (as in the entire world order)
everything still seemed certain and stabilized. It was apparent that philosophical views were changing but that no revolution threatened philosophy. Yet, some already foresaw the revolution, the abandonment of contemporary philosophy and culture.
Nietzsche wrote: "I am describing what will come and what must
come: the total victory of nihilism." He understood by this
"the overturning of all dogmas," when the ancient faith and
morality that kept humanity under restraint would fall and when
one would say "now nothing is true and everything is permitted."

OPPOSITION IN THE THEORY OF THE NATURAL SCIENCES

At the end of the nineteenth century the theory of the
sciences was developed especially by the French. This was
their philosophical specialty, just as the theory of knowledge
at this time was a German one. This theory of science was neither a synthesis of the sciences in the Comtian tradition, nor
a methodology in the Millian one. Rather, it was a critique of
scientific knowledge. As in the general theory of knowledge
the topics of liveliest discussion were the concepts of subject
and object, truth and cognition; here the debate centered on
the concepts of law and fact, theory and hypothesis. The result of this discussion was that scientific knowledge is not as
necessary, objective, and certain as laymen and some scientists
had assumed. Science also has deficiencies, just like common
sense and philosophical knowledge. This result struck at the
deepest faith of the nineteenth century, at the only dogma of
positivism. It was a sign that the scientific epoch was ending
and another era was beginning.

This criticism was partly the work of the philosophers who
belonged to the spiritualist trend and partly that of natural
scientists. Among the former were Boutroux and Bergson, among
the latter Poincaré and Duhem. Boutroux had begun his work in
the 1870s, but the others belong to the second generation of
scientific critics.

The critique of science went through two phases: in the
first it tried to undermine belief in the necessity of scientific laws, in the second their objectivity. The first phase
is known as contingentism, the second as conventionalism.
Boutroux made the greatest contribution to the first, Poincaré,
Duhem, Bergson, and others to the second.

Predecessors

As had Gailileo and Newton in the seventeenth century and
d'Alembert in the eighteenth, so now famous scientists revealed
much about the nature of science by analyzing their own work.
The result of this analysis was that scientists had to modify
their general belief in the nonrelativity of scientific knowledge. Among these scientists were Herschel in England, Helmholtz in Germany, and Sniadecki in Poland, but most of them
were in France. Although in other countries scientists affili-
ated themselves with leading philosophical trends—the English
with empiricism and evolutionism, the Germans with Kantianism,
the Poles with positivism—French criticism was generally independent of these trends: they amassed individual observations
rather than building a general theory.

The earliest of these critics was the great physicist
Ampère. He was a friend of Maine de Biran, was influenced by
him, and influenced him in turn. One line of development runs
from Biran to Boutroux, another from Ampère to Poincaré. Just
as Biran and Ampère had, now a half century later Boutroux and
Poincaré, a spiritualistic philosopher and natural scientist,
befriended and complemented one another.

1. Ampère. A. M. Ampère (1775-1836) in his *Essay on the
Philosophy of the Sciences* (1834-43) provided insights into the
activity of the knowing subject and stressed the need for hypotheses in science. He fought against the pretensions of science, in particular that science is a more perfect creation
than philosophy because it is free of hypotheses. Of course,
in philosophy the existence of God, the soul, and even matter
are hypotheses, but there are also hypotheses in science. Ampère's opinion is all the more remarkable, because it was expressed by a scientist. His critical analysis of science was
continued in the nineteenth century by Cournot and Bernard.

2. Cournot. A. A. Cournot (1801-1877), mathematician,
economist, and historian, author of many philosophical works,
especially *Treatise on the Connection of the Fundamental Ideas
in Science and in History* (1861), was perhaps the main precur-
sor of the later theory of science. In particular he stressed
the philosophical assumptions of science, the approximate nature of scientific laws, the temporal nature of hypotheses and
systems, and the role of chance in events, which science must
consider and which explains why scientific inferences are not
universal or necessary.

3. Bernard. Claude Bernard (1813-1878), physiologist and physician, also influenced the relationship of scientists to science with his *Introduction to Experimental Medicine* (1865). He asserted that science establishes only relationships between phenomena and does not offer causes. He combated the empirical theory of science and asserted that a "raw fact in itself is not scientific" and that passive observation is fruitless. On the contrary, the investigator needs hypotheses ("to make experiments, some idea taken from above is indispensable") and intuition ("a kind of intellectual sensitivity").

The Men and Their Works

These scientists prepared the criticism of science, but the first systematic development of this critique was by Etienne Emile Boutroux (1845-1921). He was primarily a historian of philosophy, but his doctoral thesis (*Of the Contingency of the Laws of Nature*, published in 1874) was a critique of science, especially, and of scientific law. This short book and the later *The Idea of Natural Law* (1895), which developed these same ideas in a new edition, exerted a great influence on French philosophy. Boutroux was an influential teacher for thirty years at the Sorbonne and the Ecole Normale, and nearly all the great French philosophers of the next generation were his pupils. At the beginning of the twentieth century, they were developing ideas he had originated.

Among the scientists of this generation who developed philosophical ideas was one of the greatest mathematicians and natural scientists of the time. Henri Poincaré (1854-1912) occupied a position in the contemporary world of science as great as his relative Raymond Poincaré, President of the Republic, occupied in the political. The philosophical criticism of science had such weight because it was pursued by a scientist with such great authority. Poincaré was only a little younger than Boutroux, but he published his philosophical works later: *Science and Hypothesis* (1902), *The Meaning of Science* (1905), *Science and Method* (1909). Unlike Boutroux's these works had no metaphysical background; they were exclusively a critique of scientific knowledge.

The physicist Pierre Duhem (1861-1916) made perhaps the most complete critique of concepts and theories in the natural sciences (*Theory of Physics*, 1906). At the same time, he was one of the most outstanding historians of science *The Scheme of the Universe: A History of Cosmological Doctrines from Plato to Copernicus*, 1913-17, five volumes); he was a scholar and apologist for medieval science.

Similar views on the nature of science were also expressed by two Parisian mathematicians, Jules Tannery (1848-1910) and

Gaston Milhaud (1858-1918), who later succeeded to a chair of philosophy. However, a distinct role was played by Emil Meyerson (1859-1933), who was born in Lublin but settled in France and was associated with French philosophy. He devoted his spare time to science, publishing his results in the book *Identity and Reality*, whose leading idea he later developed in *Of Interpretation in the Sciences* (1921) and *Of the Advancement of Thought* (1931).

Bergson occupied a separate place: his view of science was similar to that of these other scientists, but the critique of science was only a small, negative part of his vast philosophy. The mathematician Edouard Le Roy (1870-1954) developed his theory under the influence of Duhem, Poincaré, and Milhaud but also accepted the ideas of Bergson, whom he succeeded in the French Academy and in the chair of philosophy at the Collège de France. To some extent, Le Roy fused the scientific and philosophical trends in the critique of science. Simultaneously he gave this critique a more extreme form.

Views

1. Contingentism. In Boutroux's analysis of science the basic idea was that science does not discover necessary relationships. Science breaks up into many disciplines, each governed by different laws. From the laws of one discipline one cannot deduce the laws of another. The laws of logic do not lead to the laws of mathematics, mathematics does not lead to mechanics, nor mechanics to physics, physics to chemistry, chemistry to biology, biology to psychology, psychology to sociology. From logic to sociology, phenomena and laws become more and more complicated. Between each range of phenomena and the next is a leap, a break in continuity. Each discipline pictures a different form of being, which cannot be deduced from an analysis of the preceding.

This overturned the "scientistic" conception of knowledge predominant in the second half of the nineteenth century, which held that everything is subject to universal and uniform laws and that therefore everything happens of necessity. That phenomena are not related in a necessary way was the leading conviction of Boutroux. This view began to be called "contingentism" from the French expression contingence, meaning simply lack of necessity.

The laws of science are hypothetical. They can be verified only in approximation. Scientific determinism had derived its argument from the fact that laws of mathematics and mechan-

ics conform to nature, but neither mathematical nor mechanical
laws can be found in nature in pure form.

Laws do not contain the element of necessity for still another reason: they are not only dependent on nature but also on
the human mind. The mind, however, can formulate laws in different ways. Laws are its personal constructions. This subjectivistic aspect of contingentism became most important with
Boutroux's successors, but to Boutroux himself it was only secondary. His major criticism of science was that it does not
live up to the ideal of necessary relationships. Boutroux saw
the source of this imperfection in the nature of the human mind
and in the nature of phenomena themselves. Even the most perfect mind would be incapable of acquiring necessary knowledge
of them. Above all, necessity does not appear in science because it does not appear in reality. This objective justification of contingentism was Boutroux's distinct contribution.

2. *The Compromise of Nature and the Mind.* Scientific laws
are not immutable and cannot be, in view of the mutability of
things and of the mind. Science has neither fixed content,
stable form, nor stable categories as Kant had maintained. The
categories of science are partially a priori; however, they are
partially an adaptation to phenomena and therefore are also mutable. What we call categories of the mind are only a collection of habits acquired by the mind as it assimilates phenomena.
The mind adapts phenomena to its own purposes, but it also
adapts itself to their nature. Harmony between the mind and
phenomena is achieved only through compromise.

Reason is not the only instrument of the mind in developing science, but it is the most precise instrument. Scientific ideas are often as imprecise as poetic or artistic ideas,
but they are also necessary. Some saw in this view an expression of irrationalism, the "bankruptcy of science" proclaimed
by Boutroux. Such an interpretation, however, is not true to
his intentions. He was Bergson's teacher, but he did not share
his pupil's irrationalism. He laid the groundwork for later
scientific conventionalism without yet having arrived at that
position. He believed the concepts of science to be constructions that have a foundation in things; these constructions are
not wholly arbitrary. Man creates a science of nature and im-
poses his own harmony on nature, but he is "not a monster among
nature." On the contrary, he belongs to nature, and in essence
his harmony is also its harmony. Therefore, scientific concepts are not "pure convention, a simple game of the mind";
they correspond to nature. Thus, Boutroux began his criticism
of science in the spirit of compromise, but his followers later
made this criticism more radical.

3. *Freedom*.　Boutroux himself supplemented this negative
criticism with some positive conclusions.　He argued that since
reason is limited, there is place for faith.　Beside science is
a place for religion.　And since there is no necessity, there
is place for freedom.　The negative result, that there is no
necessity in the world, was complemented by a positive one that
there is freedom in it.　In any event, the result is the same:
contingentism is the negative side, freedom the positive.　Because there is freedom in the world, such a wholly mechanistic
science as people had professed in the nineteenth century is
impossible.

This idea, that despite causal relationships between phenomena there is room for freedom, impressed many modern
thinkers.　They tried to reconcile freedom and determinism in a
variety of ways.　Kant had insisted that determinism is the law
of phenomena, but freedom can reign in the world of things-in-
themselves.　The spiritualists such as Ravaisson had argued
that the law of determinism holds only on the lower levels of
development, but progress goes from determinism to freedom.
The eclectics such as Cousin emphasized that external experience points to determinism in the material world, but internal
experience convinces us of freedom in the psychic one.　Only
later thinkers doubted the universality of determinism and
whether experience really gives evidence for it.　They began to
point to the diversity and discontinuity of phenomena.　Among
these thinkers Boutroux was one of the first and most influential.

4. *Conventionalism*.　With Poincaré the criticism of science became more radical: he abandoned Boutroux's belief that
scientific laws are a reflection of reality.　Above all, mathematical axioms are not reflections of reality.　Poincaré saw as
spurious the debate between the apriorists and empiricists concerning their origin, for it was based on an incomplete dis-
junction.　Axioms are not derived from experience, but neither
are they a priori.　If they were a priori, they would be necessary, and there could be no choosing between them: for example,
different geometries would be impossible.

Axioms, then, are creations of the mind.　They are not
necessary as the apriorists maintain, but conventional.　They
are hypotheses and conventions used by science so that it can
deal with phenomena more efficiently.　The mind can make assertions in mathematics, because it is the sole legislator in this
domain; "these decrees bind science, which would be impossible
without them, but they do not bind nature."　For this reason,
many geometries are possible.　Non-Euclidean geometries exist,
but they are as conventional as the Euclidean.　They are not

objective, but neither is Euclidean geometry. No geometry re-
flects reality. One cannot demand that mathematical axioms be
true, for they are conventions; and how can conventions be
true? It suffices if they are convenient, and they are convenient if they are simple. According to Poincaré, the real virtues of mathematical axioms are convenience and simplicity.

In the natural sciences particular laws are formulated
from observation and are not conventional. But this applies only to particular laws, not to the great theories of the natural
sciences, such as the atomic theory or the wave theory. Particular laws limit themselves to ordering facts, not explaining
them. Explanation is the task of the great general theories,
but "what these gain in generality and certainty they lose in
objectivity." They cannot be directly verified, for too many
indirect elements and conventions stand between them and the
facts. These theories are not a reflection of reality, but a
translation of it into convenient language. In the final analysis, they are as conventional as mathematical principles. For
this reason there can be many dissimilar theories. There can
be no talk of their genuineness, only of their convenience.

Poincaré did not interpret this position as skepticism.
He only fought against that excessively confident dogmatism
that allowed the majority of scientists in the nineteenth century to believe that they were reproducing the world faithfully,
objectively, and totally. He initiated the conventionalist
view of the world. Poincaré did not push this view to an extreme. This would be done by his followers, especially Duhem
and Le Roy.

5. Scientific Symbolism. The conventionality that Poincaré saw in mathematical axioms and the most general theories was
extended by his successors to include all scientific laws. All
laws have conventional elements besides the real ones, subjective as well as objective elements. Verification is impossible,
for how would this make sense? Let us take such a simple and
particular law as that phosphorus melts at 44°C. Let us further assume that in testing a material identified as phosphorus
this does not prove true. Do we then concede that the law is
false? No, we only say that the body we used in the test was
not phosphorus. This means that we consider such a law as a
definition, not as an assertion that can be tested and rejected.
That phosphorus melts at 44°C is a definition by which we identify the material. "The scientist produces harmony and determinism and imagines that he recognizes this in things." All
scientific generalizations are operations that, as Le Roy said,
are as conventional as a game of chess.

Moreover, not only laws are conventional, but scientific facts as well. Of course, a directly verifiable fact remains a fact contrary to all conventions. But an essential difference between directly established facts and scientific facts is that scientific facts are not directly observed. The scientist begins from direct facts, but he passes from them to scientific facts, and this transition is often a complicated process. It depends not only on a more precise and quantitative approach to observation, but also on correction of inevitable errors and rectification of the instruments used. For a fact to be scientific it is essential that it be measured. This implies arbitrary units of measurement.

Furthermore, the establishment of every scientific fact, even such a simple one as the temperature of an object, assumes familiarity with scientific laws. The use of the thermometer implies a law for the relationship of heat to expanding bodies, for on the thermometer we do not see heat but the height of a column of mercury. In other words, a scientific fact is not the original component of our knowledge. If laws are based on facts, the reverse is also true. Facts are based on familiarity with the laws.

A fact is something with a definite beginning and end, but in nature the causes and effects of every event stretch into infinity. A fact is definite and identical with other facts of the same kind, but in nature nothing is identical with anything else. If we see identity and similarity in nature, it is only because we disregard what separates one phenomenon from another. Experience shows us reality as a "formless mass," and only in this formless mass does our mind "hew out" facts.

This was the most radical thesis of scientific criticism. It undermined the only dogma of earlier critics and scientists, the scientific fact. In light of this criticism a fact is not a part of reality but only its symbol. It connotes reality but does not reproduce it. For these thinkers symbolism was the essential feature of science, and their doctrine has been called "scientific symbolism" as well as "conventionalism."

6. *Conflict of Nature and the Mind.* What was the result of this statement of the conventionality and symbolism of science? Discouragement and abandonment of science? No, for nothing else could replace it. Its reform, then? No, for science cannot do without conventions and symbols. The critics were not concerned with improving science but with understanding it. They wished to avoid regarding as necessity what was really convention and as knowledge of reality what was only its symbol. If science is to fulfill its tasks and grasp reality, then it must deform it. Reality has a qualitative character, but sci-

ence (especially the most advanced mathematical sciences) substitutes quantity for quality. Reality is a continuum, but
science dissolves this continuity into discontinuous elements.
Reality is mutable, but science freezes reality with concepts.
Reality is diverse, but science aspires to explain it; and explanation (this was the main idea of Meyerson's works) depends
upon discovering similarity: our mind can really understand only likeness and strives for this with all the means at its disposal. What follows from this is the divergence of reality and
science and the inability of science to grasp reality. This
applies to every science, not just to science in general.

However, these critics did not wish to condemn science:
they thought of it as one of the most perfect creations of the
mind, one of the most important tasks of man. Poincaré wrote:
"I do not say that science is useful because it teaches us to
build machines; I say that machines are useful because in working for us they will someday leave us more time to devote to
science."

But the science that deviates most from reality, in other
respects the most perfect because it is the most general and
precise, is mathematics-mechanics. Of all the creations of the
knowing mind it is the most conventional. This conclusion was
of the greatest importance, signifying opposition to the mechanistic understanding of phenomena, which had already begun with
Descartes and had been triumphantly extended to embrace ever
new areas of phenomena, the first opposition from the natural
sciences themselves.

Varieties and Phases of the Criticism

The criticism of science that developed in France in the
second half of the nineteenth century and in the first years of
the twentieth was of several varieties and passed through many
phases. Initially this criticism (as with contingentism)
fought against the element of necessity in science. Later (as
with conventionalism) it combated scientific objectivity. Criticism was moderate at first; later, it became more radical (as
in "scientific symbolism").

For some (as for Poincaré) the critique of science had no
other purpose than to explain and improve science. But for others (such as Boutroux) it was directed at reducing the pretensions of science and securing an equal place for other creations of the mind: "It would make no sense to work for the
progress of a physical theory if it were not a reflection of
metaphysics," wrote Duhem. Both he and Le Roy wished to reserve a place next to science for metaphysics and for religion
(Catholicism).

Science for all critics was more of a creation of the mind
than a reproduction of reality. But for one variety of criticism it was an arbitrary creation, a convention, while for another it was a necessary creation that resulted from the eternal laws of the mind and left no place for arbitrariness. The
first (discussed above) was an original idea, the second followed Kantianism. Yet, even this second trend produced an original conception in the works of Meyerson.

This criticism of science was a reaction to the positivistic cult of science. It opposed positivistic faith in the necessity of scientific laws and the objectivity of scientific
facts. Its role at the turn of the nineteenth and beginning of
the twentieth century was similar to the role of Hume's philosophy in the eighteenth century: though a product of the Enlightenment, it simultaneously worked toward its dissolution.

Conventionalism was an intermediate stage in the views of
these last generations on science: it replaced the theories of
the Kantians and Mach and in the twentieth century gave way to
another theory connected with new discoveries in physics. At
this later stage the discovery of change in science, the conventionality and symbolism of its axioms, theories, laws, concepts, and facts had ceased to be a current theme. But this
happened because conventionalism had fulfilled its task: its
theses, at least in part, had become common property.

OPPOSITION AMONG THE HUMANISTS

Philosophical problems appeared at the same time in the
humanistic sciences. These were mainly methodological problems,
but they were quite important for philosophy, for they dis-
closed the separate structure of the humanistic sciences in
contradistinction to the natural sciences and revealed the diversity of their ideas and worlds. These problems struck at
the dogma of positivism, that all sciences have the same nature
and that the model for all of them is the natural sciences.

Investigators of the Philosophical
Foundations of the Humanities

For the most part discussions on the foundations of the
humanities took place in Germany. Thinkers from various
schools took part in the debate. The first to bring out these
problems, a kind of creator of "the theory of knowledge for the
humanistic sciences," was Wilhelm Dilthey (1833-1911), from
1882 professor of philosophy in Berlin. He had been nurtured
in the idealistic tradition, under the influence of Hegel and
Fichte, but he also grew up in the atmosphere of nascent posi-

tivism and naturalism, which through Comte, Mill, and Spencer
had tried to apply the method of the natural sciences to the
social sciences. The cross-fertilization of these various influences led him to a new conception, one that was neither
idealistic nor naturalistic. His important works were: *Introduction to the Spiritual Sciences* (1883) and *Ideas Concerning a
Descriptive and Analytical Psychology* (1894), as well as many
papers in the history and classification of intellectual
trends. Among his numerous pupils, particularly outstanding
was Eduard Spranger, from 1919 professor in Berlin, who expounded his most general view in the work *Lifeforms,* 1914 (expanded in 1921).

The Kantians of the Baden school also joined the debate.
The Baden school's main achievements were in the theory of
value and the philosophical foundations of the humanities. Its
first representative was Wilhelm Windelband (1848-1915), professor at Heidelberg. He was most famous as a historian of
philosophy, but he also investigated the distinctive features
of the humanistic sciences. He published a paper on this subject entitled *Norms and Natural Laws* 1882 (published in the
collection *Präludien,* 1884), and a book, *History and Natural
Science* (1894). His ideas were accepted and further developed
by his successor at Heidelberg, Heinrich Rickert (1863-1936)
in the book *The Limits of the Natural Science Concept* (1896-
1906) and in the compendium *The Science of Culture and Natural
Science* (1899).

To an extent the Diltheyian and Kantian schools were united in the person of Ernst Troeltsch (1865-1923), at first a
theologian and then a professor of philosophy at Berlin (*Historicism and Its Problems,* (1922). Representatives of other
schools also investigated the humanities, particularly the
relativist Simmel and the phenomenologist Scheler.

Material for the discussion was provided by the humanists
themselves, in particular by the economist and sociologist Max
Weber, professor in Heidelberg and Munich (*Collected Essays on
the Sociology of Religion,* 1920-21), the linguist Karl Vossler
(*Positivism and Idealism in Linguistics,* 1904), and such historians and theoreticians of art as Heinrich Wölfflin, professor in Berlin, Munich, and Basel (*Basic Principles of Art History,* 1921), Wilhelm Worringer (*Abstraction and Empathy,* 1908),
and Max Dvořák (*Art History as Spiritual History,* 1924).

Dilthey, Windelband, and Rickert belong to the first generation of scholars who investigated the humanities; Spranger,
Troeltsch, and the others are in the next generation: they were
active in the twentieth century during a different phase of
philosophy, and they represent a different and later position.
However, both generations are discussed here as a group in order not to break the continuity of development.

Views

1. *The Reality of Social History (Dilthey).*   Humanistic
sciences developed in the nineteenth century, but they could
not satisfy an epoch that worshipped the precise sciences.
Philosophers attempted to make the humanities similar to the
natural sciences or to say that they could not be made similar
because they were not sciences. This second alternative was in
vogue for a long time. Toward the end of the century a third
position emerged, and Dilthey was perhaps the first to take
this position emphatically. He advanced two theses: (1) humanistic sciences are genuine sciences, and (2) they are different
from the natural sciences. He began a precise analysis and
critique of knowledge in the humanistic sciences to counter-
balance Kant's one-sided critique, which concerned knowledge in
the natural sciences exclusively.
    Around 1880 Dilthey's theses seemed bold and oppositional,
but by the next generation they were taken for granted. There
was only one debatable point: what distinguishes the humanities
from the other sciences? According to Dilthey, the distinction
lay in the subject of these sciences: the subject of the natural sciences is nature and of the humanities social-historical
reality. The elements of this reality are human individuals,
nations, social structures, and cultural creations such as language, art, morality, and economy. Dilthey made several assertions about the humanistic sciences and the social-historical
reality they investigated.
    The duality of these sciences and their subject matter
does not result from a duality between the material and spiritual worlds: man and all the social-historical reality associated with him is neither exclusively material nor exclusively
spiritual; man is neither purely physical nor purely psychic,
but a complicated psycho-physical object.
    One foundation of the humanistic sciences is psychology.
But this is not ordinary psychology, which patterns itself on
the natural sciences and appeals to physiology in trying to explain psychic life. This kind of psychology is of little use
to the humanities. An analytic-descriptive psychology, one
that will analyze the structure and types of psychic life, is
necessary. There is no lack of material for such a psychology:
observers of humanity have collected such material for a long
time, especially from the time of Montaigne. This distinction
between two psychologies was important for the theory of the
sciences. Without denying the need for this former explanatory
psychology, Dilthey held that cultivation of descriptive psychology would be in the interests of the humanities.

According to Dilthey, this descriptive psychology is the
only link between the various humanistic sciences. Beyond it
are only specialized sciences, dealing with language, law, or
art. However, no one science could embrace the entire world of
man and his creations. Of course, the philosophy of history
and sociology makes claims of this kind, but for Dilthey these
were pseudo-sciences without clear problems and genuine method.
Here he echoed the empiricism of his epoch by recognizing only
scientific, not speculative, facts.

The humanistic sciences contain three kinds of assertions.
First, there are assertions about facts established by history.
Second, there are assertions about laws. These concern not
facts themselves but their abstract, isolated elements. For example, among these are laws of the composition of the state established by Aristotle or the laws of language established by
Grimm. These two assertions have their counterparts in the natural sciences, but a third category of assertions has no coun-
terpart. These are assertions about values, imperatives, and
norms. This is the distinctive feature of the humanistic sciences. To eliminate these assertions, as some of the natural
scientists had wished, is impossible. This was also an important shift in emphasis for the theory of the sciences.

The regularities that the humanistic sciences discover in
phenomena are different from those established by the natural
sciences: the latter are regularities in the sequence of events,
the former primarily in their structure. Dilthey saw the distinctness of the humanistic sciences in the fact that they establish "structural" laws.

The humanistic sciences are not only genuine sciences, but
in some way they have a more favorable position than the natural sciences. This is because the social-historical world is
more accessible to our knowledge than nature. The elements of
nature are hypothetical atoms, but in the social world they are
real individuals whom we know directly. Everyone knows himself
internally, and other people are similar; therefore, everyone
knows the elements of the social-historical world and understands them internally. The intellect is a marvelous organ for
understanding this world, but nature for us is always strange,
impenetrable, and basically incomprehensible. In this way Dilthey distinguished between the natural sciences and the humanities: in the former we strive for knowledge, in the latter for
understanding. In the former knowledge is primarily based on
discursive thought, in the latter on direct experience.

Further differences between the two kinds of sciences resulted from this. Knowledge in the natural sciences touches
only phenomena, behind which reality is hidden. Facts in the
natural sciences are only given externally. The elements of
nature are only hypothetical. The atoms and mechanisms with
which the natural sciences operate are only symbols the mind

uses to grasp phenomena. The situation is different in the humanities. Here knowledge touches reality itself. Knowledge grasps reality directly and internally. These arguments imply that the humanities have scientific value which equals or even exceeds that of the natural sciences. Dilthey emphasized that this applies to the humanistic sciences, which have been developing for millennia, but not to impetuous philosophical-humanistic syntheses like those made by Comte and Spencer, which despite their pretensions remain only scientific fantasies.

But every understanding of the world, either that of nature or the social world, is dependent on the knowing mind. In particular, this understanding is dependent on the time in which this takes place. There is no philosophy; there is only the history of philosophy. With this Dilthey admitted historicism. This historicism was not without Hegelian influences, but it had completely different features. For Dilthey the stages of history were not as rationally connected as for Hegel. Still further, they were not stages of truth but of untruth, for truth does not change nor is it ever wholly reached at any given moment. The historicism of Dilthey was very influential, and toward the end of the nineteenth century his influence surged through Germany at about the same time as the wave of renewed Kantian apriorism.

The consequence of Dilthey's view of human reality was irrationalism. Events do not develop according to general laws. The concrete lives of individuals and groups overflow these laws. Philosophy is not universally binding knowledge, but a view of the world that depends on the personality of the individual who declares it. "The ultimate source of a view of the world is life." History is a live process; the knowledge it gives is a reproduction of this process in experience. Dilthey thought that the humanities should avoid schemata and hold to life: their real task is to discover the typical forms of life; therefore, it was natural for his followers to place the concept of life in the foreground of their deliberations. Their philosophy became a "philosophy of life."

2. *The Ideographic Sciences (Windelband and Rickert)*. At about the same time as Rickert, Windelband expounded a different view concerning the distinctness of the humanities: this distinctness is not in their subject, but in their method. The most essential difference between the sciences is that some of them establish laws, others facts. Some of them speak of things that repeat themselves many times and are always the same; others of things that occur only once. The former have a general character, the latter an individual one. The first, as Windelband expressed it, are nomothetic, the second ideographic.

The same subject can be investigated scientifically in both
ways. For example, the systematics of plant life proceed nomo-
thetically in organic nature, but the theory of descent proceeds ideographically. This methodological difference is essential, but it leads to further consequences. A science that
establishes general laws is more abstract, one that establishes
individual facts is more concrete; in the former there is more
construction, in the latter more reality.

Thus, in the natural sciences the main concern is with
laws, and individual phenomena are of interest only as illus-
trations of applied laws. But the majority of the humanistic
sciences have a historical character, and they try to grasp individual, nonrepetitive phenomena—the history of a definite
individual or nation, the development of a definite language,
religion, art, or science.

Rickert accepted this division of the sciences from Windelband, but he combined it with Dilthey's division. He thought
that the sciences were primarily distinguished by their method,
but their subject is also different. Only two intersecting
divisions—method and subject—can precisely delineate the
place of the humanities among the sciences.

Science can assume either a generalizing or an individualizing approach. In the first case it treats its subject natu-
ralistically, in the second historically. Reality becomes nature when it is viewed in its general aspects, history when
viewed in the particular and individual. How can the same objects take on different form in different sciences? If science
were simple copying, then reality could have only one form, but
a copying science would be preposterous and purposeless. There
is no such science. Science transforms, simplifies, and selects from reality with the help of general or individual scientific concepts. The natural scientist and historian both
make selections from reality, but each of them selects something different: the former picks from reality what is general,
the latter what is individual.

Sciences are also divided into studies of nature and studies of culture. Here the criterion of division is no longer
method but the subject matter itself. We call nature that
which has arisen by itself and culture that which has been created by man.

Rickert introduced his division of the sciences—sciences
of nature and sciences of culture—in place of the traditional
division into sciences of nature and sciences of the soul. Another of his ideas was: the material division must be combined
with the formal division into generalizing and individualizing
sciences. For Dilthey these two divisions were not identical;
they crisscross and create four kinds of science. History in
the usual, narrow sense is an individualizing science dealing
with culture. The most developed naturalistic sciences, such

as physics or chemistry, are generalizing sciences dealing with
nature. But there are also individualizing sciences of nature,
such as geology, and generalizing sciences of culture, such as
sociology.

   3. Sciences of the Soul (Troeltsch, Spranger, and others).
The theories of Dilthey, Windelband, and Rickert interpreted
phenomena in various ways, but they always held to phenomena;
they did not go beyond phenomena into a transcendental sphere.
These theories originated in a time of positivism and remained
true to this philosophy. Meanwhile, a change began in German
philosophy at the beginning of the twentieth century that was
fully evident after World War I. This was a retreat from both
positivism and criticism. It was not only the phenomenologists
who departed from these views, but also some of Dilthey's pupils, and even Rickert in his old age.
   In the background of earlier deliberations on the humanistic sciences was the opposition between physical and psychic
phenomena. It was axiomatic that there are no other objects
for science. This axiom was now questioned: a belief developed
that the alternatives "body or soul" did not exhaust all possibilities. Both possibilities lack spirit, for spirit is
something different from either body or soul. It is nonmaterial but objective, nonpsychic, and nonindividual. Scientific
truths, legal norms, and religious dogmas all belong to the
world of spirit. If they were psychic phenomena, they would
appear only in the psychic consciousness of the individual, in
his internal experience. Yet they are common to many individuals and appear in both internal and external experience. They
endure, even though the individuals who created them disappear.
Of course, we only know about spirit through psychic experiences; but just as material things exist beyond the experiences
and ideas that conscious individuals have of them, so, too, do
spiritual objects.
   Hence, the spiritual world is an object of the humanistic
sciences. Psychology deals with psychic phenomena, but the humanities deal with something else: language, religion, or social structures, which are not elements of the subjective psyche, but of objective spirit.
   Such linking of the humanistic sciences with the world of
spirit sprang up at once in many quarters: not only the phenomenologists favored it, but also Spranger, Rickert, and other
specialists in various areas of the humanities. Spirit, which
until now had been regarded as something either below or above
science, now was included among its concerns. The proponents
of this view tried to represent it as thoroughly scientific, as

the result of scientific analysis, but the spirit of Hegel and
metaphysics seems to stand behind it.

Dilthey asserted that the knowledge of individuals depends
on their "reasoning." The new position accepted this thesis
but interpreted it differently: we understand the spirit, not
the soul. We can only understand what is objective, general,
and lasting. People's experiences are subjective, individual,
and changeable. Hence, we can only indirectly, partially, and
approximately understand these experiences. There always remains some elusive "psychic remnant." We only understand these
experiences to the extent that they contain spirit. Such a
view was the total reversal of the existing one: the way to
knowledge of spirit does not lead through the soul, but, contrariwise, through spirit we come to knowledge of the soul.

We understand things because we grasp them in a priori
forms, categories, and ideas. These are forms of the spirit,
and for this reason they permit us to understand spirit. We
understand things when we recognize some form or idea in them.
To understand the beauty of some things means to recognize the
idea of beauty in them: whoever associates beauty with some
other idea, usefulness for example, does not really understand
it. Spranger distinguished six leading "forms of life"—cognitive, aesthetic, economic, social, political, and religious—
which correspond to six a priori ideas—truth, beauty, usefulness, love, freedom, and sacredness.

How is it possible for the humanities, which are empirical
sciences, to treat nonempirical spiritual objects? This they
can do indirectly: spiritual objects, though nonempirical, represent empirical entities. The humanities, then—as the phenomenologists stressed in particular—investigate the essence
of things. To put it another way, they investigate the ideal
types of things. This view, that the task of the humanities is
to establish ideal types, was now echoed by both philosophers
and specialists. To be sure, not all of them understood "ideal
types" (and the "essence of things") in the spirit of Plato.
Some of them understood these things subjectively, convention-
ally; they say in these ideal types a construction of the mind.
Yet, it was not this view, but the objective, Platonic view
that dominated Germany at the beginning of the twentieth century and expressed the main tendencies of the epoch.

Related to this were the concepts of "whole" and "form" in
the humanistic sciences, psychology, sociology, and philosophy.
They expressed the idea that the phenomena of culture are something more than the sum of chance elements, that they have unity
and lasting sense. This spiritual factor gives sense and unity
to social products, religion, morality, the state, and art.

The essential thing in this new position was the recognition of objective values. Not only was it asserted that value
judgments are necessary in the humanities (as Dilthey had al-

ready stressed), but also that they have an objective foundation. To be sure, there were deviations from this view (for
instance, the famous sociologist Max Weber believed that all
value judgments are subjective, and science should therefore
refrain from making them). Nonetheless, this was the most typical and widespread view.

Spranger stated in 1923 that the three leading philosophical schools in Germany—phenomenology, the Baden school, and
Dilthey's school—though they had started from different traditions and assumptions, had finally joined to defend two most
important theses: the supratemporal nature of some elements of
history and the objectivity of value. These theses were even
defended on Kantian grounds or on the grounds of historicism
itself (Troeltsch). And all of these schools combated positivism, psychologism, and a relativistic understanding of values,
the doctrines that, in the nineteenth century, had seemed to be
the greatest contributions of science.

This new position also influenced the understanding of the
basic concept of the humanities—the concept of culture. This
led to the view that besides material and psychic components
culture also contains spiritual ones. These latter are the
most important. Neither material forms nor the experiences of
particular individuals are most essential to such things as the
state, science, art, and all forms of culture in general. Cultures cannot be understood as purely psychological or material.
Opposition to psychologism was initiated by Husserl in logic
and was also applied in ethics by Scheler, in economics by
Sombart, in social history by Weber and Troeltsch, and in the
history of art by Worringer.

Such an understanding of culture had a number of consequences. First, whereas elsewhere explanation of the development of culture through material factors was considered proper
scientific procedure, here culture was explained by nonmaterial
factors. The idea that culture develops autonomously became
quite popular: for example, the development of one dogma or another depends more on other dogmas than on the material conditions or psychic moods of the epoch. Likewise, every discovery
depends on previous discoveries, every social order on previous
social orders, every style on preceding styles. Only such an
immanent explanation of dogmas by dogmas, social orders by social orders, and styles by styles can truly explain culture.

Further, in every epoch the forms of culture, though externally different, are basically identical, for their spirit is
common: scholasticism has a hierarchical warp identical with
feudalism and with Gothicism, Cartesianism is identical with
absolutism, Calvinism with capitalism, deism with liberalism
and free trade. Moreover, this belief that spirit is the most
essential thing in culture acted to dissuade theorists of culture from purely factual investigations: facts are not impor-

tant, for they are only an external expression of reality.
This also reduced the role of the individual in the creation of
culture; as with Hegel, a universalistic understanding of culture assumed prominence.

This new position also influenced the understanding of history. Shortly before this, even Dilthey and Rickert had understood history as the investigation of events in their unique-
ness and nonrepetitiveness. Their successors stressed that
there are lasting elements in events, and that only these are
essential. Before, the task of history was to discover the
genesis of phenomena; now it was to discover their essence.
Earlier, historicism had reduced systematics to history and
equated a humanist with a historian. Now it emphasized that
the historian is dependent on systematics, for he must use the
concepts that history has developed. A short time ago, the explanation of ideas in history was psychological: to understand
history one has to understand the people who have created it.
Now this view was reversed: historical events are not grasped
through an understanding of people but through understanding
events one gains understanding of people.

Summary

The deliberations on the humanistic sciences begun by Dilthey and Windelband after 1880 played an important role in German philosophy for at least half a century. During this time
they went through two phases. The first lasted until the end
of the nineteenth century; the second occurred in the twentieth
(it has been discussed here to show the continuity and contrast
between the two centuries). The first phase expressed nascent
opposition to nineteenth-century positivism; the second phase
departed from positivism still further.

During the first phase investigations were made in the
spirit of criticism and empiricism. They were methodological
in character and were primarily concerned with the distinct
method of the humanities. They inspired the idea of the ideographic sciences, descriptive psychology, psychic structures,
and philosophy of life.

In the second phase, however, the slogans were anti-his-
toricism, anti-psychologism, and idealism. Now investigations
stressed the ideas of spirit, universal categories, and objective values. If the first phase was permeated by the spirit of
Kant, the second was filled with the spirit of Hegel. Similarly, even general psychology passed from an epistemological to
an ontological treatment of problems. From analysis it passed
to speculation, from methodology to metaphysics. This second
phase, though it began somewhat earlier, really began to develop after World War I, a period of crisis in Germany. The at-

mosphere there was such that even the followers of Kant and Dilthey passed to metaphysics. "It is impossible to detach the sciences from a view of the world," wrote Spranger. Troeltsch and Spranger even passed to a religious understanding of philosophy. They began to say that only in religion, not in science or metaphysics, could one grasp the sense of the world as a whole. The religiosity to which they appealed was, in its abstractness and subjectivity, specifically Protestant and frequently clearly opposed to Catholicism.

This second phase of investigations on the foundations of the humanities, history, and culture deviated from the empirical, concrete, scientific, and methodological problems of the first phase. It entered the domain of religion and metaphysics and ended with imprecise concepts and theories. It broke not only with what was bad, but also with what was good in the philosophy of the nineteenth century.

But this phase was not uniform and assumed two different forms in Germany: rationalistic and irrationalistic. The rationalistic was the philosophy of neo-idealism represented by Troeltsch, Spranger, Rickert, and others. The irrationalistic trend was known as the "philosophy of life"; it derived from Dilthey and Nietzsche and was intensified still further by the influence of pragmatism and Bergsonism. This second trend was the more popular, but among scholars the rationalistic trend predominated. However, this entire movement with its intensive studies on the foundations of the humanities did not last long: after 1930, when National Socialism came to power, it was interrupted, as was all of German philosophy.

This movement in the humanities was specifically German. In Anglo-Saxon, Romance, and Slavic countries the philosophical orientation at the end of the nineteenth century and beginning of the twentieth continued to favor the natural sciences, not the humanities. There the humanistic sciences were not an object of such intensive philosophical investigations, but neither did they pass through such a crisis as in Germany nor did they link their problems with metaphysical ones.

ANGLO-SAXON IDEALISM

At the end of the nineteenth century, the time of minimalism, a surprisingly active phase of metaphysical idealism appeared in England. Of all the opposition movements occurring at this time, this was the least expected and furthest from prevailing views. Directed against the naturalism of the minimalists, it was initiated around 1865 by the writings of Stirling and Green and depended on Hegelian idealism. This trend was called "Anglo-Hegelianism," but it soon developed its own position. In England, Bradley and Ward became its most outstanding representatives at the end of the century. In America, the wave of idealism was weaker but continuous from the time of Emerson. The leading idealist philosopher there at the turn of the nineteenth century was Royce.

Main Representatives

1. *Emerson*. Ralph Waldo Emerson (1803-1882) was one of the few American philosophers in the nineteenth century with a world-wide reputation. He was descended from a family of Unitarian clergymen, that most secular of Protestant sects which proclaimed freedom of religious thought. For a time he, too, was a clergyman. Later, he retired to the countryside around Boston and devoted himself to writing. He was ideologically associated with the Bostonian socio-philosophical Transcendental club, founded in 1836. His public appearances were rare but important. In his memorable speech of 1837 on "The American Scholar" he opened the eyes of Americans to distinctness of their culture and announced, as it was said, its "declaration of independence." In the following year his address at Harvard Divinity School was again a kind of "declaration of independence," that of the individual in his relationship to God: he asserted that everyone can and should create his own religion. His most mature work was his *Essays* (two series, 1841-44). Mickiewicz corresponded with him and was one of the first to discern his importance, calling him "the philosopher who best reveals the needs of our century." Other more outstanding Anglo-Saxon idealists were at least a generation younger than Emerson and belong to the last thirty years of the century. Chronologically the first of them was Green.

2. *Green*. Thomas Hill Green (1836-1882), professor at Oxford from 1878, was most influential in causing idealism for a time to become the official English academic philosophy. He drew his inspiration from Carlyle and his model from Kant and Hegel. His philosophical activity was quite polemical. He did not so much develop idealism as criticize empiricism and naturalism: he came out against his contemporaries, Darwin, Spencer, and Buckle, but his most scathing criticism was directed against Hume, the initiator of empiricism. The only work published during his lifetime was a critical one, *Introduction to Hume* (1874). After Green's death his second book appeared, *Prolegomena to Ethics* (1883). He lived only a short time, wrote little, but accomplished much with his pen, and even more

with his oratory. With him Oxfordian idealism begins. The only earlier exponent of idealism in England was J. H. Stirling,
a private scholar of Scotch descent, who in 1865 published a
huge (1200 pages) and tedious work, *The Secret of Hegel*, which
began the English cult of Hegel. At first English idealism was
simply Hegelianism. It became widespread at Oxford as well as
in Scotland. Whole families devoted themselves to its service:
Edward and John Caird, professors at Glasgow, and Andrew and
James Seth, professors at Edinburgh. Soon, however, Bradley,
Ward, McTaggart, Sorley, and others gave English idealism an
original turn.

   3. Bradley. Francis Herbert Bradley (1846-1924) studied
with Green at Oxford and then spent his life there at Merton
College. Though he lived there for more than half a century,
he did not perform any pedagogical function. He had poor
health and lived in isolation, entirely devoted to research.
Early in his career (1876) he published a book on ethics, in
1883 *The Principles of Logic*, and in 1891 his main metaphysical
work, *Appearance and Reality*. Above all else, he was a dialec-
tician with the ability to discover unexpected relationships
and unnoticed contradictions between concepts. His dialectic
had a destructive character; it dissected philosophical theories but did not construct them as did the Hegelian dialectic.
Not without cause was Bradley called the modern Zeno Eleatus.
What he shattered by his dialectic he later complemented partly
by experience and partly by mystical intuition.

   4. Ward. James Ward (1843-1925) from Cambridge gave another tone to English idealism. In his youth he was a clergyman, then later gave up this profession. His philosophy, however, retained a religious orientation. In contrast to Bradley,
who was always only a philosopher, Ward was first a natural
scientist, biologist, psychologist, and only rather late in his
career a philosopher. In 1886 he published a famous article on
psychology in the ninth edition of the *Encyclopaedia Britannica*,
universally acclaimed as ground-breaking in the history of this
science. He assumed the chair of philosophy at Cambridge in
1897. Of his two philosophical works, one deals with the world
of nature (*Naturalism and Agnosticism*, 1899), the second with
the world of purposes (*The Realm of Ends, or Pluralism and Theism*, 1911).

5. *Royce*.   Josiah Royce (1855-1916) was the leading representative of idealism in America, at the same time that Bradley
and Ward were active in England. He was even farther from Hegelian idealism than they. Educated on Mill and Spencer, on
friendly terms with the pragmatist James, he retained certain
naturalistic and empirical inclinations to the end of his life.
His interests were diverse; they included mathematics, music,
and literature. He studied both Indian and European philosophy,
the scholastics as well as Kant and Schopenhauer. From 1882 he
was a professor at Harvard, where he associated with James.
His major metaphysical work, *The World and the Individual*, was
published in 1900-01 (2 volumes), and his main ethical work,
The Philosophy of Loyalty in 1908. He imposed religious purposes on philosophy: like many American thinkers he tried to
discover a philosophical interpretation of Christianity. He
pursued his philosophy, though abstract, transcendental, and
absolute, with fantasy and even humor, as Socrates and Plato
had once done.

Predecessors

German idealism is regarded as the source of English idealism; this movement of English idealism is known as the "Anglo-
Hegelian movement." This name is only partially correct, however. Coleridge and Carlyle, the first idealists in England in
the nineteenth century, simply developed from the romanticism
of their own country. The Germans suited their romantic taste,
and they were enthusiastic about German philosophy, but they
hardly differentiated Hegel from Kant. The Americans did not
read the Germans at all; they knew German philosophy only from
the remarks of Coleridge and Carlyle. Stirling and Green were
really quite taken with Hegel. Stirling expected that what
Hegel had said would be the last word for succeeding centuries
on all the great questions of mankind. However, the Anglo-Hegelians retained very little of Hegel because they rejected
what was really his most distinctive idea: a system that un-
folded dialectically and panlogically. A. Seth, who first worshipped Hegel, quite soon began to criticize him. Bradley
called Hegelianism a "ballet of bloodless categories." Berkeley and the theologians exerted a greater influence on Ward's
idealism than Hegel did. This was natural, for philosophy in
England had long been either empirical or theological. But Plato also influenced English idealism at the end of the century.
The mediator of this influence was the famous Oxford philologist B. Jowett, professor of Greek from 1855 to 1893 and trans-
lator of Plato. The majority of English and American supporters of idealism changed it into spiritualism, a personalistic,
monadistic, and theistic philosophy. They remained true to the

national tradition rather than to Hegel when they tried to retain the union of idealistic metaphysics with experience.

Views

1. *Forms of Idealism.* The name idealism has been given to various views, especially to Berkeley's conception; everything that the mind perceives is of the same nature as itself. What has a nature different from the mental cannot be apprehended, and there is no evidence for its existence. This view is a particular interpretation of the perceived world. It is the opposite of realism, which asserts that in acts of cognition the mind apprehends something different from itself, something that is not mental by nature. These two theories developed as the result of epistemological analysis and are the two basic possibilities in the theory of knowledge.

But there is another view that is also called idealism. This view, which comes from Plato or Hegel or Schelling, also states that being is intellectual in nature, but stipulates that this refers only to genuine being. It argues that the perceived world is not genuine being, but only a phenomenon. Genuine being is beyond perceptions and beyond phenomena. It is made up of ideas, either unchanging ones as with Plato or developing ones as with Hegel, but these ideas are always absolute in contrast to relative phenomena. This view, claiming the ability to recognize genuine being, is metaphysical. It is the opposite of naturalism, whose most distinct form is materialism. Idealism says that only ideas exist and nature is their phenomenon: naturalism says that only nature exists and ideas are fictions. These are the two basic possibilities of metaphysics.

In the time of positivism, idealism of the first type, epistemological idealism, was the most widespread and harmonized with positivism. But metaphysical idealism, Platonic or Hegelian, opposed all of the deepest contemporary beliefs. Carlyle and Emerson were able to advance such a philosophy previously, but they were not academic philosophers. Green's success in espousing this position in a scholarly Oxford environment after the greatest triumphs of Mill was wholly unexpected.

2. *Sources of Idealism.* By its very nature metaphysical idealism has other sources and arguments than epistemological idealism. Green appealed to the theory of Kant, that under analysis what we call reality turns out to be a construction of the mind. For the most part, other Anglo-Saxon idealists used

two arguments: first, although the world is a coherent whole, matter always disintegrates, so in its foundations the world cannot be material; second, spontaneous activity, freedom, and creativity—which are properties of spirit—appear in the world.

Nonetheless, idealists themselves often admitted that they had arrived at their doctrines not through theoretical deliberations alone, but also with regard to the needs and desires of people. Above all, these were moral needs and desires: that good and beauty could prevail in the world. They thought that naturalism afforded no grounds for distinguishing between good and evil, beauty and ugliness. Thus they inferred that moral needs dictate a conception other than a naturalistic one.

Still other needs inclined philosophers to idealism, namely the need for continuity, the desire that death not be the end of existence, the need to assure certainty, that perfect and eternal forces govern human fate and give sense to existence. In short, these were religious needs which naturalism could not satisfy. In view of this, religious needs no less than moral ones are the source of idealistic doctrines.

These two sets of needs are not always equally apparent among people. When they become vivid and insistent they also force their way into philosophy, and then philosophy passes through periods of intensified idealism. But other periods guard against making philosophy dependent on life needs. These periods are usually suspicious, if not hostile, to idealism. This was generally the case in the second half of the nineteenth century, with the exceptions of the Transcendental club and the Oxford Anglo-Hegelians.

3. *The Idealism of Emerson and the Transcendentalists.*
American idealism attempted not so much to understand the world as to satisfy the moral needs of man. It made no effort to hide this: Emerson said that he was primarily concerned with rehabilitating man in man's own eyes and with instilling in him self-respect and pride.

These Americans, like Plato and the German idealists, differentiated the "essence of things" from phenomena and were convinced that this essence was spiritual. This already made them idealists. Moreover, they placed spiritual values above material ones, contrary to the inclination of their times and their country. They also placed lasting values in religion, morality, and politics above all current, transient forms. In opposition to the empiricists and skeptics they believed that the highest spiritual truths and values were accessible to everyone; "common sense" or intuition can know them. Thus they recognized every individual as an authority in his own right and in this connection proclaimed freedom of thought. But the foundation for all their views was a mystical and pantheistic faith in the spiritual unity of the world and the presence of the divine spirit in every individual. From this faith they derived their individualism, their opposition to tradition, authority, and hierarchies as well as their optimism, faith in progress, and faith in the possibility of perfecting man.

Emerson understood all of material nature as "the method of God" for teaching us truth, but not as truth itself (in this he was dependent on Carlyle). Nature is only the embodiment of thought and turns into thought again just as ice turns into water and steam. And nature develops in the direction given it by the world-soul. The individual is the instrument of cosmic purposes, feels this, and through this senses the bliss of complete security.

Even so, all human efforts to express truth and realize the ideal are imperfect. For this reason, Emerson, despite his pantheism, was a relativist. This was also the source of his anti-dogmatic, rebellious attitude. Yet he was not a fatalist; on the contrary, he recognized the moral mission of the human individual. Emerson's moral individualism was an important addition to the ideology of liberalism in the nineteenth century. European liberalism developed from the spirit of empiricism and utilitarianism, but American liberalism sprang from the spirit of idealism, pantheism, and apriorism.

4. *The Critical Idealism of Green.* From the outset Anglo-Saxon idealism posed negative problems: it wished to eliminate what it considered erroneous. With Carlyle it was directed against the Enlightenment, rationalism, unbelief, criticism, utilitarianism, and common sense. It retained this attitude half a century later with Green. He also combated naturalism and empiricism, which were then predominant in England. He saw their main error as disregard for the role of the subject in cognition. In other words, they ignored the discoveries of Kant: Kant had corrected Hume, and the English empiricists who still wished to philosophize in the manner of Hume were already an anachronism. Reality is not composed solely of impressions, as Hume had maintained. Also integral to reality are relationships between phenomena, which are no less real than impressions. And even when some impression does belong to reality, we know it only because it is related to other impressions. Hence, the interconnectedness of impressions verifies reality. But because all relationships are by nature mental, all of reality itself must be of the same nature. Green in this way arrived at an idealistic conclusion.

He was unable to develop this position, but it could have led to a Kantian, Hegelian, or Berkeleyian view. In any event, it did lead to a break with naturalism and empiricism, and this was the direction in which English idealism proceeded.

   5. *The Empirical Idealism of Bradley*. The dialectic played an important but negative role in Bradley's philosophy; it did not construct an authentic picture of the world but demolished a false one. Bradley himself said that dialectic thought is incapable of grasping any truth because it entangles itself in unavoidable difficulties, even when making assertions of the simplest kind, like "S is P." Such assertions can be interpreted in two ways: either S and P are the same thing, in which case the assertion says nothing, or they are something different, in which case the assertion is false, since S is not P.
   Bradley demonstrated such dialectical difficulties in the most general concepts, such as things and qualities, cause and action, movement and change, things-in-themselves and the self. There are similar difficulties in the concepts of time and space, matter and energy. Physics operates successfully with them, but they lead to difficulty and contradiction when philosophy analyzes them. They are useful auxiliary constructions of the mind (here the idealist Bradley agreed with the positivists), but metaphysics cannot use them. Neither can it benefit from the concepts of psychology, for even they would be contradictory should they claim to reconstruct reality. Above all, the leading concept of psychology, the self, is contradictory. At the same time it is supposed to be unified and plural, lasting and changeable.
   Reality is characterized by noncontradiction, unity, wholeness, harmony, lastingness, nonrelativity, and the absolute. Where this is lacking—where there is plurality, relativity, diversity, changeability, chaos, disharmony, and especially contradiction—we are dealing with phenomena not reality.
   The dialectic convinced Bradley that contradictions arise wherever thought reaches; therefore, the dialectic always operates in the sphere of phenomena not reality. The fruit of the dialectic was the ruin of our knowledge: things and qualities (primary as well as secondary), space and time, substance and movement, good and evil, even the self and God were only phenomena.
   Yet, Bradley's final conclusion was not negative. To be sure, dialectic thought does not reach reality, but experience does. Bradley was an idealist, but he trusted experience and was true to the empirical tradition of his country and his time. He believed that even an absolute philosophy can and must be empirical. Experience had led him to idealism, for wherever experience reaches is the sphere of the mind. Whence the con-

clusion: "Beyond the spirit there is not and cannot be any reality."

But experience only deals with what takes place in time; therefore, when we speak of absolute reality we clearly go beyond experience. Bradley's premises did not permit him to speak of the absolute, yet he did speak of it. He was dishonest to the extent that his idealistic metaphysics, though it was supposed to be based on experience, really aimed at realizing certain longings: it had its foundation in needs rather than in its conclusions. Bradley himself said that metaphysics consists in finding bad reasons for what we instinctively believe, and also that their discovery is a matter of instinct. Yet, Bradley thought that even such a metaphysics was better than none. What would we have left if we did not have this? As he said there would be only either the dogmas of theology or the dogmas of materialism. So ended this most empirical and skeptical idealistic philosophy.

6. The Pluralistic Idealism of Ward. Above all, Ward was a psychologist. He initiated a new era in English psychology by pointing to the dominant role of will and feelings in psychic life, which led psychology away from intellectualism, atomism, and mechanism, more characteristic of English psychology than any other.

Later, he passed to philosophical deliberations that concentrated on one question: the antithesis of mechanistic nature and the organic world with its purposes and values. Mechanism and organism are the two possible aspects of the world. Philosophy has to reconcile these positions and judge which of them is the first and most essential. Ward's conclusion was detrimental to mechanism: it is too one-sided to be the foundation for a view of the world. A philosophy based on this is naturalism, agnosticism, evolutionism, and psychophysical parallelism. But all of these views are incomplete and omit the greatest part of reality. Such a philosophy owes its triumphs and failures to its one-sidedness. "There are more things in heaven and earth," said Ward paraphrasing Shakespeare, "than are dreamt of in naturalistic philosophy." In its latest discoveries science has indicated that the organic factor plays a greater role than previously assumed. It is fair to say that all of nature has organic, individual, and psychic features. For this reason spiritualism expresses its essence better than materialism.

Ward thought that the world is made up of many individual existences: his view was pluralistic, or to use Leibniz's term—monadistic. But Ward also thought that plurality was not the ultimate world view: only a philosophical view that has not been thought through to its conclusions confines itself to plurality. Of course, the unity of the world cannot be verified scientifically. This unity cannot be found among facts, and empiricists will always have the right to question it. However, for philosophy it is enough that this belief does not conflict with experience. A theory that permits reality to be understood as a unity, though not verified empirically, is philosophically justified. Theism is such a theory. Unity is given to the world only in the concept of God.

   7. The Universalistic Idealism of Royce. Some idealists recognized only the existence of individual spirits about which something can be stated from experience. Others, however, further posited the existence of a universal spirit, noting that individual spirits are not enough to explain all the phenomena and problems of the world. As Green remarked, we regard nature as a creation of spirit, but not of individual spirit, for it would then have to be limited in its possibilities.
   Such a conception of a universal spirit, a "universalistic idealism," was developed by the American thinker Royce. He reasoned that we regard the external world as different from ourselves, as our opposite, but it is only a complex of our ideas. It is external to every individual mind, but not to mind in general. If the external world were not intellectual in character, then it would not be knowable. The two go together: either it is spirit, or it is unknowable. Everyone knows only his own self, but he has the right to assume that other selves are like his. However, all of these selves enter into one wider, universal self. In this universal self ("logos"), which includes all selves, lies the only possible solution to the difficulties of metaphysics. The universal spirit alone explains everything: the order of nature and spirit, the physical and moral order, the human and the divine, necessity and freedom.
   Royce's system was idealistic in limiting all knowledge to that of ideas; monistic in recognizing only one principle of being; spiritualistic, for this one principle was spirit; universalistic in understanding spirit as something above the individual; pantheistic, for all individual spirits were contained in the universal spirit; and absolutistic in holding its assertions to be absolute truth.
   In a universalistic system the most difficult question to resolve is that of individual freedom. But Royce thought that his system left enough place for the freedom of individuals. At the same time it offered them a moral idea, the idea of loyalty, devotion to the community and its affairs, which are more important than the affairs of the individual.

8. Personalism. Personalism began in Europe and became a school in America, where it was started by B. P. Bowne (1847-1910) of Boston University. His view of the world was Berkeleyian: the world is composed of a plurality of free beings, and above them is an infinite being who has created them. After Bowne, personalism became the name for many doctrines, quite different from one another, but having in common the belief that the nature of the world is personal, creative, free, moral, and social. Its principles were: Persons, individual sources of consciousness, are the highest form of existence. They are active and creative: God created the world, but they transform it still further. They are free and therefore responsible. They are subject to moral principles. They are social and create a moral system out of the world. Of all forms of philosophical idealism and spiritualism this one most suited the religious rather than the philosophical inclinations of people.

The Character of Anglo-Saxon Idealism

Idealistic metaphysics appeared unexpectedly in England at a time when it was being discarded on the continent. It quickly gained a number of supporters: idealists assumed chairs of philosophy at Oxford, Glasgow, and Edinburgh. Ward and McTaggart lectured at Cambridge, and Bosanquet was active at London. In the year 1883 alone Green's ethics, Bradley's logic, E. Caird's work on Hegel, and a collective work of the idealists entitled *Essays in Philosophical Criticism* were published. Later the range and activity of the English metaphysical idealists spread around the world: among them, A. E. Taylor became a professor in Canada, H. Wildon Carr in California, and R. F. A. Hoernle in South Africa.

The English idealists concentrated most on metaphysics, but they also devoted their attention to ethics. In addition to Green and Bradley, the results of A. Seth, W. R. Sorley, and H. Rashdall were important from more than an idealistic point of view. They published works in the history of philosophy, mainly of Kant and Hegel. In these works they appealed to earlier philosophy and to a large extent followed well-established guideposts. Some of them only wished to propagate Hegel; Bradley's manner of philosophizing reminds one of Plato; in his universalism and pantheism Royce approached Plotinus; Ward was related to Leibniz and Berkeley. But some details were new: even those who wished to hold to the doctrines of Hegel almost against their will transformed them into a more empirical, more English philosophy. Even if their positive inferences can be questioned, the negative results, such as the critique of naturalism, remain. This critique has survived them and influenced the thought of the twentieth century. At least in this respect, then, these basically conservative philosophers were predecessors of the new era in philosophy.

These thinkers represented various types of idealism. Some of them, such as the transcendentalists, stressed practical aims, while others, such as the Hegelians of Oxford, set theoretical ones. Some of them remained rationalists to the end, while others ended in mysticism, like McTaggart who wrote that every genuine philosophy had to be mystical, not in its method of course, but in its conclusions. Some thought that being was patterned on thought, others that it resembled the will; intellectualistic idealism predominated at Oxford, voluntaristic idealism at Cambridge. Pantheistic idealism was professed by Royce, theistic by Ward, and atheistic by McTaggart.

In their view genuine being was composed either of abstract ideas or concrete selves; some, like Royce, took a universalistic and monistic position, others an individualistic and pluralistic one; in the world they saw only selves and beings similar to selves. This last view was called "personal idealism." In America G. H. Howison applied this name to his philosophy, but there were similar thinkers in England, a group that included Ward, McTaggart, and the pragmatist F. C. S. Schiller, who published a book entitled *Personal Idealism*.

This latter view is generally called spiritualism. It is not identical with idealism in the strict sense. For the latter genuine being is composed of general ideas, for the former individual souls; the first inclines to pluralism, the second to monism. But they have much in common, especially an antagonism to naturalism. In the great struggle of world views they are on the same side. For this reason, they were treated as one group of theories and included under one common, very broad title.

Influence

Idealism in America exerted wide social influence. The idealism of Emerson and the transcendentalists became, as R. Dyboski says, a powerful element in the shaping of the national character; with it came something like spontaneous optimism and radical individualism, which opposed all authorities and hierarchies. It increased America's faith in itself and the future. It was a declaration of independence of American civilization from Europe and generated the idealistic trend that produced famous works of social philanthropy and intellectual organization.

In America it had still another result. It began there from Hegelianism, but with the development of American intellectualism, it also led to mysticism. It was the medium of European as well as Asiatic influences. Before long a mystical and magical movement developed, New Thought and from 1875 Christian Science, "the scientific system of divine healing" based on Mary Baker Eddy's doctrine that the world in its entirety is spiritual and good.

Idealism in England had fewer practical aspirations and wished only to be a philosophical doctrine. It influenced only philosophy and for a time at least dampened the spirit of empiricism, naturalism, and utilitarianism that dominated English philosophy.

Opposition

Idealism, which had been designed to satisfy metaphysical, moral, and religious needs, did not entirely satisfy scientific ones: for the most part its conclusions were arbitrary and foggy. Beyond the Anglo-Saxon countries it was regarded as an anachronism and ignored, and in these countries it encountered a reaction before the end of the century. James wrote in 1880 to Renouvier that the resurrection of Hegel in the United States and in England after his burial in Germany was incomprehensible. And he added that "this movement cannot last long." James became a leader of the opposition. Radical empiricism, realism, pragmatism, and pluralism were different trends in American and English philosophy constituting a reaction to idealistic metaphysics. They charged that idealistic metaphysics is incompatible with the spirit of science, that it investigates things inaccessible to our knowledge at the cost of things that are accessible to it, that it introduces miracles by excluding man from the universal laws of nature, and that it ends in subjectivism or mysticism, the manner least desirable for science.

FRANZ BRENTANO

One of the most important opposition movements in the last part of the nineteenth century was initiated by Brentano. He built on experience no less than the positivists and scientists and was an enemy of speculative metaphysics, but he was not an empiricist.

Life

Franz Brentano (1838-1917), a German of Italian descent and later naturalized in Austria, was originally a Catholic priest. He was a professor of philosophy at the University of Würzburg from 1866 to 1873 (when he left the Church), then for

a few years in Vienna, but during this short time he attracted
a large number of students. He resigned his post in Vienna,
then lectured there as a private tutor. He later gave this up
and settled in Florence. Despite his loss of eyesight in old
age he never stopped working and improving his views.

His attitude toward knowledge and life was extremely intellectualistic: like the classical Greek philosophers he thought
that falsehood and evil were the results of faulty thinking.
This attitude inclined him away from mysticism and revelation,
and this was one reason for his break with the Church. His
Christianity was deistic without secrets. Full of respect for
the human mind, he was convinced that all the contradictions
and difficulties of philosophy could be resolved, that there
was no opposition between thought and experience, and that Leibniz and Locke could be reconciled.

Writings

Brentano wrote much but published little. *Psychology from
an Empirical Standpoint* (1874), of which only the first volume
appeared, remained his major and most extensive work. But with
this unfinished book he was able to influence the history of
psychology. In similar fashion he influenced the history of
ethics with a short treatise, *The Origin of Moral Cognition*,
published as a brochure in 1889. Most of his published works
were about Aristotle: he devoted his first two books to him in
1862 and 1867, as well as his two final ones published nearly
half a century later in 1911. The legacy of his manuscripts,
published from 1924 by his pupils, greatly exceeds the importance of the works published during his lifetime: these publications are not only a complement to but also an essential
modification of his earlier views.

Predecessors

Brentano, with his independent mind, did not subordinate
himself to contemporary philosophical trends. But he did refer
to views that were closely related to his from other centuries.
As a theologian he studied Aristotelian and scholastic philosophy: more precisely, he studied the scholastics, then went back
to their source, Aristotle. He accepted their manner of thinking and many concepts that had gone out of use, and when he revived them in the nineteenth century they seemed new. His
whole manner of thinking was a novelty for his contemporaries,
even when he only returned to old views.

The Aristotelian-scholastic base was common to his philosophy and to the nascent neo-Thomistic trend, but the latter

simply tried to continue earlier views, whereas Brentano developed them in his own way. He had been nurtured in scholastic
culture, but he had a modern, empirical mind. Brentano was far
from positivism, but even further from speculative metaphysics.
The main task of his life became the struggle with German metaphysics and with Kantianism, which was a wholly incompatible
view to this realist. "I regard all of Kantian philosophy," he
wrote, "as an error that has led to still greater errors and,
in the end, to complete chaos in philosophy."

Views

1. *Descriptive Psychology*. For Brentano, all knowledge is
based on experience. If there are genuine a priori assertions,
they are only *ex terminis*, that is, they result from the terms
themselves and are purely formal and analytic. Real general
assertions can only be arrived at through induction. Knowledge
can be based only on individual statements. If it is to represent honest knowledge, philosophy also must be empirical.
He was convinced that this is possible, for philosophy can base
itself on psychology, which relies on introspective, internal
experience.
     Brentano began to work on empirical psychology almost at
the same time as Wundt, but his psychology was of quite another
character. It had a different view of the object of internal
experience. It distinguished between content and act in experience (for example, between the sound heard and the act of
hearing the sound) and thereby stressed acts. But the majority
of contemporary psychologists, those led by Wundt, had placed
sole emphasis on the content of psychic acts. They asserted
that acts are unobservable, hence cannot be made the subject of
science. This had been the prevailing viewpoint since Descartes and Locke: from their time psychology had concerned itself solely with the content of consciousness (for example,
perceived colors, heard sounds); it understood consciousness as
a combination of such contents. However, for Brentano colors
and sounds did not belong to psychology; they were physical objects to which psychic acts are exposed. He saw consciousness
as a combination of acts, not contents: it was composed of acts
of seeing or hearing, not colors or sounds.
     Brentano distinguished two branches of psychology: descrip-
tive and explanatory. He asserted that the descriptive had
been neglected; this was bad because psychology tried to explain facts before it had accurately stated them. Much has
changed since the time of Brentano, and pure description of

facts has gained a place in psychology. However, this came
about in large measure because of Brentano.

As Brentano understood it, psychological description was
not to represent the concrete experiences of any definite individual. Rather, this description was to be general and synthetic, stressing the constant forms of psychic life and the general character of each of them. For this reason Brentano's psychology ascribed particular importance to general definitions
and classifications. This was the Aristotelian spirit: to base
concepts on experience, but to strive for the most general concepts.

    2. The Intentionality of Psychic Phenomena. Brentano,
above all, established what all psychic phenomena and acts have
in common. They are all directed toward some object: we see
colors, hear sounds, and always make assertions about some object or other. This characteristic of psychic acts had already
been known to the scholastics, and Brentano used the scholastic
term "intentionality" (from *intendere*, to direct) to define it.
Every psychic act has an "intentional relationship" to its object; this feature, common to all psychic acts, differentiates
them from physical phenomena. Every act of consciousness directed to an object goes beyond consciousness and has a transcendental relationship to it. This fact is without analogy in
the external world. The theory of knowledge should state this
as a fact, rather than claiming (as has most frequently been
done) that the existence of things is a hypothesis and that
consciousness does not encounter them.

This simple assertion had far-reaching consequences.
Namely, only "intentional" acts are psychic, but the objects of
these acts are not intentional and are not psychic. Only acts
belong to consciousness, not their objects. Only acts are immanent to consciousness; their objects are transcendental.
This assertion negated subjective idealism by demonstrating the
falsity of its argument (which had seemed irrefutable to many
modern thinkers): objects perceived by us are our perceptions,
belonging to the consciousness and therefore psychic. The
analysis of psychic acts led Brentano to realism in a period
that inclined to subjective idealism.

Brentano thought that psychic acts could have the most diverse objects, ideal as well as real and abstract as well as
concrete. But in his later years he unexpectedly limited this
view: he began to assert that the objects of acts are always
real and concrete. We know nothing else and have no evidence
for its existence. Only real things exist. Brentano joined
nominalism to epistemological realism: what is not a concrete
thing is only an empty word.

3. *The Division of Psychic Phenomena*. Because intention is the common feature of psychic phenomena, there are as many phenomena as there are intentions. Brentano classified psychic phenomena on this basis. The results were quite unexpected: his division was totally different from the one that had long since been universally accepted. This earlier division had divided psychic phenomena into phenomena of cognition, feeling, and will. It had originated in the eighteenth century and was popularized by the writings of Kant. Until Brentano, it had not been questioned.

First, he pointed out that what is usually called "cognition" includes two different kinds of psychic acts: representation and judgment. These are so different that one cannot be reduced to the other. The opposition of truth and error does not apply to representations. They can be neither true nor false, because they assert nothing. If they are sometimes called true or false, it is only in the sense that a person expresses the content of his representations as judgments. Even the person who imagines chimeras still does not commit error; error is made only when we state that chimeras exist in reality; he states the truth who asserts that chimera is his idea. Hence, truth and error arise only in judgment: judgment is an act of acknowledgment or rejection, assertion or denial, in which one pronounces truth or falsehood. This difference makes it necessary to separate representations from judgments as different kinds of psychic phenomena.

On the other hand, what the traditional division had treated as two different things—feeling and will—for Brentano were one and the same. Joy and sadness, resolution and indecision, though the first are usually called feelings and the second acts of will, are basically the same, namely acts of positive or negative interest in an object, inclination or disinclination. Therefore, Brentano combined these under the name of emotional phenomena or "acts of love or animosity." Like judgments these are acts of choice: they acknowledge or reject the value of things, as judgments either acknowledge or reject their existence.

Brentano in this way arrived at a new tripartite division of psychic phenomena: representations, judgments, and emotional phenomena ("phenomena of love and animosity"). To these three kinds of phenomena he subordinated three traditional ideas: beauty, truth, and good. Beauty he regarded as perfect representation, truth as perfect judgment, and good as the proper relation to love and animosity. There is also a different philosophical science corresponding to each of these: aesthetics, logic, and ethics. In Brentano's opinion they deal with norms, not with facts: aesthetics with the norms of representation, logic with norms of judgment, ethics with norms of love and hate. Therefore, Brentano ascribed a normative character to the philosophical sciences.

4. *Self-evidence.* In order to demonstrate the norms of truth one must have some criterion differentiating it from falsehood. What then is the criterion of truth? The natural answer is proof. Truth is a verified judgment. But every proof assumes premises, which it often accepts without proof. To be sure, these premises can be proven in turn, but finally one must accept premises without proof, for otherwise the process stretches into infinity. Thus, some kind of criterion must exist that would enable one to recognize certain unproven premises as true. This criterion must be in the premises themselves, for if proof gives no guarantee of their truth, they must be convincing in and of themselves.

At first Brentano accepted the most usual "adequate" criterion of truth, that truth is agreement of thought and thing, or an assertion is true if it corresponds to reality. Later, however, he saw that this criterion leads to a vicious circle: a judgment is true when it corresponds to things, but we only know the nature of a thing when we have a true judgment of it. This same difficulty is also encountered in another widespread criterion in the theory of knowledge, namely in the Kantian criterion that truth is conformity of a judgment with the laws of the mind. If to establish the truth of a judgment this judgment must be compared with something else, then circular reasoning cannot be avoided. It can only be avoided if this criterion is in the judgment itself, or if the judgment itself leaves no doubt as to its veracity. Or to put it another way, if the judgment is self-evident. Therefore, the criterion of truth lies not in the agreement of a judgment with reality, but in its self-evidence. In the light of this criterion self-evident judgments are true, as well as those derived from self-evident ones.

This was one of the most essential, if not the most essential part of Brentano's philosophy and, at the same time, the one that separated him from the majority of contemporary philosophers. At that time it was almost universally recognized that self-evidence was a question of intuition, which was not trusted. For this reason another criterion was sought and this most natural one was avoided. But Brentano saw that this criterion was not only the most natural, but the only possible one. Self-evidence is not a question of the intuition of the subject, but a feature of certain judgments.

Some judgments are essentially self-evident: we can neither deny their veracity nor even understand how they could not be true; there is an internal compulsion to recognize them as

true. But if they are self-evident, it makes no sense to require their justification: at most this would consist in appealing to other certainties. One can simply either accept
them or not accept them: this is a question of confidence in
the mind. However, if we do not accept them, there is no way
of identifying truth. On the other hand, acceptance not only
affords a criterion of truth, but also saves one (as Brentano
believed) from eternal Protagorean relativism. Not every person is the measure of truth, as Protagoras maintained, but only
the person who derives judgments from self-evidence. Among
such persons there is no divergence of opinion. This is the
"point of Archimedes." Brentano based his entire philosophy on
this.

Like Leibniz Brentano distinguished two classes of judgments: judgments of facts and judgments of relationships,
verités de fait et de raison. But both of these classes contain self-evident judgments. Self-evident judgments of facts
are those concerning internal experience, one's own acts. We
imagine or feel something we know with complete certainty and
irrefutable conviction. Every experience is accompanied by a
consciousness of one's own act: for example, in perceiving a
horse I am simultaneously conscious of the fact that I perceive
it. Certain judgments of relationships and logical principles,
such as the principle of contradiction, are as self-evident as
judgments of internal experience.

Extreme empiricism incorrectly limited self-evidence to
experience, and extreme rationalism incorrectly limited it to
principles: in both cases self-evidence amounts to the same
thing.

But judgments of external experience are not self-evident.
It is always possible for us to derive the wrong perceptions
from the working of external causes. For example, when I see a
horse it is not self-evident that a horse is standing before me;
it could be a hallucination. However, although nothing is self-
evident about external perceptions, they are (as Brentano said)
"a self-evident probability": it is self-evidently probable
that our perceptions are derived from external causes, from the
real world and not from our own minds, for this is precisely
what distinguishes them from acts of will or imagination. It
is also self-evidently probable that the external world is not
chaos, but that it is subject to the law of causality, and this
probability increases with experience. We assume the regularity of the world hypothetically, but experience verifies it.

In this position Brentano had many predecessors: his view
was compatible with that of Aristotle and Descartes, who used
the criterion of self-evidence in assuming that truth is what
is clear and distinct. But Brentano disagreed with Kant and
the Kantians, who were predominant in his time. Not only were
his answers different from Kant's, but his problems were dif-

ferent as well. In deriving his concept of cognition from mathematics, Kant understood knowledge as a creation of the mind—
hence, he also had to ask how such a creation could conform to
reality. For Brentano this question was superfluous. In essence it reduced to this question: on what do I base the belief
that my convictions are true? To answer this one could again
appeal only to convictions.

　　5. *The Reform of Logic*. Judgment is usually understood as
the joining of two representations, that of the subject and
that of the predicate. This apparently simple and natural understanding of judgment was questioned by Brentano. He came to
doubt this through his analysis of existential judgments (for
example, "*A* exists" and "No *A* exists"), which have no predi-
cates. In such judgments we recognize or reject the existence
of *A* itself, not its connection with a quality of existence.
However, if some judgments do not imply a connection between
representations, then the connection of representations cannot
be a basis of judgment. The basis of judgment can only be what
also appears in existential judgments and all judgments in general—recognition or rejection of some object or other. This
means that judgments are "thetic" (establishing the existence
of something), not synthetic (reconstructing what something is).
　　This understanding of judgment implies that every categorical sentence can be transformed into an existential one without changing its sense. The sentence "A certain person is
sick" means the same thing as "There is a sick person"; the
sentence "No man is mortal" the same thing as "There is no mortal man." This leads to a peculiar consequence: no affirmative
judgment is universal, and no negative one is particular.
Hence, traditional logic was wrong in debating the affirmative
nature of universal judgments and the particular nature of negative ones. Yet, this is not very important: it also leads to
the fact that all a priori judgments (as general ones) are contradictory, even the principle of identity. If this seems otherwise, it is because, linguistically, they are stated in affirmative form. When I say "For all triangles, the sum of the
angles is 180°," this means that no triangle exists that does
not fit this description. This judgment says nothing about the
existence of a triangle, but states that if such a triangle exists it must have this quality. This is true of all a priori
judgments.
　　This was the first revolt in centuries against Aristotelian logic. It turned out that what had seemed definitely established could be understood differently.

6. The Reform of Ethics. Value judgments are a parallel phenomenon to propositions: they also imply taking a positive or negative position in relation to things. As with propositions only one attitude can be correct: if delight in a particular thing is correct, then antipathy toward it cannot be correct at the same time. That which evokes a correct proposition we call truth, and that which calls forth correct liking we call good. As not all of our propositions are correct, so neither are all our predilections. But among them, some are accompanied by an irresistible feeling of correctness. What self-evidence is for the theory of truth and knowledge the feeling of correctness is for our own behavior and the theory of good. Only when we possess this feeling can we be completely certain that our predilection is correct. In ethics, then, self-evident and irrefutable belief is also the measure of all correctness and the foundation of all our knowledge.

This feeling appears infrequently, but we do have this feeling toward fundamental goods, namely toward moral, intellectual, and hedonistic ones. Sometimes we even have this feeling with regard to the placing of some goods above others: with a feeling of certainty we place every good above every evil and a good composed of many goods above any single one of its components. But we never have this feeling when we compare qualitatively different goods: no one is able to say whether knowledge is better than unselfish love. This cannot be otherwise, for all goods are finite and their value also depends on their quantity.

The moral task is simply a matter of increasing goods—one's own and others, present and future ones. Acting to intensify goods in the world is the obviously correct aim of life: "This is the only categorical imperative on which everything else depends." Brentano treated ethics and the theory of knowledge in a totally different way from Kant; his approach was more simple and not only in the formal sense.

7. Philosophy and Psychology. At his graduation Brentano elected to defend the thesis that the method of philosophy is the same as that of the natural sciences: *vera philosophiae methodus nulla alia nisi scientiae naturalis est*. His intention was not to defend naturalism, but to attack the view that philosophy had a speculative or transcendental method not used by the other sciences. His opinion was that there is only one genuine method for all the sciences, a method that can to a certain extent be adapted to the distinctness of the object of investigation.

In any event, psychology is the natural science with the natural method. Only psychology can resolve logical and ethi-

cal philosophical problems, for in internal experience it discovers obvious facts that are the measure of truth and good.
In basing itself on psychology, philosophy does not become subjective and relative. On the contrary, it is precisely in psychological certainties that one finds a defense against subjectivity and relativity. Derivation of the measure of truth and
good from the analysis of psychic acts by no means implies that
truth and good are dependent on psychic acts. To base oneself
on psychology does not lead to psychologism.

Psychology is the foundation of philosophy. The zenith of
philosophy could be metaphysics, and Brentano's realistic position opened the way to this. However, Brentano himself did not
take up metaphysics. He limited himself to preparatory, descriptive philosophy in which he analyzed the leading concepts
of metaphysics—existence, substance, and causality.

8. The History of Philosophy. Brentano was one of the
many nineteenth-century thinkers who tried to find a general
formula for the development of philosophy, that is, to approach
the history of philosophy philosophically.

According to him, philosophy in each of its great periods
passes through four phases: first a phase of flowering, then
three phases of decline. In the first declining phase it loses
theoretical interest and subordinates itself to practical goals;
in the second it loses faith in its own prowess and lapses into
skepticism; and in the third, having no other way to satisfy
its desires for knowledge, it escapes into mysterious intuition
and falls into mysticism.

Brentano applied this schema to the three major periods of
European philosophy. The ancient period had its phase of flowering until Aristotle; then it passed through a practical phase
with the stoics and Epicureans, through skepticism with the
Pyrrhonists, and through mysticism with the neo-Pythagoreans
and neo-Platonists. Likewise medieval philosophy had its period of flowering until Thomas Aquinas, its practical phase with
the Scotists, its skeptical one with the Occamists, and its
mystical one with Eckhart and Nicholas of Cusa. In the modern
period the flowering of philosophy lasted from Bacon to Leibniz,
then followed the practical period in the French Enlightenment,
the skeptical period with Hume, and the mystical one with Kant,
Fichte, Schelling, and Hegel. In Brentano's opinion these last
thinkers signaled the bottom of the decline.

Summary

Brentano's philosophy was distinct in that it began from a subjective opposition and ended with objective results. Brentano was convinced that he had resolved the eternal debate about subjectivism—the debate of Protagoras and Plato. His solution was based on the fact that not every person is the measure of all things, only the person who pronounces self-evident judgments. Brentano accomplished something exceptional for the philosophy of the nineteenth century: he avoided a minimalistic limitation without falling into speculative metaphysics. His role was like that of Maine de Biran at the beginning of the century. Though quite different in their manner of thinking, both had the ability to find an intermediate solution in a century that was characterized by the struggle between minimalism and maximalism. Biran followed Augustine, Brentano returned to Aristotle.

Brentano tried to reverse the main trend of nineteenth-century philosophy, and he also stimulated debate on many particular questions: separating descriptive from explanatory psychology; separating psychic acts from their content; basing knowledge on the criterion of self-evidence; reviving sciences that dealt with the intentionality of psychic acts; stating a classification of psychic phenomena, a new interpretation of formal logic, a new ideogenetic theory of judgments, and a new foundation of ethics.

Development

In the years 1905 to 1910 a basic change took place in Brentano's views: his thesis of the intentional character of experiences was narrowed in the sense that he now stated that experiences are intentionally directed only toward real, concrete things. Experiences can be directed to fictions (as when we think of centaurs), but these fictions also have the shape of things and not abstractions. Brentano took a position which T. Kotarbinski has called "reism." Only real objects can be known. Unreal objects are only names to which nothing either materially or psychologically corresponds: in accepting their existence we fall victim to language. There are no ideal forms of being. The concept of thing is the most general and embraces everything that exists.

School

Among his contemporaries Brentano was at first regarded as an anachronism, a medieval remnant. Nevertheless, he attracted a group of pupils, and in time his influence grew rather than decreased. The main center of his influence was Austria, especially the universities of Graz and Prague, but these influences went even further. Various philosophical trends at the end of the nineteenth and beginning of the twentieth century are derived from him: "phenomenology," the "theory of objects," and other theories that pursued descriptive psychology, attempting to precisely analyze facts without engaging in metaphysical questions.

His pupils split into two opposing trends. Some of them emulated the earlier Brentano, who had stimulated debate on diverse, unreal objects with his theory of intentionality. Others followed the later Brentano, who disapproved of these deliberations more strongly than anyone else. Among the first group are A. Marty, C. von Ehrenfels, and A. Höfler, three Prague professors who developed Brentano's earlier views in the philosophy of speech, the theory of value, and psychology, respectively. The leading representative of this group was A. Meinong (1853-1920), professor at Graz, who tried to create a new philosophical science called the "theory of objects." This theory was to be even broader in scope than metaphysics, for it was to include unreal as well as real objects. The psychology of K. Stumpf and the phenomenology of E. Husserl also bear the stamp of Brentano's earlier views. But other pupils of Brentano became proponents of his later reistic theory. The most active of these was O. Kraus, professor at Prague, who founded a Brentano archive in Prague and a society in Brentano's name. Kazimierz Twardowski was also a pupil of Brentano. Through him, Brentano's views exerted influence in Polish philosophy at the beginning of the twentieth century even greater than in the philosophy of other countries.

NIETZSCHE

One part of Nietzsche's activity was an expression of his epoch: he represented its scientism, naturalism, evolutionism, and relativism. Yet, another part of his work struck at his epoch and all of its culture. He revealed the features of his age and was one of the first to rebel against it.

Life

Friedrich Nietzsche (1844-1900) was a classical philologist. He matured at an unusually early age. Shortly after finishing his studies, in 1869 he assumed the chair of philology in Basel. His interests quickly changed to philosophy, and after ten years he gave up his chair to devote himself to writ-

ing.   But this was also the end of his normal, quiet life.   He
left Basel and began his *Wanderjahre*.   Driven by anxiety and
plagued by illness he continually changed his place of resi-
dence.   He stayed at various places in Italy and Switzerland,
living in hotels and boarding houses and growing ever more home-
less and lonely.   In 1889 he contracted a mental illness from
which he did not recover.   He lived for eleven more years,
cared for by his mother in Weimar.

This admirer of life and strength, this apostle of harshness, was personally frail and sick and, in his relations with
people, unusually considerate and delicate.   He was a German of
Polish descent, coming from a Germanized family named Nicki.
He was aware of his background and valued his Polish blood.   He
wrote, "My ancestors were Polish nobility and my instincts are
inherited from them, among these perhaps even the *liberum veto*."
In describing his attitude toward music he said, "I am enough
of a Pole to give up the music of the whole world for Chopin."
The Germans regard him as their great philosopher.   To be sure,
he was born a German and wrote in German, but he ran away from
Germany, despised Germans, and no one so violently and passion-
ately pointed out their vices.   He stated that the Germans were
retarded culturally by two hundred years and would never catch
up.

Writings and Development

During the short twenty-year period of his creativity Nietzsche lived with the continual pressure of thought and wrote a
great deal.   But with the exception of his first two books his
writings are only collections of aphorisms and detached
thoughts.   Such a way of writing suited his mind, which could
generate the most splendid thoughts but could not spin a continuous chain of ideas.   Moreover, unendurable physical suffering did not permit him to concentrate on his ideas for a long
time.   In his later years he could only write while walking.
He wrote down his thoughts while roving in the Engadine moun-
tains.

The swarm of continually new ideas caused him to change
his position many times.   Three distinct periods can be distinguished in his writings.   Each of these was characterized by
a different cult, a new enthusiasm.   In the first period this
was the cult of art, in the second of science, and in the third
of life, strength, and individuality.   During the first period
he was influenced by Wagner, in the second by Darwin and the
ideal of exact scientism, and in the third period he expressed
ideas that were mostly his own.   To the first period belong:
The Birth of Tragedy from the Spirit of Music (1872) and *Un-
timely Meditations* (1873-76).   To the second: *Human, All Too*

Human (1878), *The Dawn* (1881), and *The Happy Science* (1882).
To the third: *Thus Spoke Zarathustra* (1883-84), *Beyond Good and Evil* (1886), and *The Genealogy of Morals* (1887). Published posthumously were *The Will to Power* (1906) and *Ecce Homo* (1908).

Predecessors

Engrossed in his own thoughts, Nietzsche had little time to study the thoughts of others. His erudition was limited both in the natural sciences (which he worshipped for a time) and in philosophy. But he knew Darwin and Spencer, who supplied the most material for his theories. He also knew F. A. Lange with whom he shared a liking for the precise sciences and empirical thinking. In the previous generation Schopenhauer and Stirner were close to him. In Schopenhauer Nietzsche found the point of departure for his philosophy: in time he overcame Schopenhauer's pessimism, but to the end retained his voluntarism and irrationalism. However, very closely related thinkers congenial to Nietzsche can only be found in antiquity: Heraclitus' theory of nature and the sophists' theory of man. If anyone announced the idea of the superman (*Übermensch*) before him, it was only Callicles and Thrasymachus described by Plato. There are also similar ideas in Carlyle.

Views

1. *Relativistic Theory of Knowledge.* Impressed by the biological theories of his time Nietzsche was convinced that human acts and creations are conditioned by life needs. Knowledge is no exception; it also serves practical aims. Truth for us is only what life demands. Objective and absolute truth is an illusion. Therefore, all truth is subjective and relative. "What are ultimate human truths? They are only human errors that cannot be abolished."

Nietzsche went further than anyone else in his relativistic theory of knowledge. Not only did he believe that the mind does not grasp reality faithfully, but he thought that the mind definitely falsifies it. This is so because reality is continual change: to embrace reality and subject it to life needs we must stop it and ossify it. Reality is chaos, which we must order and seek laws for. It is inexhaustible richness, but we must simplify it for our needs. Our truth is always fixed, ordered, and simplified. Our truths are illusions to which we have become accustomed and the falsity of which we do not remember. Because we have become accustomed to these truths, in the end we ourselves believe in the false image of reality we have created.

For us this image is true because we live in it. "We have made the world so that we can live in it. We have introduced bodies, lines and planes, causes and results, movement and rest, form and content. . . . But this does not prove them. Life is not an argument: among the conditions of life one can find error." For centuries we have been using metaphors, and we finally forget that they are only metaphors. We use words and forget that they are only words. "Words obstruct our path; in every act of cognition we encounter ossifed, prescriptive words."

Each of our concepts deforms reality, because each one generalizes it. The more general it is, the more false it is. Hence, philosophical concepts are most false: nothing corresponds to such concepts as absolute or substance; they are exclusively schemata of thought.

2. *The Relativistic Theory of Value.* Even more relative, subjective, and biologically conditioned are our value judgments and everything that we regard as good, as valuable. This is particularly the case with moral values. There is no universally binding objective morality; everyone has the kind of morality necessary for his life needs and suitable for his feelings and affections. One has a morality that justifies everything for which he has a desire; another has a morality that gives him the peace he longs for; still another has a morality that permits him to retaliate against his enemies. People do not even have to be conscious of this, but such indeed are the sources of their morality.

Everyone has the kind of morality that corresponds to his nature. And Nietzsche saw as the most essential difference between people that some have a weak nature and others a strong one. The morality of the strong (master morality, in Nietzsche's term) is different from the morality of the weak (slave morality). The strong value personal eminence and dignity, decisiveness, efficiency, certainty of action, and uncompromising effort to carry out their intentions. The weak value what helps their weakness: compassion, softness of heart, love, altruism, and consideration.

At one time the "masters" were in control; they fashioned concepts and created the ideas of good. These they understood as dignity or courage. But then came the rebellion of the slaves; they were indeed weak, but they were more numerous and therefore victorious. Now their opinion prevails. What suited their interests began to pass for good: a soft heart, altruism, humility, gentleness, and self-denial, qualities imposed on slaves, which they afterward raise to the dignity of virtues. A complete reversal of judgments took place. We live in an epoch after the rebellion of slaves, and our morality is the slave morality.

Nietzsche wanted to assume an impartial, scientific, naturalistic, and descriptive position toward human morality. He noted that all is as it should be when slaves have the morality of slaves. It is bad only when the masters submit to this morality. This is already, as he said using biological terms, degeneration and decadence.

However, Nietzsche did not retain this objective and impartial attitude. He felt that he belonged to the race of masters, and he felt that their morality was incomparably higher, that it was the only proper one. And he took their side. Here the relativistic ethic, with the thesis "everyone has the kind of morality that suits him," ended and the absolutist ethic, with the thesis "only one morality is correct, the morality of masters," began. This second, wholly different part of Nietzsche's philosophy, was neither naturalistic nor relative.

3. *Critique of Contemporary Morality*. Nietzsche had an unusually astute understanding of the contemporary morality he opposed. His opposition was not systematic, but we can reconstruct this opposition in the spirit of his arguments.

The dominant contemporary morality bases itself on three main assumptions: (1) the assumption of equality: everyone is equal with equal rights and responsibilities; (2) the assumption of freedom: everyone should be free as long as he does not harm the freedom of others; (3) the assumption of moral value: moral value is absolute, and there is no need to verify it by indicating that it is necessary for life or health, for morality is not a means but an end.

The principles of contemporary morality are based on these assumptions, above all such principles as: (1) The principle of justice: everyone has a right to the same laws and goods. (2) The principle of utility: one should act to produce the most good. (3) The principle of altruism and love of one's neighbor: one should also remember the good of others. (4) The principle of mercy: in producing good for others one should above all help the unhappy and the weak. (5) The principle of the superiority of spiritual goods: spiritual goods are higher than material ones and should be most valued. (6) The principle of the primacy of the commonweal: the good of the people as a group is more important than the good of the individual. (7) The principle of intention: the most essential value of behavior is not what it attains, but what it intends, whether it really aims at the good of others, spiritual good, or the commonweal. (8) The principle of education: no effort should be spared for this good and one should educate oneself and others to be mindful of it. (9) The principle of rewards and punishments: moral behavior is rewarded, if not in this life, at least in the succeeding one, and it even carries its own reward in the form of internal satisfaction; immoral behavior is punished and carries its own internal punishment in the form of pangs of conscience.

Nietzsche saw Socrates and Plato as the source of this morality with its disastrous (as he believed) idea of good. Christianity, "Platonism for the masses," accepted this idea; it consolidated the prevailing morality. Also influential in this process of consolidation was the new democratic movement, which Nietzsche saw as corresponding to Christianity in almost every particular. Nietzsche was an opponent of Socrates, Plato, Christianity, and democracy.

4. The Transvaluation of All Value. Nietzsche's own position, the master morality, was almost directly opposite to the prevailing morality in every particular. Its main assumptions were: (1) the value of life: only life has absolute value and gives birth to everything else that has value; (2) the freedom of the strong: freedom belongs only to the person who is strong enough to secure it for himself; (3) inequality: people are not equal; they are better or worse depending on how much life and strength is in them.

These assumptions are the source of Nietzsche's opposition to the principles of contemporary morality. The principle of justice is bad: laws and goods belong to the most dignified, active, strong, but not to the weak, incompetent, and abortive creations of nature. True justice does not base itself on the principle of equality; everyone should get as much as he deserves. "Equality is a signal of collapse." The principle of utility is bad: to produce the most good is not important; life, the greatest good, is most important. The principle of altruism is bad: if one has great aims, these aims are more important than other people's. One should not spare one's neighbor; everything belongs to the best person. "Egoism of the eminent is a holy state." Finally, altruism is also egoism, but egoism of the weak. The principle of mercy is bad: it wastes energy on the weak and degenerate. The strong should have the "pathos of remoteness," or the feeling of their position of superiority. The principle of the primacy of spiritual good is bad: the basis of everything is the body; life is primarily a physical matter, and spirit is only a superstructure above it. The principle of the commonweal is bad: only great individuals have value, and if the masses have value it is only as a copy of great people or as their instrument, or as a resistance that stimulates the great to action; finally, as Nietzsche said, "May the devil take statistics." The principle of education is bad: what is not in the organism and life forces, what is not in the instincts cannot be replaced by any education. Finally, the principle of rewards and punishments is bad: reward is understood as happiness, punishment as unhappiness, and it is more important to live a full and dignified life than to feel happy. Happiness is an ideal of the prevailing morality, a work of slaves that should be overturned.

In particular Nietzsche combated all limitations, all asceticism, and all escape into the sphere of ideals: only degenerate life needs renunciation, prohibitions, asceticism, religious and moral ideals.

Nietzsche's indictment of contemporary morality was threefold: that it bases itself on false psychology and therefore disregards natural instincts, compelling people to follow principles incompatible with nature; that it is built on fictions: it talks of altruistic deeds, free will and moral order, which do not exist; that it has negative practical consequences: it educates people to mediocrity.

Nietzsche, as he himself said, undertook a "transvaluation of all value." This means demonstrating the worthlessness of everything that is commonly regarded as valuable and replacing this with genuine values. Nietzsche also said that his philosophy was to be "beyond good and evil," meaning that it was to be beyond "moral" good and evil based on principles of altruism, the primacy of spirit, the commonweal, intention, and education. Nietzsche called himself an amoralist. Above all, he opposed the prevailing morality, but also any morality placing spiritual values above life and subordinating life to them.

But in the wider sense, what Nietzsche himself proclaimed was also a morality, for it applied norms and value judgments to human actions. One can say that Nietzsche was not just the creator of a new ethic or a new theory of morality, but also the creator of a new morality. No thinker of the past—Plato, Aristotle, Augustine, Aquinas, Kant—aspired as far: they created a new ethic, not a new morality. They only tried to conceptualize the morality of their times and their environment, to reveal its features, assumptions, and consequences. When one critic reproached Kant for giving only a "new formula" of morality, the latter answered that such had been his intention. Morality has not been created by philosophers but by religious and social movements, and philosophers have only developed the details of the existing morality. But Nietzsche went further: he undertook the task of creating a new morality.

The foundation of this new morality was life: life is the first and absolute value. Therefore, this morality based itself on instincts, not on conscious thought. The slogan of life was a motif running through Nietzsche's philosophy from beginning to end and forming a connecting link between the various periods of his thought: everything in his philosophy changed, but this motif remained. Nietzsche took his inspiration from the biological thinking of Darwin and Spencer, but his understanding of life was different in at least two respects. First, he understood it dynamically, not mechanistically. Second, he did not see its function in the struggle for existence. Only in exceptional cases is life a struggle for existence. More usually it is something more; it wishes not only to remain in existence but also to develop.

However diverse the moral ideas known to European thought, one belief was common to all of them: human life has purpose. Many people thought that such a purpose was as yet unknown and undiscovered, but few doubted that such a goal exists. This belief was weakened in the nineteenth century, as expressed in the philosophy of Schopenhauer: life has no goal; it is an aimless, irrational forward thrust. Nietzsche appealed to this: he admitted that Schopenhauer was partially right, for man does have an essential goal within himself: the goal of life. Here Nietzsche went beyond the nihilism and pessimism of Schopenhauer.

Nietzsche created his ideal of man (called the superman) against the background of such beliefs. Such a man does not exist in contemporary reality, but one can and should, using Nietzsche's biological phraseology, rear him. Humanity began from master reality and would return to it. Then the ideal of superman would be realized. Above all, this is an ideal of biological perfection: vitality. But it also contains spiritual perfection: dignity and firmness with respect to others and toward oneself as well.

5. *The Apollonian and Dionysian Attitudes*. In his first works Nietzsche contrasted two basic human attitudes. At that time he was a philologist and derived his metaphors from antiquity: a symbol of one of these attitudes was Apollo, another Dionysus. The Apollonian attitude values what is clear, transparent, composed, sedate, closed, perfect, harmonious—passive. The Dionysian values fullness and exuberance of life, its drive to demolish all barriers and harmony; dynamism is the greatest of all perfections. Naturally, Nietzsche favored the Dionysian attitude. He argued that everything great, powerful, and creative has had its source in this attitude. Even Greek culture, according to Nietzsche, which seems Apollonian, was basically Dionysian.

This contrast, Dionysus and Apollo, was changed by Nietzsche in his last years to an even sharper one: for him Diony-

sus was the symbol of life as the highest good, whereas God on
the cross was a symbol of sacrificing life for other goods.
Nietzsche was Dionysian with all his heart: he was an enemy of
religion and Christianity.

Summary

Nietzsche's most deeply held belief was that physical life,
a biological fact, is the basis of human existence, and spiritual life is only its offshoot. This conviction led him to naturalism and epistemological and ethical relativism. Also derived from this was the conception of a new morality, the transvaluation of all values, going beyond good and evil, the opposition of masters and slaves, Dionysus and Apollo, the superman,
the struggle against decadence. All of these ideas and expressions passed from Nietzsche to the mental makeup of the nineteenth-century intelligentsia.

Only on occasion did Nietzsche turn his attention to the
philosophy of nature, but when he did make chance statements
about it he applied what he had found in analyzing man: he
thought that just as in man the essential element in nature is
will. The presumption that spiritual factors are primary and
essential he regarded as an egregious error. His favorite idea
was the ancient idea of eternal recurrence: when the history of
the world reaches its peak, the process begins again and will
trace the same course. This was Nietzsche's surrogate for eternity.

Nietzsche was an extraordinary psychologist, not in the
sense of systematically elaborating and describing psychic life
as Locke or Wundt had, but in the sense of a Pascal or La
Rochefoucauld: he had the ability to discern the most hidden
human motives and intentions.

He was also a sociologist. He was able to derive human
views and actions from the conditions in which they originated,
from their environment, from their membership in either the
group of masters or of slaves.

Above all, he was concerned with ethics. Though he emphasized his amorality, he was the creator of a morality. He was
conscious of this, for in later years he saw the task of his
philosophy not in the investigation of culture but in its creation. In this sense he distinguished "philosophers" from "philosophical workers," as he contemptuously called them. Among
these latter he included many who had been regarded as great,
even Hegel and Kant. He called contemporary impoverished philosophy "epochistic" (from the Greek ἐποχή—forbearing), for
instead of posing great problems it caused philosophers to refrain from them.

Influence

When insanity darkened his mind and stopped his work in 1889, Nietzsche was still relatively unknown, although Georg Brandes, a Danish historian of literature, made him the subject of his lectures in 1889. But when he died eleven years later, he was famous. He influenced philosophers. Many became interested in him, and some accepted his position. He had still greater influence on the intelligentsia, on men of letters and publicists, and not only in Germany. A testimony to his influence are the stories of Gide in France, d'Annunzio in Italy, and Przybyszewski and Berent in Poland. Nietzsche also influenced politicians: Mussolini was an enthusiastic reader of his writings. When the National Socialist German Workers' Party came to power, it made Baeumler, a Nietzschian, its official philosopher. But if Nazism acknowledged Nietzsche, he himself would doubtlessly have rejected this homage: perhaps this adoption by the party resulted from his writings, but certainly not because they were understood. For Nietzsche the characteristic of the "masters" was not only strength but, even more important, dignity.

There are two elements in Nietzsche. One is romantic: this is the cult of Dionysus, the exuberance of life. This has had the greatest influence on philosophers. The other was a realistic element: the will to power, authority, and domination. This has influenced politicians as well as political philosophers.

The liveliest discussion in German philosophy at the beginning of the twentieth century was connected with Nietzsche. For example, when L. Klages defended subjective and emotional "spirit" against objective, universalistic, and rational "spirit" (*The Spirit as Adversary of the Soul*, 1929), or when O. Spengler argued the inexorable decline of European civilization (*The Decline of the West*, 1918-22), they were beginning with Nietzsche.

Nietzsche foresaw that someday his philosophy would have great influence. "I know my fate," he wrote.

Someday my name will be associated with the recollection of a crisis the likes of which has never been seen on earth, the greatest conflict of conscience, the reversal of everything that has hitherto been believed in, which has been required, which has been worshipped. I am not a man, I am dynamite.

Summary

Problems

Twice in the history of modern philosophy the same change took place: as at the beginning of the eighteenth century, now in the middle of the nineteenth there was a retreat from metaphysical problems to epistemological and psychological ones. Metaphysical problems did not disappear completely, but they receded into the background. To many people of that time they seemed anachronistic; up-to-date, progressive philosophical trends posed quite different problems. These were epistemological problems—the forms and content of knowledge, truth and probability, objectivity or subjectivity, cognition and the sciences, experience and thinking, intellection and explanation, concepts and judgments, axioms and postulates, principles and criteria, individual facts and general laws.

At any rate the diversity of problems remained great: philosophers analyzed the sciences, investigating their most general laws (Spencer), their logical structure and method (Mill), their leading categories (the Kantians), their assumptions (the positivists), their cognitive value (the contingentists and conventionalists), or descriptions of what takes place in the cognizing mind (the psychologists).

Problems of the theories of value, ethics, aesthetics, and religion, as they were then understood, were most frequently reduced to psychological ones: the question was not what has value or how we know that it has value, but rather what happens in consciousness when we evaluate things or how the mind arrives at one valuation rather than another. Thinkers even appealed to biology and investigated the dependence of our value judgments on the needs of our life and organism. This was particularly the case in the main philosophical trend of the epoch, positivism. Representatives of other trends asked not only how we arrive at value judgments, but also what possesses value. They went beyond the question of how we think, feel, and live to ask: how should we feel, think, and live?

231

Positions

The nineteenth century was a period of estrangement from philosophy; but despite this, philosophy looms large in it. There was no lack of philosophers; only the public was disinclined to philosophize. But even those who did not listen to philosophers and condemned philosophy philosophized in their own way: the philosophy of the philosophers was combated, but at the same time a philosophy of the natural scientists and a philosophy of men of letters was developed.

The outstanding feature of the philosophy of the entire century, beginning from 1830, was minimalism, especially in its positivistic form. It was the leading motif of the century, but not in the statistical sense, for through inertia representatives of earlier trends still had the statistical majority. Neither was this leading trend a novelty; after the eighteenth century it was no longer new. It was a main trend because of the continuity of its development: it developed gradually and continually, gaining increasing recognition.

There were also other trends. Materialism had supporters in the middle of the century and even later in Haeckel's time; at the end of the century idealism flourished in England and Kantianism in Germany. Materialism had supporters especially among natural scientists and social activists, idealism among men of letters, and Kantianism among philosophical specialists.

Other features, motifs, and trends were also characteristic of thought in the nineteenth century, some of them unexpected and seemingly mutually contradictory but nonetheless characteristic of the times. For instance, the social motif (from Comte and Marx) in a century of exhuberant individualism; the aesthetic motif (from Ruskin and Walter Pater) in a century exceptionally lacking in taste; the motif of pessimism (from Schopenhauer and von Hartmann) in a century of exceptional prosperity, peace, and advantageous conditions just for those classes who philosophized.

Philosophy in the nineteenth century was more uniform than in other periods. Nevertheless, in many important matters it was inconsistent; there were varied opinions and the debate between them filled the century. One debate centered on whether the development of society and nature takes place in a continual manner or by leaps: typical for the nineteenth century seems to be the belief in continuity of development, but Marx and Boutroux favored the view of discontinuity. There was a debate between the evolutionary and revolutionary conceptions of development: Cuvier believed that development takes place in the form of catastrophes, Darwin in the form of evolution; a similar duality was manifest among the philosophers. Debate also continued on the understanding of history: the idealists saw profound sense and purposefulness in history, but to the

positivists the belief that history has sense and goal appeared
to be unsophisticated anthropomorphism. Characteristic of the
epoch was reducing phenomena of a higher type to a lower one,
but this same epoch produced Boutroux who opposed this view.
Under the influence of the development of machines and technology, a typical attitude was seeing the world as a mechanism,
but this same time produced anti-mechanistic theories like
Guyau's. Kantianism was typical in Germany and other countries,
even in France, long opposed to it, where it attracted Fouillée
and Renouvier. On the other hand, even in the German countries,
mechanism was opposed by Brentano and Mach. A typical view of
the nineteenth century was relativism of various kinds, but
this same nineteenth century sought evidence for absolute laws.
In philosophy, battle raged between the rule of law and anarchy:
the spirit of law seemed to predominate, but against it were
Stirner and Kropotkin. A spirit indifferent or even hostile to
religion seemed predominant, and yet the century produced new
religious impulses—Newman, Kierkegaard, neo-Thomism. As never
before the cult of science seemed supreme, and yet this century
was the first to use the words "the bankruptcy of science."

Concepts and Terms

The philosophy of positivism, in contrast to the philosophy that had preceded it, expressed itself in the simplest
everyday language. It had neither the desire nor the ability
for linguistic innovation. There were few terminological novelties. Some universally accepted terms such as "positivism,"
"altruism," and "sociology" were derived from Comte. Others
came from Darwin, Spencer, and their supporters: "evolution,"
"development," "struggle for existence," "adaptation," "natural
selection," "ontogenesis" and "phylogenesis," "agnosticism."
These terms passed from the biological sciences to philosophy.
The expression "philosophy of science" was begun by Ampère.
The term "voluntarism" was originated by Paulsen. In the theory of knowledge, particularly characteristic for those times
were terms condemning or deprecating scientific progress, such
as "anthropomorphism," "animism," "hypostasis." Psychology introduced a few new terms—"introspection," "synesthesia," "iden-
tification," "psychophysics," and "ethnopsychology." In general, however, the new terms were psychophysiological and psycho-
pathological. General psychology retained earlier, common expressions, only distinguishing them more precisely and consoli-
dating them. Even such original thinkers as Carlyle and Stirner did not use original terminology. The original terminology
of Newman and Kierkegaard was not used by others. Marx's vo-
cabulary influenced economics and the language of political
parties rather than philosophy. Nietzsche's expressions—

"Apollonian" and "Dionysian" attitudes, the "transvaluation of value," and "master morality"—became widespread, but these expressions belonged to a widely attacked position or, at least, not to a terminology in daily use by the philosophers of that time. In general, terminology did not develop in this epoch but rather became stabilized and standardized. The ordered terminology that we now use is, in general, the work of the nineteenth century.

Chronology

The philosophy of the nineteenth century from 1830 went through three phases. The first phase (1830-1860) was rich but indecisive. Conservative positions such as Hegelianism in Germany and messianism in Poland were still important, but during this period the new conceptions of the century were formulated. In the second phase (1860-1880), one of these conceptions, positivistic scientism, became public property. However, even before the end of the century (1880-1900), opposition to it had begun. These years comprise the third phase of the philosophy of the nineteenth century.

This is the general schema, but the activity of many thinkers of the nineteenth century, especially the most important ones, transcends the framework of any one phase. Comte and Mill had formed their views before 1830, but they became influential only after 1860. The activity of Carlyle and Newman, which began about 1830, lasted for more than a half-century. The work of Spencer and Renouvier embraces the entire second half of the century. Marx and Engels announced their views shortly after 1830, but the first volume of *Das Kapital* did not appear until 1867 and the second volume much later.

Each of these three phases contained a great variety of philosophical events. The dates of the main works of the nineteenth century point to this.

1. Comte began to publish his *Course of Positive Philosophy* in 1830 at about the same time (1833) that Newman, an opponent of positivism in every particular, began his activity. Ampère's theory of science appeared in the same year (1834) as the Carlyle's metaphysical narrative. The main work of the materialist Feuerbach was published in the same year (1841) as Lotze's *Metaphysics* and the Emerson's first essays, which were inspired by spiritualism. The year 1843 is marked by the appearance of the empiricist Mill's *System of Logic* and by the existential writings of Kierkegaard and the spiritualistic system of Lamennais. Stirner introduced his philosophy of individualism in the same year (1845) that Marx and Engels were formulating the philosophy of socialism in *The Holy Family*. In Poland Wiszniewski's book on Bacon, in the spirit of empiricism (1834), appeared at about the same time as a major messianic

work of Wronski (1831). In Germany, a leading representative of Kantianism, Helmholtz, made his debut in the same year (1855) as the most popular materialist, Büchner. In England, the lectures of the aging Hamilton were published in the same year (1859) as Darwin's *On the Origin of Species*. In the first phase of the nineteenth century, many diametrically opposed views found expression at the same time.

2. In the second phase the situation was not much different. Spencer's *System of Synthetic Philosophy* appeared in the same year (1860) as Fechner's psychophysics and K. Fischer's work on Kant, which became one of the main pillars of neo-Kantianism. In 1865 the work of Stirling was published, marking the beginning of English neo-Hegelianism; in 1867, the first volume of *Das Kapital* of Marx; and, between them, Lange's *History of Materialism* (1866), which was anti-Hegelian and anti-materialistic. Du Bois-Reymond popularized the slogan of agnosticism in the same year (1876) that von Hartmann began to publish his metaphysics. In 1873 Wundt's *Physiological Psychology* appeared and, in the following year, Franz Brentano's *Psychology from an Empirical Standpoint* which represented the opposite point of view. Avenarius announced his philosophy of empirio-criticism in the same year (1876) that the positivist Kantian Riehl and the idealistic metaphysician Bradley expressed their positions. Renan also published his skeptical dialogues in the same year. During this phase, both Nietzsche and the positivist Laas began their careers in Germany.

3. In the third phase the diversity of philosophical positions was perhaps even greater. The standard works on positivism, Kantianism, and evolutionism appeared at the same time. In Germany, the anti-materialistic movement became widespread at the same time that the materialist Haeckel became popular. In England, the anti-metaphysical Bible of scientism, Pearson's *The Grammar of Science*, came out at the same time as the metaphysical works of Ward, Bradley, Royce, and McTaggart. Nietzsche was already famous, and Brentano had a considerable school. Bergson, James, Husserl, Le Roy, and Freud—all celebrities of the coming century—had already begun to publish their works. The general public still lived according to the positivistic ideas of its century, but the leading slogans of the coming century had already been announced.

Society and Culture

The philosophy of the nineteenth century (from the year 1830) should be seen against a background of life that was exceptionally peaceful and stabilized. Cataclysms, which had afflicted people in the past and were to come in the future, avoided this century. The only shattering events of this time were: the year 1848, with its Paris, German, and Hungarian revolutions; and the years 1870-71 with the Franco-Prussian war and the Paris Commune. There were other wars, such as the Russo-Polish war of 1831, the Crimean war of 1853, the battles of Magenta and Solferino in 1859, the battles of Custozza and Königgrätz in 1866, the Russo-Turkish war of 1877, the Balkan wars of 1885 and 1897, but these events did not adversely affect the main sources of European culture.

In this era the great political powers were formed. Great Britain was experiencing its Victorian era (1837-1901). France had a brilliant epoch during the Second Empire (1853-70) and the Third Republic (from 1870). In 1861 united Italy became a monarchy. Germany became united after a series of victorious wars and became an empire in 1871. Under Bismarck (1862-90) she had strength such as she had never known before. And beyond Europe, the United States embarked on a period of rapid development after the Civil War (1861-65).

The simultaneous flowering of several continental powers with few conflicts and the peaceful cooperation of many sources of culture formed the background against which the philosophy of the nineteenth century developed. International cooperation was greater than had ever been known. And knowledge of the world was unprecedented. The macro symbol of this was the great world's fairs (the first in London in 1851), the micro symbol was Baedeker's guide books (in German from 1832, in other languages from 1846). Europe spread itself over the entire world. The first international undersea telegraph was installed in 1846. The Suez Canal opened in 1869, and in 1876 the English queen became Empress of India.

Socially and economically one should regard the philosophy of the nineteenth century against a background dominated by the Third Estate, rapid industrialization, the growth of capitalism, and the development of small and large industries and banking firms. The industrial capitalists grew rich, while the working class and the intelligentsia lived near poverty, especially the mass of scholars and writers. The end of this era was in America already the era of gigantic concerns and trusts. In 1870 J. D. Rockefeller created the Standard Oil Company, in 1872 Vanderbilt and Morgan began the monopolization of the railroad industry, and in 1882 the first trust was formed. In England liberalism made rapid progress from 1832, and parliamentary order entered government, although it did not by any means embrace all countries. Socialistic ideas appeared from the beginning of the century, first in utopian form, as represented by phalangists and the phalanstery, the dreams of Cabet, Fourier, and Owen; but these dreams were realized only as small and transient colonies in North America, such as New Jerusalem (1824), New Harmony (1825), and Icarus (1858). With Marx and Engels, however, socialism passed from an ideal to a real form.

The Communist Manifesto appeared in 1848. To the end of this century, however, socialism remained only an opposition party and was illegal in many countries. It did not yet assume power.

Demographically one should regard the philosophy of the nineteenth century against tremendous population growth, which had been unknown for centuries. The population of Europe, whose number had not greatly increased through the centuries, now in the course of one hundred years rose from 190 to 520 million and the population of the United States from 5.3 million to 123 million. So, at the end of the century philosophers already had a much greater number of listeners and readers than at the beginning of the century.

One should also view the philosophy of this period against the lessening role of religion, the secularization of life. From 1871 the Church lost its last lands, Rome became the capital of Italy, and the Pope shut himself in the Vatican. In 1871 the *Kulturkampf* began. The Church found itself on the defensive even in some Catholic countries: France, for example. But this defensive role increased its coherence and activity. In particular, it led to the development of Catholic philosophy. In 1870 the doctrine of Papal infallibility was proclaimed, in 1879 the Papal encyclical *Aeterni Patris* was announced, and in 1897 the Index was reformed.

One should also regard the philosophy of the nineteenth century against a background of tremendous technical advance, particularly in the area of communications. This century built railroads and steamships. Almost at once, a railway network as well as paved roads began to cover the world. This was possible through inventions such as the steam engine and through an advance in metallurgy—the invention in 1858 of the Bessemer process for cheap production of softer steel. In many areas machines replaced human hands. Innumerable inventions were perfected, from the telegraph by Gauss-Weber in 1833 and Morse in 1836, to the telephone, by Bell in 1876, and the wireless telegraph in 1896. Of particular importance for scientific work were advances in the art of paper making, printing, and lighting. In 1854 the Americans Watt and Buyers discovered a method of obtaining wood fibers for the production of paper. In 1879 Edison invented and began producing light bulbs. Some new machines had particular importance for the sciences. An improved typesetting machine—monotype—was invented by Lanston in 1887 and was being sold from 1897. The first typewriters were produced by Remington in 1874, an improved Underwood in 1898.

Science in this era expanded along with philosophy and even beyond it. Far-reaching discoveries were perfected, and important scientific concepts were developed. We have already spoken of some of them, and now will mention others. In 1828, Wöhler first synthesized an organic compound. In 1831 Faraday's theory of magnetism was announced and in 1839 Schwann's discoveries about the living cell. In 1843 J. R. von Mayer formulated the theory of the conservation of energy. In 1851 C. Bernard began the science of endocrinology. In 1859 spectrum analysis was perfected, and in the same year Darwin published *On the Origin of Species*. In 1865, G. Mendel discovered the basis of genetic inheritance. In 1873 Maxwell formulated the electromagnetic theory of light, and in 1874 van't Hoff began the science of stereochemistry. Becquerel discovered the phenomena of radioactivity in 1896. Roentgen discovered x-rays in 1895, and in 1898 Maria Curie-Sklodowska published her discoveries on radium. These were all discoveries of great scientific importance, changing the concepts of matter, life, and development, and they were important for philosophy as well.

This was also an age of momentous medical discoveries, the age of Pasteur, the discovery of the tuberculosis bacteria by Koch (1882) and a serum against diphtheria by Behring (1892), the discovery of antiseptics and anesthetics, the age of "the battle of man with death."

This age was also a time of flowering in history and philology. Bopp's comparative Sanskrit grammar appeared in 1833, Mommsen's *History of Rome* in 1854, Renan's *History of the Beginnings of Christianity* in 1854, and Taine's *Origins of Contemporary France* in 1875-93.

Externally, however, this age retained rigid and unchanging social forms. The strangest and most uncomfortable clothing, starched shirts, corsets, top hats, and bustles, was bravely endured. A breach in social customs could place a person beyond the pale of society. In the days of nascent revolutionary movements, particularly conservative and demanding views prevailed. Apostasy was stigmatized not only in ideology but even in external social forms.

Fiction, especially narrative prose, also flourished at this time. The year 1830 marks the approximate end of romanticism in literature (Byron died a year earlier and Scott in 1832). Further developments in fiction paralleled developments in philosophy. The most ambitious efforts belong to the first half of the century. This was the era of national poets—Mickiewicz and Slowacki in Poland, Pushkin and Lermontov in Russia—and of great novelists: Stendhal, Balzac, Gogol, and Dickens. After the half century, even earlier than in philosophy, new genres appeared in fiction. In 1857 Baudelaire's *The Flowers of Evil* and Flaubert's *Madame Bovary* appeared. Rimbaud's *The Drunken Boat* dates from 1871 and Mallarmé's *Afternoon of a Faun* from 1876. In 1864 Zola began his career, and his collected short stories, *Les Soirés de Medan*, marking the highest point in the development of naturalism, were published in 1880. This movement was a transient but real reflection of positivism. It gave rise to opposition, for in 1867 Dostoevski's *Crime and*

Punishment and Ibsen's *Peer Gynt* made their appearance. In 1887 the avant garde Theatre Libre of Antoine was opened and in 1891 Die Freie Bühne. Wilde's *The Picture of Dorian Gray* (1891), Hamsun's *Hunger* (1890), and Maeterlinck's *Princess Maleine* (1889) were far removed from naturalism, just as the contemporary philosophical writings of Boutroux, Bradley, or Dilthey were far from positivism. More or less at the same time plays that were social and revolutionary in content were staged, works with no predecessors in literature: Hauptmann's *The Weavers* (1892), for example. In this same year Gorki, the first great representative of proletarian literature, began his literary career.

The nineteenth century was a peculiar era. It was the age of decline in architecture and decorative art; only old forms were reworked, and this gives proof of an exceptional lack of taste. At the same time painting developed rapidly. Especially in France, one can find parallels to developments in philosophy. In 1855 "realism" was begun by Courbet. In the 1870s the impressionists appeared—Manet (1832-1883), Monet (1840-1919), and Renoir (1841-1920); in 1886 Seurat and the neoimpressionists attempted to reproduce impressions on canvas by "scientific methods." All of these currents can be regarded as reflections of positivism in philosophy. But in art as well, other than positivistic currents appeared before the end of the century. The symbolistic painting of Puvis de Chavannes started in the 1880s as did the synthetic painting of the post-impressionists Cezanne (1839-1906) and van Gogh (1853-1890).

Even in music one can find analogies to developments in contemporary philosophy; at the very least one sees the same tremendous variety. The romantics like Chopin and Schumann composed in the first half of the century, and Wagner (1813-1883) in the second half; but composers of a completely different style were also popular—Gounod (*Faust*, 1859), Bizet (*Carmen*, 1875), and Verdi, and on another scale Offenbach (*Orpheus in Hades*, 1858), and Johann Strauss.

In all areas of life the same peculiar phenomenon that appeared in philosophy repeated itself—almost total two-track development. Discoveries were made, ideas were born, but for a time they had no effect. Everything remained as before. The chronology of the origin of thoughts in the nineteenth century is entirely different from the chronology of their acceptance. This was especially so in art. The impressionists gained great fame only after their work had existed for several decades. In those days, which we now call "the days of the impressionists," exhibitions were entirely composed of old-fashioned, offical art. The exhibition by Manet of *Picnic on the Grass* was commonly regarded as a scandal. But the situation was also the same in some areas of science. In mathematics, for example, the mass of scholars went on in the old way, not paying any at-

tention to the discoverers, the precursors of new disciplines,
such as Cantor, Frege, Rieman, and Peano. One must state that
philosophers coming out with new ideas in the nineteenth century found relatively earlier acceptance than artists and scientists.

Index